Narrow Gate
Churches

Narrow Gate Churches

The Christian Presence in the Holy Land
Under Muslim and Jewish Rule

by Atallah Mansour

Hope Publishing House
Pasadena, California

Copyright © 2004 Atallah Mansour

For information address:

Hope Publishing House
P.O. Box 60008
Pasadena, CA 91116 - U.S.A.
Tel: (626) 792-6123 / Fax: (626) 792-2121
E-mail: hopepub@sbcglobal.net
Web site: http://www.hope-pub.com

Printed on acid-free paper
Cover design — Michael McClary/The Workshop

Library of Congress Cataloging-in-Publication Data

Mansour, Atallah, 1934–
    Narrow gate churches : the Christian presence in the Holy Land
under Muslim and Jewish rule / by Atallah Mansour.-- 1st. ed.
        p. cm.
    Includes bibliographical references and index.
    ISBN 1-932717-02-1 (trade pbk. : alk. paper)
    1.Christians--Palestine--History.2.Chrisitans--Jerusalem--History.
3. Palestine--Church history. 4. Jerusalem--Church history. I. Title.
    BR1110.M36 2004
    275.694--dc22

                                        2004005042

Dedicated to my parents, Nijmeh and Botrus Mansour;
to Evelyn, my wife; and our children and grandchildren.

Contents

1

Introduction

"May the God of steadfastness and encouragement grant you to live in harmony with one another, in accordance with Christ, Jesus, so that together you may with one voice glorify the God and Father of our Lord Jesus Christ. Welcome one another, therefore, just as Christ has welcomed you, for the glory of God" (Rm 15:5-7).

For the last half century, the overwhelming political ideology dominating my generation of Israel's Arab minority has been basically secular, anti-imperialist and left leaning. This tendency was typical in most ex-colonies – or "Third World" countries – including Arab states.

We, as an Arab community of Israeli citizens, endure the additional predicament of being caught in the crossfire. We feel deep sympathy and strong solidarity with our Arab people – especially the Palestinian refugees – for the natural reason that they are our parents, sisters, brothers, uncles and first cousins. At the same time, contrary to any logic, we are quite alienated and ostracized by the Arab "fraternal" regimes outside Israel. Worse, we are considered as collaborators with the enemy for no other crime than the fatal sin of holding fast to our homes in our homeland. Yet anti-Zionist feelings are so overwhelming in Arab nationalism that they blind almost the entire Arab nation to the fact that we only did the natural thing. As farmers, we could not run away from our olive trees and grain fields to go into exile. Since Israel was willing to tolerate our presence in 1948 under our tragic conditions, was taken as conclusive proof that we are traitors and collaborators.

Israel was perceived merely as an imminent danger confronting the Arabs—a spearhead for the old colonial powers in the area. This feeling was substantiated beyond any doubt by the 1956 British-French-Israeli attempt to invade Egypt and topple the national pan-Arab leadership of that state. The Arab consensus began then to consider the Jewish state as responsible for any Arab suffering— including the military regimes of those Arab juntas whose excuse for seizing power and decreeing emergency laws was as "a necessary step towards recovering Palestine from the Zionists." Because we lived in an uneasy but peaceful coexistence with that devilish power, we had to suffer from the poisoned atmosphere that dominated Israeli-Arab relations.

Since we take part in Israel's public life, like voting for parliament or earning our daily bread in Jewish enterprises, this is enough for our Arab neighbors to denounce us as despised agents of the enemy. These hate feelings are so intense and overwhelming that rarely do Arab writers notice or even care to preserve themselves from the evil of Anti-Semitism (including that of the Nazis) simply because the Zionist Jews are the enemy who humiliated them in the battlefield. The Jews were the cause of the Palestinian refugees' tragedy, people who stubbornly—and contrary to the UN's resolutions—prevented them from returning to their homes.

During the period of pan-Arab nationalism when young Arabs in the 20th century aspired to unite all Arab states from Morocco in the west to Iraq in the east into one strong state restoring Arab golden days of the past, Israel was blamed for a physical reason. Since it was located between Asia and Africa, Israel was seen as "dividing" the Arab world between its Asian and African parts.

I remember vividly a moving article in the Egyptian weekly *Al Mussawar* which appeared during the 1960s trial of Nazi criminal Adolph Eichmann in Israel. At that time most Arab commentators were hurling accusations at Israel for kidnapping a German old man from Argentina and claimed Israel's leaders would stand accused of crimes more heinous than those of the Nazis. Ahmad Baha al Din, the editor of this publication, chose rather to write a lengthy review of William Shearer's *The Rise and Fall of the Third Reich* and used this piece as a means to call Arab writers not to play into their enemy's hands by "defending" Nazi criminals who, he reminded them, considered Arabs also as Semites, like the Jews, and thus at the bottom of the race list along with the most "inferior" nations. Baha al Din concluded for his Arab readers that those posing as pro-Nazis injured the Arab cause and they would reap no benefits by associating themselves with such criminals.

This piece moved me deeply at the time and I took it as a sign of hope that my people could prove stronger than their pain and remain rational. Despite their suffering from injustices wreaked at the hands of the 20th-century colonial powers, they could keep themselves from drowning in squalid ponds of hatred. Unfortunately this article proved to be an isolated episode, not a turning point. The Arabs and Jews were to suffer a lot more enmity before arriving at a reasonable new path.

During most of the epoch of British rule, the Palestinian leadership (1918-1948) had been under the firm leadership of the Grand Mufti Haj Amin al Husseini whose main characteristic, noted by foes and followers alike, was always to say "No." He never agreed with another's point of view and seldom trusted anyone, believing most proposals were mere fronts for a conspiracy (A'omar 1999:510).

His suspicious reign was bound to fail, as it did with the disaster of 1948. After that catastrophe, it was easy for young activists in Marxist cells to promote an anti-clerical public opinion. Amidst the tense and heated arguments about a course of action for the new cultural-political discourse, a general consensus among the young Arabs in Israel was to regard religion as an irrelevant factor in public life.

Many young people, especially in the Christian camp, felt such behavior was natural and also essential in building a national solidarity between the Arabs. Downplaying religion was a the first step towards class solidarity and international friendships, especially for our Muslim compatriots, since the term "Arab" was often synonymous with "Islam." Granted, some 80% of the Arab population are nominal Muslims and Islam is a major component of the Arab heritage.

The fundamentalist revolution arrived almost unnoticeably before the end of the 20th century. Many had looked to the Soviet Union for support of the Palestinians' dream to return to the status quo – or at least to demand that Israel (and the USA) implement the UN's original resolution of November 1947, often referred to in political circles as the "Partition Scheme." This Scheme was to have divided Palestine into two national states, but sadly, only the Arab side adopted these goals after launching and being defeated – in spite of the fact that Arab leadership had rejected them out of hand in 1947. The collapse of the USSR and the Communist bloc crushed these illusions.

The Pan-Arab movement, under the popular leadership of the charismatic Gamal Abed al Nasser, had lost its drive earlier after its military defeat in the 1967 Six-Day War. Soon came Nasser's unexpected early death in 1970 before he could restore his authority. Anwar al Sadat, his successor, changed course and his relative victory in the Tishreen-Yom Kippur round of the Arab-Israeli War in 1973 enabled him to negotiate and regain all the Egyptian-occupied Sinai in the talks facilitated by Carter at Camp David in 1978.

Among the many effects of this war, one far-reaching result went almost unnoticed. The backward oil-rich Arab countries, especially in the Arab peninsula, became the region's most influential Arab force. The Saudi sheikhs either took over as publishers of important reputable Lebanese publications or they established new media outlets, even buying TV stations in London and Paris and installing Palestinian and Lebanese journalists to direct them. The civil war in Lebanon that had raged between Muslims and Christians had impoverished some of the region's leading newspapers making them vulnerable to takeover by these new millionaires, who began now to mold and dominate the Arab cultural scene, spreading their community's conservative values and rejecting any half-baked modern ideas that were not completely internalized by most Arabs in the Middle East.

The sudden disappearance of the Soviet Empire weakened the followers of the Communist line and drove many Arabs who were striving to change the miserable status quo to lose their compass. In despair many looked for a substitute and "returned" to ask for help from the heavens. These began to reconsider their religious beliefs, and in less than a decade after the dramatic tearing down of the Berlin Wall we were witnessing a massive religious revival in most Arab states and in Israel.

The Muslim fundamentalist elements that had appeared to be dying embers turned out to be raging flames. Suddenly these rabid fundamentalists were welcomed and embraced by proponents of a ready-made ideology with its catchy slogan: *Islam is the solution.* This battle cry was coined in 1928 when the Muslim Brothers Movement was established in Egypt). So today we find that many of our younger generation in the region claim to place religion first in the list of what identifies their beliefs and cultural values.

Many good (and some not) books have been written to cover in the most comprehensive and detailed way, the history of the Promised Land. These tend to place special interest on the events of the last millennium, concentrating on the holy sites and their legal status. As might be expected, a multitude of writers have discussed the authenticity and archaeological status of such sites. Venerated historical shrines remind us of the Bible stories: the Annunciation, birth, miraculous life, death on the Cross and the glorious Resurrection of our Lord. Some refer to these sites as the "Fifth Gospel" because they add another dimension to the four canonical gospels of the New Testament.

These sites were witness to how the Holy One raised the human race from the earthly life to the sublime. They are the locales where our salvation was forged and the miracle of the ages took place. The humble unknown village of Nazareth ("Can anything good come out of Nazareth?" [Jn 1:46]) was chosen as the location where the divine Lord of the universe became human in the womb of a humble Nazarene virgin. In this land, the Lord of Lords was born in the midst of the cows in a Bethlehem stable. Here the Almighty was killed on the Cross like a mean thief in the company of two thieves outside Jerusalem. Here we saw Christ's glory: the Resurrection.

It was in this land that the "Church" was born – not the buildings or the stones but the congregation of faithful Christians – who make up the Sixth Gospel and are the topic and substance of this book. I have no intention of arguing for the primacy of any of the official churches or even against other religions. I have no laboratory to test and prove one faith superior to another – aside from my conviction that religious beliefs are a set of rules and values meant to make the human race superior to the jungle beasts. I judge religions by their fruits and their teachings, for I believe the Almighty, who created this universe and every living being in it, doesn't need us. Rather the test is how we treat each other and those around us who need our help.

This book makes a humble appeal to all those who receive Jesus Christ as their Lord and Savior to accept all and any of their fellow believers in the faith as genuine kin. It is not a book written for a theological debate. We all need to remember our Lord's teachings about our duties to love our enemies and bless those who curse us. Thus we must stop hurling pejorative terms and even gunpowder at those with whom we differ on interpretation or understanding of trivial issues and keep in mind the command of Jesus that we are to "love one another" (Jn 15:17).

For me the term *Christian* is proper and correct for anyone who accepts Jesus Christ as Lord and Savior, whether that person attends a Catholic, Orthodox, Protestant or Hebrew-Christian church. All quotations used from the Scripture are derived from the *New Revised Standard Version* of the Bible which was blessed by an ecumenical approval from Catholic, Orthodox and Protestant churches. My hope here is to make a modest contribution to the ecumenical movement we have been blessed to witness in these last decades. As the heads of the Eastern Churches stated in their pastoral message from Nicosia:

We all believe that Christ is God and Man, Lord and Savior, Shepherd and Leader in the darkness of life and especially in these days in which we see many of our children stripped of their basic human rights. They are forced to look for refuge in terrifying numbers, from Southeast Turkey. (In the case of this steady painful movement of immigration) we want to tell you that our Lord Jesus Christ wants us and wants you, to carry the yoke of this burden, the mission, to this East. The mission is to keep high the banner of the Gospel ideals (Jan. 24, 1998).

But in no way is this book an official enterprise of any organization. Rather it is an entirely personal endeavor and no individual or group offered me any help in it. On the contrary, I made a special attempt to keep some distance from the church officials to ensure that I would not be party to their tragic squabbles.

During the Muslim-Arab Empire, Christian natives also contributed to the culture of the Arab peoples by translating classic books of medicine, science and philosophy from Greek or Persian to Arabic. I feel I should give a short summary of this history in order to give the necessary background on some of the squabbles between different churches. Already there are too many books on this sad issue. Though I want to refrain from an in-depth study of the long, sad theological wars, it does seem necessary to mention these squabbles briefly, if only to point out their absurdity.

This book is meant to tell at length and in detail the story of all Christians in the home of Christianity during the last two centuries of the second millennium and to examine their future prospects in the new century. My main concern remains the future. Thus we shall focus on Galilee (the land of the Annunciation), the first miracles and the faithful apostles, concentrating on the Christian population in Palestine within the borders of the British mandate (between 1918-1948 within the generally accepted political borders of Israel/Palestine) and also look in detail at the relevant official statistics on the natural increase of Christians and their socio-cultural position plus their role in the general population.

Since Palestinian Christians are part of the larger body of Middle Eastern Christians it is important to look at the Arab Christian communities living in neighboring states – the area of present-day Syria, Lebanon, Jordan, Iraq and Egypt. Abraham, the patriarch who first introduced monotheism to the area, was born in the city of Ur in present-day Iraq. Also the divine infant Jesus with his family found refuge in Egypt immediately after his birth. As an adult, Jesus visited Tyre and Sidon in Lebanon (Mt 11:21; Mk 7:24) and Caesarea Philippi (currently called Banias in the Syrian Golan occupied by Israel since 1967 [Mk 8:27]). Thus the title *The Narrow Gate Churches: Christians under Muslim and Jewish Rule in the Holy Lands.*

The term Narrow Gate Churches is not an arbitrary one. The number of church faithful is dwindling in some cases and the share of Christians in the general population is impoverished in all these countries. The withdrawal of the Christian communities is demonstrated in the physical shape of the buildings of the church. The gates become narrow. The Nativity Basilica, one of the most venerated churches in Christendom, failed to be a sanctuary for two dozen Palestinians who fled from Israel's vengeful wrath. The Israeli army did not respect this sanctuary and in their military incursions to force them out, they killed the church's verger and wounded others. Only "foreign" intervention solved the problem.

Visitors to the Nativity Basilica in Bethlehem note that the only entrance to this shrine is so narrow all must stoop to enter. But it was not built purposely to force anyone entering to pay due respect to this venerable spot (Mt 7:14). On closer examination it can be seen that this entrance was originally wide and majestic. Built during the days of Christian emperors that dominated the Holy Land, beginning with Constantine in 326-330, after Samaritans rebels destroyed this church in 529, the existing building was put up by Emperor Justinian I. When Bethlehem fell to the Persians in 614, they plundered the entire country and all the churches except this one because in it they found a mosaic depicting the Magi as Persians. Later, Muslim conquerors saved this church and other Christian shrines in Palestine because of their respect for Jesus and his mother.

The narrowing of this church's entrance took place after the European Christian soldiers lost Palestine at the end of the Crusades. The intent was to keep the Mameluk Baybars and the Ottoman horsemen from riding into the churches as they pillaged the country. In 1500 two of the church's gates were entirely closed off and the third was lowered to its current size. This pattern was repeated throughout the Holy Land to make it impossible for a mounted rider to enter sacred sites.

In addition, we have included relevant remarks on the many (I feel too many) Arab Christians who found it beyond their capacity to go on living in the Middle East and moved to calmer shores in the Americas, Europe or Australia. Rather than discuss the problems facing these emigrants, we will focus on the problems created within the communities they left behind, for our Christian community is impoverished by their absence while the rest of the world enjoys the fruits of their Christian labor.

I first became aware of this issue when I was privileged to study in Oxford on a British Council scholarship. My family was with me and my son attended elementary classes in a Church of England school where his classmates called him "Paki" (short for Pakistani) because of his dark olive skin and foreign accent. When I suggested to the teacher that this might be resolved were she to introduce my son to his schoolmates as a cousin of Jesus Christ, she was so furious she almost fainted. When she managed to regain her composure, she advised me in most polite terms that she understood we were Jewish. When I explained that we were native Galilean Christians, she was flabbergasted, for she had never imagined that native Christians still lived in the Holy Land.

This young teacher in Oxford was not the only Westerner who confessed to me sheer ignorance that such a group existed – which contributed impetus to my wanting to tell this story of Arab Christians, natives of the Holy Lands. There are many variations among the rituals and Christian practices of the different Arab Christians – as there are throughout Christendom. We come from long separated Eastern traditions: some use our own national ceremonies, some practice Byzantine-Greek rites, some use rituals of the Roman Catholic church, the Church of England, the Southern Baptists, among others. Some worship in our native Arabic, others in Latin, Armenian, Syrian or English – but all of us accept Jesus Christ as God and Savior.

We have had to endure peculiar experiences. Even keen Christian clergy from the West who have lived in our midst don't fully grasp our own unique ways of worship. Once I had to explain a basic symbol to an old friend, a retired Presbyterian pastor from Michigan, who had attended a Greek Catholic mass with me in Nazareth. Walking back to my home, he shocked me by asking why we "cross ourselves" in church—a gesture he perceived as a public declaration of our faith in a pagan custom. I had to calm his fears and explain that this little ritual, "drawing the sign of the Holy Cross" as we call it, was an essential identification mark for Christians in the dark days of our forebears' persecution.

The last millennium was a period of great progress in every aspect of human life, but it saw many misunderstandings as well. In the middle of that millennium, Johan Gutenberg's invention, the printing press, made books available to a thin segment of the secular society, leading many to believe it was a major step in creating more understanding among human societies. Unfortunately not all that was printed was very good. Thus in reports about their visits to the Holy Lands, foreign travelers offered their readers both positive and negative comments about our Middle Eastern homeland. So these visitors often skewed how their European and American readers perceived us, often creating stereotypes about the East that ignored its Christian population.

I would suspect the failure for many of those commentators to even mention such Christians may have arisen from their inability to communicate in a common language plus their anxiety to hurry from one biblical site to another. Having spent four decades as a journalist, I understand the pressures of short trips, imminent deadlines and related hazards. So these compounded factors have often turned a hope for understanding into a curse of misunderstanding.

Certainly the story of these Christian communities deserves the attention of those who care about human relations, about Christianity and the Holy Land and about how Islam, Judaism and Christianity interact. Islam dominates some 50 nations with a billion adherents and Judaism has played a major role in religious history. In this context the inter-faith issues raise intriguing points:

The mere fact that native Christian (and Jewish) communities survived under Muslim rule for most of the last 1,400 years, keeping their faith and their public worship, is remarkable. In contrast, during the almost 500 years prior to this when Holy Land Christians were subject to the Byzantine Christian Empire, they were often mistreated for refusing to accept Greek supremacy. The 200 years of Crusader domination did not afford them equality either since they did not adhere to the Latin or Roman Catholic rites. Thus we are justified in calling the native Christian history a prolonged story of suffering because of prejudicial treatment.

Since Arab Christian communities survived under different Muslim governments for a thousand years on their own, they deserve an honorary degree in survival skills, endurance, cross-bearing and continued faith in the teaching of Jesus' love, charity, passion and forgiveness. This alone should entitle them to special recognition throughout Christendom. But then credit should also be allowed the Muslim majority for their tolerance and humane treatment toward Christian minorities in their midst. These Muslim "saints" deserve to be lauded. Unfortunately, such miraculous behavior did not happen universally. Although native Christians survived in some areas, they disappeared in others.

Why no Christians survived in other Arab-Muslim states in the Arabian peninsula and, excluding Egypt, in North Africa is an important question. On the Arabian peninsula there is a facile answer: the second Muslim caliph, Omar Ibn al-Khattab, issued an edict of deportation for all Christians, basing his order on ambiguous teachings attributed to the Prophet Mohammed. But no one drove the Christians from North Africa. So why, in less than 100 years under Muslim rule, was the homeland of St. Augustine deserted by entire Christian communities that had flourished there for hundreds of years? What allowed Egyptian Copts, Lebanese Maronites, Syrian Arabs, Iraqi Assyrians and Chaldeans survive while the Christian communities in North Africa disappeared?

In discussing this issue of Christians' survival in Arab society we should remind all parties concerned that a Christian presence is an essential component to our national future as a pluralistic civilized nation, just as the existence of any of its other cultural-religious components is vital to our future as Arabs. Clearly pluralism is an educational, cultural and political need for any society today. Young people must meet and exchange ideas with others to prepare themselves for future encounters with totally different cultures; all this is essential in the third millennium as the global village becomes ever more a reality. Thus the mere existence of our Christian community in Arab countries is a national service to other Arabs.

Jews and Muslims share many practices and beliefs – such as restrictions and prohibitions on how to prepare food, what food should be eaten by the faithful (kosher and *halal*) and in venerating some of the same sites and historic persons. But there are tenets separating them, such as the Muslims' belief that Jews (and Christians) have distorted the Bible and the Gospel in order to deny Mohammed's recognition as a prophet. This gap is easier to bridge on the Christian front because of the blood relation that Christian and Muslim Arab neighbors usually cherish. Obviously, Christians have cultural links with the Jews as well, since the Christians' Old Testament is the Jewish *Tanakh*. Thus the claim may be made that a Christian presence, as a third side of this triangle, may be helpful especially in these days when we hope to end the military confrontation between Israel and the Arab world.

Such coexistence may prove essential to our future as an Arab minority inside Israel (Arabs are a million strong in a general population of six million). But the Christian presence is also significant to those Jews in Israel who aspire to live in real peace and cultural harmony in the region.

The question as to whether the Christian Arab community is on a path to extinction is critical. When asked if I feel we are about to disappear, I always express my fervent hope that we are not on the way out, but I know many have their doubts and fears. The dwindling Christian presence in the holy town of Jerusalem sound a loud warning of a looming and imminent danger. If the 21st century Middle East is to be part of the global village and not the isolated world it has been in the past, accommodations must be made. No country on earth today can maintain such a state of isolation as was possible 50 years ago.

In the age of Amnesty International, CNN and the internet, any political regime must be measured in its policy and treatment of religious or national minorities. Thus NATO's intervention in Bosnia and later in Kosovo to rescue Albanian Muslims spurred more interventions by the international community in East Timor to save the Indonesian Christians from disguised terror gangs. Such international actions signal a new era of global policy aimed at forcing recognition of the human and national rights of minorities and persecuted communities.

As a member of a peaceful Christian minority, I feel more protected in this open society than my ancestors were. The fact that my Christian community is made up of loyal citizens makes me feel even more secure – and we *are more peaceful, productive and law-abiding than our neighbors.* This well-known fact is appreciated by friends and envied by adversaries.

Strangely, we have had opposition from some "born-again Christians" and fundamentalists, mainly Americans, who voice doubts about our rights as Christian Palestinians to inherit the "Jews Promised Land" – the homeland of our ancestors and our Savior. They make this claim on racist lines, saying this land is Jewish – as it was during King David's kingdom, and so today Jews exclusively are entitled to this land, just as they were during the days of Joshua. Somehow they've decided we native Christians are simply another Gentile nation similar to the heathen nations of the Old Testament and thus we deserve similar treatment.

This falls on my ears as sheer blasphemy, based on a wrong understanding of the Gospel, the Scriptures and history. King David himself was not a "pure" Jew. His grandmother was Ruth, the Moabitess, and his heir, King Solomon, was the son of Bath-sheba, widow of Uriah the Hittite (Mt 1:1-6). Moabites and Hittites were not Hebrews or Jews.

Only the God of Isaac and Ishmael knows what happened in the last 2,000 years to the "pure" race of the Jewish people. The Bible itself doesn't insist on the claim for a "pure race." Many historians are convinced that Job, from the land of Uz and one of the most pious and heroic characters of the Bible, was an Arab. Certainly we Christian Arabs are no less Jewish than the Jews of Israel with whom we live these days–as anyone can see, for Yemeni and Ethiopian Jews bear little physical resemblance to the Jews from Russia, Germany, or Poland. Often eastern Jews look similar to their Arab and African neighbors with whom they lived for many hundreds of years. Most Christians and Muslims in great Syria look so similar, that it is hard to differentiate them from the Jews who have lived in their midst for centuries.

Recent scientific research supports this claim. A team of mainly Jewish scientists from Tel Aviv and Arizona carried out research on Y genes that are transferred directly and solely from father to male offspring. When Jewish males who immigrated to Israel from a variety of countries were compared to their non-Jewish compatriots, their genes, according to Bat Shiva Boneh-Tamir from Tel Aviv University, showed that the Palestinian Arabs' Y genes were quite similar to those of the main Jewish groups of the neighboring states, while the Ashkenazi Jews' Y genes were similar to those of Greeks and Turks. Ethiopian and Yemeni Jews' genes were quite different from the other two groups (Ha Aretz:May 9, 2000).

As Christians we ought to remember that "He came to his own home and his own people did not accept him. But to all who received him, who believed in his name, he gave power to become children of God, who were born, not of blood or of the will of the flesh or of the will of man, but of God" (Jn 1:11-13). It would seem that the shame complex of the European's collective conscience is so bad–because of the Nazi's anti-Jewish crimes–that many are blinded to what this Gospel message means.

Besides, why should my people pay the price for the Nazi atrocities? Is it right to ask the Palestinians, both Christians and Muslims, to compensate for the anti-Jewish pogroms, anti-Semitic feelings and the maltreatment of the Jews by the rest of the world?

Perhaps the entire body of Christ, at the dawn of the third millennium, needs to hear again the words of Saint Paul, the great apostle to the Gentiles:

> Now before faith came, we were imprisoned and guarded under the law [of Moses] until faith would be revealed. Therefore the law was our disciplinarian until Christ came, so that we might be justified by faith. But now that the faith has come, we are no longer subject to a disciplinarian, for in Christ Jesus you are all children of God through faith. As many of you as were baptized into Christ have clothed yourselves with Christ. There is no longer Jew or Greek, there is no longer slave or free, there is no longer male and female; for all of you are one in Christ Jesus. And if you belong to Christ, then you are Abraham's offspring, heirs according to the promise" (Gal 3:23-29).

Another motivation for exploring this topic comes from our Muslim neighbors–especially those who show some eagerness to carry on a dialogue with us. In that blessed ecumenical atmosphere initiated in this past century by various resolutions of the Second Vatican Council and the World Council of Churches on relations with non-Christians, these Muslims often ask why Christians failed to respond to their "good will." They claim that despite their acceptance of our Lord as a great prophet born from the spirit of God and their acceptance of his holy mother as a unique woman who conceived without knowing sin, still we refuse adamantly *their* prophet and his teachings as if they were satanic.

Tragically, for most of the 1,400 years of Islam, Muslims have been in a state of war and conflict with Christian powers and communities. This has driven many to believe there can be no coexistence between the two religions. However, based on my understanding and my community's experience, there is much common ground and interest on the part of both parties to make rapprochement possible.

Many Westerners tend to lump all Arabs together, so their anti-Muslim sentiments sweep over all Arabs. Often little attention is paid to Arab history. The "official" Roman Catholic guide for pilgrims to the Holy Land, published by the Franciscan Press with the blessing of the *Custos del Terra Sancta,* "summarizes" the history of our people before the Muslim era in one sentence. "The Arab race up to Mohammed's day had been in the main, pagan." (Hoade 1962). That some of the most prominent Arab tribes – including the family of Mohammed's first wife Khadijeh – were Hebrew Christians and that many Arab bishops attended the first Christian councils is simply ignored.

This lacuna needs to be filled and I am hoping this labor will lead us to some positive conclusions. One main misconception I want to address is the prevailing sentiment that my Palestinian-Arab people are backward, divided, totally obsessed with side issues and forever limping behind the forward-galloping nations on this earth.

Others point to the easy rationalization from the common slogan some sources introduce as a *hadith* – or a traditional Muslim saying, "The world became hell for the faithful and heavens to the heathen" (Choueiri 1999:16, 19). This explains why Muslims are indoctrinated with the concept that they should not feel bad for any suffering in this life while the heathen succeed, for they shall be well compensated in heaven.

I do not come to this sensitive and complicated topic as a disinterested bystander. Religious belief was the main cultural-spiritual experience of my early childhood, for I was raised in a mixed Muslim-Christian village in the mountains of Upper Galilee. As the only son in a happy family of three children, I was raised by parents of Maronite and Greek Catholic backgrounds. We knew our life was earthly and holy, and we worked hard to earn our bread and enjoyed the pleasures of coming near to God in church. Our lives revolved around our church – we wore our best clothes, "our church dress," on Sunday and worked hard during the week to survive. Always our church was the bright side of our life – the warm, happy, festive part.

Al Jish, our village, was divided into two equal communities: Muslim and Christian. The division was as roughly geographic as it was religious. The eastern quarter, around the mosque, was Muslim; the western quarter was Christian and built around as-Sayyidah (the Lady) Church of the Maronite Catholics. On the top of the hill on which our village stands is al-Dair, a Greek-Catholic monastery dedicated to St. Peter and St. Paul and – according to St. Jerome – our village was home to Saint Paul's family before they moved to Tarsus in Celica.

During my childhood, our mixed village had a population of fewer than a thousand. All the other neighboring villages around ours were totally Muslim aside from some Christian neighbors to the west in Kafr Bira'am. The relations in our village were normal – with the usual amount of bickering and misunderstandings between neighbors. Occasionally we heard about some *zua'ran* (uncultured, savage and violent youngsters) who would misbehave, but such persons and acts were always easy to contain. The *awadim* (the respected ones) of the village would interfere and decide on the proper justice. A few times acts would be brought to the police or the state courts, but mostly the "punishment" by our local traditional justice system meant that compensation was given the victim for the loss or injury while the wrongdoer was made to apologize publicly to the victims in a ceremony we called *Sulha*. The state of public peace in my village was by far better than in most similar communities that I came to know of later.

To sum up, my childhood days were happy ones. We lived peacefully and enjoyed warm relations with our Muslim neighbors. My father was a farmer like most everyone else in our village, but he was also a mason who helped other farmers build or repair their homes. My father's clients, like everyone else, tended to want their repairs done in inclement weather, but paved roads and motor transportation were nonexistent in our neighborhood, so this meant that many times my father would stay overnight at a client's home so he could finish a task. Since many of these clients were Muslims, in time my father had made many Muslim friends in our region – and was grateful for them.

When our village became the site of a weekly open market for nearby villages, many of my father's friends came to the market and then stopped by our home. Thus on market days my mother's work doubled because she had to prepare food for these guests. It was my job, as the only male in residence, to be ready to entertain these guests whenever my father was away on a job. This entertainment was taken very seriously because not only were we returning their hospitality, but these clients were important to our economic welfare. Although we had no metal beds to sleep on, laying our mattresses on the floor, we always had a special carpet to offer our Muslim guests for performing their prayers.

One fond memory especially stands out. Sometime in the mid-1940s my father felt we had to replace our home's traditional roof made of wood and earth with a concrete roof that would better protect us from the rain and snow that occasionally penetrated the muddy ceiling of our house. When he went to begin the project, he discovered he could not buy cement in the open market because the military efforts of the Second World War had tied up the entire available stock. Through the mysterious ways of the marketplace and my father's good Muslim friends, the Hlaihil family from Qadita, we not only secured the needed materials, but one bright morning I remember vividly we found a dozen men singing and working on our roof. By noon the concrete roof was finished and the lamb in the oven was ready for the festive meal that we gratefully served to our deserving guests.

This Hlaihil family, I am happy to say, managed like ours to stay in Israel after the 1948 war that turned most of our people into refugees. Our family was able to facilitate this because our homes were wide open to welcome them, and we offered them a temporary shelter during that war when they were forced to desert their homes in Qadita.

My mother also befriended a Muslim woman, Um Mahmoud who, like herself, had lost her firstborn son. The bereaved mothers became sisters in grief. I was born some two years later as was her second son, Mahmoud Yaseen Saa'd. The now happy mothers visited each other frequently, calling each other "sister." Mahmoud and I went to same school and parted ways only when my mother passed away forcing me to look for a new home and he lost his father, thus becoming the new head and provider of his family.

On the other side, my family also had fraternal relations with Jews. My mother's father, Jiryes Mansour, was partner with a

Jewish man from the nearby town of Safad shepherding a small herd of animals. Grandfather looked after the cattle in the spring and summer when the pasture was lush on our side of the Galilee mountains. During the autumn rainy seasons the cattle were moved to the land of another partner, a Muslim farmer who lived in the warm Jordan Valley. (In World War I my mother's only brother was killed in the service of the Ottoman sultan and his family needed urgent help. A Jewish partner helped my mother find work and she was forever grateful for this favor.)

So growing up, my experience of inter-faith relations in our village was clearly positive. Besides being the market town for the region, our rather large school offered seven years of schooling in an area where most villages had no schools of any kind. Some villages had a four-year primary school, but their pupils were not taught English – the most prestigious and career-promoting subject at the time – so our village eventually attracted hundreds of pupils who would walk five to ten kilometers daily to attend classes. Some, from a more distant area, rented rooms in our village so they could attend school. It was here that we as teenagers met students from surrounding Muslim villages who told us how often violent "troubles" erupted in their villages that were divided by clans and extended families.

All of us, however, were raised on the stories of our elders who remembered bitter experiences from their childhood under the Ottoman-Turkish rule. They described for us the rough anti-Christian policies and treatment of those years. During the dark days of Ottoman rule, members of my family were forced to cut their precious olive trees and carry the wood all the way to the Full and Afoul railway station to burn in the furnaces of Turkish trains. Since my father was too young to be drafted into the sultan's armies (unlike his unfortunate brother-in-law) he could study and he survived to tell about the *frareyyeh* – the military deserters who had lived in caves in the forests near their villages.

One of these deserters was my Uncle Fayyad who managed to escape the Turkish tyranny and move all the way across the Atlantic Ocean. His children and grandchildren still live in Lansing,

Michigan, but I don't know if my cousins have heard about the solemn funeral held for Uncle Fayyad in the village church before he left to set off for freedom. Afraid that he might be arrested and killed by Turkish soldiers, robbers or die from one of the many epidemic plagues that were common in those days, my father's family was unwilling to risk the possibility of an unconsecrated death so they arranged for Uncle Fayyad to have a Christian funeral, just in case – some 50 years before he actually passed away.

Later in my youth I developed strong anti-clerical feelings, coming under the influence of the great Lebanese-American writer, Jobran Khalil Jobran (famous as Kahil Gibran to English readers). Most Christian clerics around us in Galilee were Westerners whom I felt were foreigners. My protests tended to be verbal or passive, but once I did stand up to these clerics. As a newspaper reporter I was obligated to be objective and neutral in pursuing a story. This neutrality was tested when I was assigned to cover a rare public sermon in Nazareth by Billy Graham, one of the most famous preacher of the 20th century.

This famous American evangelist was the first person to arrive in Nazareth – the town where Jesus was raised modestly and where people continue to have modest means – in his own private plane. Most members of the small Evangelical communities in Nazareth and the neighboring villages gathered in the YMCA woods to listen to this guest, who had briefly walked the streets of this old city before his sermon, mainly to give the accompanying American photographers photo opportunities for their reports.

He opened his sermon by extolling his experience of walking the same roads Jesus had passed along and then, in what I felt was a rather theatrical style, be began to recite the Sermon on the Mount and finished by asking the entire gathering to kneel and repent.

I internally fumed. How could this extravagant American, swooping in his private metal bird over the tents of the truly hungry and poor, give lip service to the Sermon on the Mount? This self-centered American had no right to preach to our people.

But I was the only rebel in the crowd. Everyone else dutifully knelt and prayed. Even when those around me innocently asked me to join them, I refused, feeling it was my duty to protest against this towering man on his high platform overlooking the sloping valley where Jesus had humbly walked in bygone years.

I doubt anyone noticed my unbending knees. But it saddened me to feel that my silent protest against these over-fed Christians who preach to the poor and the oppressed went unnoticed. How dare these foreign Christians ignore my ancestors' share in spreading the faith and their sacrifice in holding up the banner of Christianity? They had paid a heavy price in preserving our faith – in obedience and love for our Redeemer – and I trust this book will contribute a modest share in lifting up their story.

My first hope with this book is to impress on all Westerners – believers, agnostics or atheists – that whatever they do or contemplate publicly vis-à-vis the Muslim world, their behavior is interpreted as a Christian act. This is especially true when they take a negative stand or look as if they are threatening Muslim interests.

This is equally true for Muslim fanatics who call an Arab Christian "a Crusader" any time they disagree with him or when they don't approve of something said by an Arab Christian. All too often Westerners have been ignorant of even the existence of Arab Christians, in some cases because colonial powers used us or failed to remember us when they concluded new alliances. Some missionaries embraced us warmly when we fellowshiped with them – and then reported us back home as their "gains" – especially since they were unable to talk to Muslims (by the law of the Ottoman state) or to Jews (as a result of the long history of animosity that created a huge gap dividing Old and New Israel). But soldiers and missionaries alike failed to report back home how they were perceived here: travelers, colonial soldiers, merchants or missionaries were all perceived primarily as Christians.

Basically, I am attempting through my personal experiences and observations to describe the historic experience of Christian Arabs along with their miraculous survival in the Holy Lands. I would also like to lift up the practical dimensions and potentials of interfaith dialogue among Christians, Jews and Muslims in the land that was privileged and sanctified by being chosen as the theater to the divine salvation of the human race. This miracle began when the angels announced to the virgin in Nazareth that she was chosen to be the mother of her Savior. That miracle continued up to his Resurrection and the angel's second announcement to the women: "Do not be alarmed; you are looking for Jesus of Nazareth, who was crucified. He has been raised; he is not here. Look, there is the place where they laid him. But go, tell his disciples and Peter that he is going ahead of you to Galilee; there you will see him, just as he told you" (Mk 16:6-7).

And in the Galilee of our days this miracle is still going on. Christian communities survived for 2,000 years under the rule of Roman and Byzantine, Muslim and Crusaders, under Arab and Turk, with Hebrews and Christians. They dream of a peaceful life under Jewish rule, just as they lived for centuries under Muslim rule. They continue to worship and expect Christ's Second Coming.

Therefore the first question that we must address, naturally and adamantly, is this: "Who are these Christians and where did they come from?"

2

Native Christians

*"A thorn was given me in the flesh, a messenger of Satan to tor-
ment me, to keep me from being too elated" (2 Cor 12:7b).*

Their historic narrative is not what unites native Arab Christians; rather it is their future prospects and fears that bring them
together as one tribe. Their story is not that of a closed, tightly
knit or well-identified community, for in their history they have
participated in various cultures and nations, playing myriad and
sometimes contradictory roles in these encounters. Generally you
find that native Christians have played an integral part in the entire history of the many cultures and political forces that have
roiled the Holy Land for the last 2,000-plus years.

At times these external forces proved almost fatal to the native
Christian population, but others had only marginal effect. For our
purposes we will explore the following churches: the Punic North
Africans, the Egyptian Copts, the Lebanese Maronites, the Syrian
Arabs, the Syrian Orthodox, the Iraqi Assyrians, and the Chal-
deans; we will trace how all these merged into forming the native
Christian populations of Israel/Palestine and Jordan.

The dawning of Christian history began with the Annunciation in Nazareth and the Nativity in Bethlehem, and culminated with Christ's death on the Cross, the Resurrection and Pentecost in Jerusalem. All these events took place in a small confined area called the Holy Land – also known as the land of Canaan, Eretz Israel, Palestine or the Promised Land. Its geography has long played a major role in its long history. Palestine for its entire history was the only natural strip of land bridging between the great cultures of the ancient Middle East. This land bridge was the only choice possible for armies charging from one of the surrounding regional empires in hot pursuit of conquering another army.

This small and relatively poor country between the Mediterranean Sea and the river Jordan was always too small to mount the necessary military force to stop the passage of these mighty armies coming from the basins of such major rivers as the Nile, the Tigris and the Euphrates. The Egyptians crossed this bridge on their way to Persia, and the Assyrians returned the favor when they advanced on Egypt. The Romans and Greeks found no other road, nor did the Muslim Arabs, the Turks or the Mameluks. The Fatimid Muslims, having left their home in North Africa, crossed this bridge to Damascus and Baghdad. Yet in these forays all these armies left their mark – greatly contributing to the natives during those many centuries, forcing them to learn and exchange ideas with others from the four corners of the known world.

From a military viewpoint, the Holy Land was an essential pathway and a necessary bridge, but it was far from being prosperous enough to provide for a major community to dwell there or maintain a military impediment to block invasions. Jerusalem, capital of this semi-arid land for the Jebusites, King David and the Crusaders, was one of those rare historic towns built far from any sea or river. David chose Jerusalem not only for its geographic centrality to his kingdom but also because it was a sacred site.

The pre-Christian history of Galilee is even more modest. This poor area had no economic significance nor could it boast any cultural fame. A mountainous zone between the kingdoms of Phoenician-Lebanon and Canaanite-Israel, Galilee failed to leave any apparent mark on the spiritual, political or military history of the Hebrew-Jewish kingdoms.

The Bible tells us Solomon gave Hiram, the Phoenician king in Tyre and his neighbor and ally, 20 cities in Galilee as a token of appreciation for his help in building the Temple. When Hiram visited these cities, he was not impressed and asked Solomon, "'What kind of cities are these that you have given me, my brother?' So they are called the land of Cabul to this day" (1 K 9:11-13). Later, in Isaiah and the Gospels we find further disparaging comments about this area. Christ's critics in Jerusalem told the admiring crowd to remember he came from Galilee and that "Surely the Messiah does not come from Galilee, does he? ... Search and you will see that no prophet is to arise from Galilee" (Jn 7:52).

But Galilee was the humble, happy land destined to be made holy by the Lord, who chose it for the first steps towards reconciliation between God and humankind. Here Jesus grew up and began bringing the good news to those in darkness. Here he began to build his church and to choose his first disciples in and around Nazareth, a city so humble and unimportant it is not mentioned in any Jewish historical or rabbinical text before his birth. In the same manner, for disciples Christ picked humble fishermen to become the proclaimers of the good news and the teachers of all humanity.

"In former time he brought into contempt the land of Zebulun and the land of Naphtali, but in the latter time he will make glorious the way of the sea, the land beyond the Jordan, Galilee of the nations. The people who walked in darkness have seen a great light and for those who sat in the region and shadow of death, light has dawned" (Is 9:1-2).

Galilee (or *Galil* in Hebrew) simply means "region." Why was the area called by this common name? One plausible explanation is to be found in Isaiah (9:1-2) where the area is called the Galil of the Goyyim (or the region of the nations – Gentiles, not the Jews). This leads us to speculate that the name Galilee is a shortened form of "Galil of the Gentiles." The nature of the area confirms such a name. It is a mountainous area, divided by steep valleys and narrow plains. These features made it a welcoming, warm nest for small, proud tribes who looked for refuge or wanted to build a castle to make themselves feel secure.

This area extends from the Great Sea, the Mediterranean, in the west to the river Jordan in the east and from Mount Carmel, Nazareth and the Sea of Galilee in the south to Solam Tsur (or Tyre Ladder) and Mount Hermon in the north. It borders with Syria in the east, Lebanon on the north, the open sea on the west and the fertile valleys in the south. The main and only reason for the fame of this area stems from the gracious honor bestowed on it by the Lord's life here some 2,000 years ago.

No longer can anyone claim this is an isolated area, forgotten by God. Here, as the Gospel tells us, Mary and Joseph had lived and back here they came after fulfilling their duties in Bethlehem and Egypt. "They returned to Galilee, to their own town of Nazareth. The child grew and became strong, filled with wisdom; and the favor of God was upon him" (Lk 2:39-40).

Here Jesus lived most of his time on our planet, laid the foundation for his church and chose his disciples. Here our race heard for the first time the eternal Sermon on the Mount; here was the Transfiguration on Mount Tabor and here he taught the people that the Messiah had indeed come and that peace was accomplished between God and humanity. Jesus did all that in this most humble theater, though, granted, the cornerstone for his Church was laid later in Jerusalem.

The birth of the church happened in Jerusalem:

> When the day of Pentecost had come, they were all together in one place. And suddenly from heaven there came a sound like the rush of a violent wind, and it filled the entire house where they were sitting. Divided tongues, as of fire, appeared among them, and a tongue rested on each of them. All of them were filled with the Holy Spirit and began to speak in other languages, as the Spirit gave them ability.
>
> Now there were devout Jews from every nation under heaven living in Jerusalem. And at this sound the crowd gathered and was bewildered, because each one heard them speaking in the native language of each. Amazed and astonished, they asked,

"Are not all these who are speaking Galileans? And how is it that we hear, each of us, in our own native language? Parthians and Medes, Elamites and residents of Mesopotamia, Judea and Cappadocia, Pontus and Asia, Phrygia and Pamphylia, Egypt and the parts of Libya belonging to Cyrene, and visitors from Rome, both Jews and proselytes, Cretans and Arabs – in our own languages we hear them speaking about God's deeds of power" (Ac 2:1-11).

So here the book of Acts tells us that 2,000 years ago people from all over the Middle East were firsthand witnesses of the birth of the Christian faith. This group, of course, included our Arab and Jewish ancestors who both listened to the Word and spread it.

Later on, Acts tells us, those first Jewish-Christians were divided into a multitude of sects. Some established the Universal Christian Church. Others, insisting on keeping the Mosaic law, formed the Church of Circumcision. There were also the Nazarenes who believed that Jesus Christ was just a divine person, not the Son of God, and the Ebonites who accepted him as a messiah, leader and teacher for his own people only (Briand 1984:10-11).

These sects were so fractious in their different points of view that they perceived the others as enemies. The Hebrew-Christians, for example, refused to defend Jerusalem during the siege in the year 70 and abandoned it to move to Pella in Transjordan. When Titus conquered Jerusalem, we are told the Jews were "exiled." What this actually meant is uncertain. Did the Roman fleet amass hundreds of thousands of Jews on board a fleet that sailed across the Great Sea, did their troops lead them like cattle for thousands of miles all the way to Rome or what?

Most probably this deportation of "the Jews" means the Romans selected a large sample from the leading (or potential) rebels and led them as slaves to Rome. Most Jews never left that land and the Jewish spiritual center moved to Yavneh (Jamnia or Janeh). About 70 years later there was another Jewish revolution against the Romans which was quelled by Hadrian in 135. At this point they were deported and enslaved in a huge multitude; many were killed in battle, others were sold in Hebron, Gaza or Egypt. "The price of a Jewish slave was no more value than a horse," writes

Emil Schurer in his classic book, *The Jewish People in the Times of Jesus*. Schurer says that although the Jews of Palestine during the second century were defeated, most of them continued to reside in that land, albeit many of them as slaves.

David Ben Gurion, Israel's first prime minister, when writing on this issue rejected the traditional theory that *all* Jews who lived in Palestine during the first-century rebellion were deported. According to Ben Gurion, this revolt, which resulted in the destruction of the Temple and the exile of the Jews by Titus in 70 AD, did not in fact exile most Jewish farmers. They never went into any exile but managed to cling to their land and survived in their villages. Some of them joined one of the many Christian groups or were converted to Islam at later stages; a few of them, certainly, managed to keep their Jewish faith (1931).

Eusebius, the bishop of Caesarea (265-340) and church historian writes of a flourishing Christian community in Jerusalem during the first century that, because of the Jewish anti-Roman revolt, was forced to move to Pella across the Jordan River. He also talks of a Christian community established in Sebastia. Acts tells us that St. Peter and other apostles were preaching, doing miracles and laying the foundation for the Christian communities in Lydda (9:32-35), Joppa – Jaffa of today (9:43), and Caesarea (21:8). "And all bishops were of the circumcision," or of Jewish birth.

In Nazareth and the neighboring Sepphoris we know about "relatives in the flesh of our Lord," who tilled the land and were also at the center of the young church. At the end of the first century two of these relatives, Zocer and James, sons of Jude, were sent to Rome for questioning but proved that they did not pose any danger to the Roman Empire and were released. One of their descendants, Conon, was not so lucky in the year 249. He was arrested and martyred in Pamphylia – Turkey today (Briand 1984:20).

Father Emmanuel Testa from the Franciscan Biblical Stadium of Jerusalem conducted the last archaeological digs in Nazareth in 1955-1960 just before the new Basilica of the Annunciation was built. These digs supplied us with added evidence supporting the idea that Christians, especially those of Jewish origin, have lived in Nazareth and Galilee since the days of our Lord and that Hebrew Christians were far more numerous than was previously assumed.

Testa wrote in his classic *Faith of the Mother Church* that the archaeological discoveries of the Stadium Biblicam Franciscanum of Jerusalem and the studies of Judeo-Christian theology done by J. Danielou changed the outlines of the church's primitive history. Now, he adds, it is well accepted that the Hebrew Christian church existed from the first to the eighth centuries. The many oven-like tombs (*kokhim* in Hebrew) of Dominus Flevit and the Jerusalem region are archaeological proof of this (Testa 1992:12).

There is good evidence that since the first century there have been Christian communities in the Lord's homeland. Today, 2,000 years later, when I look at historic maps from the first and second century showing those communities of Judeo-Christians in Palestine (Briand 1984:20), I shiver with excitement, for they include virtually the same towns and villages where Christians dwell today – beginning in the north with the village Al-Jish (historic Gush Halav, or Giscala), the village my ancestors were born and buried in. An identical map with the same Christian locations found a thousand years later during the Crusades is included in Joshua Prawer's book *The Crusaders: A Colonial Society* (1975:240). Against all odds, Christians have survived here down through the centuries.

Christian communities of local Syrian-Arabs were later found all around the country. In the 20th century one of these communities in Syria, the village of Maa'lula, proudly pointed out they still exist and speak the language their fathers shared with the Lord 2,000 years ago. Yet the most impressive location today is also a significant tourist site – Petra, the pink city carved in rock in southern Jordan. This capital of the Nabatean Arabs – and its minor sisters, Avdat and Shivta in the Israeli Negev – testifies to an ancient Christian culture.

The latest digs in these sites show the ruins of their churches. The official history of the Church adds more evidence to the spread of Christianity to the Arab clans. In the Council of Nicaea (in 325) a delegation of 14 bishops represented Palestine. In the

Chalcedon Council (in 451) the number doubled. We know that by then, an Arab Christian kingdom had risen on the Byzantine borders.

The Gassanid and Lakhmid dynasties of this region served as allies, vassals and guards against the desert frontier of that empire. Interestingly, the Greek contemporary historian and cleric Chrysostom Papadopoulos affirmed and recorded for us the theory of another Greek historian, Theofanos, who blamed Byzantine's minister of finance and his rude treatment of the Arabs for the fatal rift between Byzantine and the Arabs that drove the famous Christian Gassan horsemen to back the Muslim fighters against Byzantine in the battle for Syria. This also may explain why the tribal kings of Gassan Arabs have fought side-by-side with their Arab Muslim neighbors against Byzantine since 634 "out of rage and to revenge an insult" (1984:534).

Arab historians like Al Tabari support this theory, offering additional details about the Christian tribe of Gassan and their contribution to the swift advance of their Muslim allies into Syria and Iraq. He writes that thousands of brave, skilled Christian horse riders from Gassan took part in the decisive battle for domination of Syria: al Yarmuk in 636 (Nau 1933:100). Gassan knights also fought on the Persian front along with other Arab Christian tribes (Heyer 1995:94).

This alliance of Arabs – both Christian and Muslim – let F. Nau conclude that if the Byzantine political leadership had been wise enough to win the Arab Christians to their side, Syria would have been in a position to stand against the Arab-Muslim assault because he felt the Bedouins of Hijaz were less of a threat than those from Persia. German historian Fredrich Heyer, at the University of Heidelberg and author of a book on church history in the Holy Land, offers additional compelling evidence. He claims the 13,000 Christian knights who came to help the Muslims at the Yarmuk battle were "Monophysite" opponents of Byzantine – in other words, they were members of a group in conflict with the official Byzantine Christianity and were followers of the Church of the East (the Nestorians).

As a sidelight, the Greeks' pejorative term for Arabs was "the slaves of Sara," referring to the story of the patriarch Abraham's "marriage" to Hagar, the maiden servant-slave of his wife Sarah. It was Hagar who bore Abraham's son Ishmael, the "father" of all Arabs. Thus the reasoning that the Arabs, Ishmael's "children," are therefore slaves of Sara, the lady for whom their ancestress was a slave (Al Masa'oudi 1968:143), and called them *Sarakenoi* in Greek, a term that mutated in time to "The Saracens."

So did the Arab Christians betray their comrades of the faith, and if so, why? To answer this question we must examine the relationship between the two factions within the church in the East—a community that has been divided since the first century. The leading force in the region—the Byzantine empire and its church hierarchy (since Constantine)—failed to dominate the region; their weakness enabled the Persians to occupy Jerusalem in 614 and capture the Holy Cross. The legendary Byzantine Emperor Hercules succeeded, after lengthy efforts, in forcing the Persian Zoroastrians to free the Cross. In 630 the emperor himself brought the Cross back to its proper place in Jerusalem, just a few years before the Islamic Arab invasion of the land and their decisive triumph in the battle of Yarmuk.

Some ten years after the Cross was returned—and two years after the Yarmuk battle—Jerusalem was again facing an imminent danger. The fear of Muslim forces had already affected life in Jerusalem during the years of siege on the Holy City. On Christmas 634, Sofronious, patriarch of Jerusalem, complained that because Muslims were endangering the region's public peace, Christians were unable to march in their traditional procession from Jerusalem to Bethlehem (Papadopoulos 1984:535). The Byzantine Empire, in fact, had only a very short time in which it could attempt to heal its wounds from wars and recover its health (especially from the war in Persia) and to make peace with the Assyrians and the Arab Christians.

The schism that had caused severe damage and valuable loss of blood for the Christian church for centuries turned the diversity between kindred peoples. The Syrian Monophysite historian Abu al Faraj Ibn Al Ibri (1226-1286), known by the name Ber Hebraus, wrote: "God the almighty and vengeful Lord sent us the Arabs to rid us from the Greeks. They (the Muslims) did not strip us from our Churches, and every one maintained his own property. We became free from the cruelty of the Greeks and their hatred toward us" (Rabatt 1981:26).

The German historian Friedrich Heyer concludes, "The Syrians saw the Arab occupying forces as their saviours. The Armenians were granted a favorable treatment from the Muslim rulers, as compared to the way Muslims treated Byzantine Christians, the Muslims main enemy and the Armenians' traditional adversary" (Heyer 1995:97-98). Our contemporaries Bishop Yateem and Archimandrite Deek conclude, "The schism in the church was, at first, limited to the usage of different terms and did not touch on the theological substance. The schism came, later on, out of cultural and national motives" (1991:102).

There seems no reason to doubt it was more than religious beliefs that brought division to church ranks. Since these happened along national-cultural lines, it would be rational to assume that local patriotism and linguistic affinities played a major role in creating the warring camps. Of course, the schism added to and escalated polemic arguments and violence when the Monophysites were persecuted and later expelled from the Byzantine sphere of influence in the Persian Empire. This tragic story was repeated later against the Egyptian Copts and Arius (250-336) of Alexandria. Both Nestor and Arius were not in a powerful enough political position for them to challenge Constantinople's strong arm and domination.

The distinguished American-Lebanese historian Philip Hitti agrees, "There is no room for arguments about the motives of the dissenters. The inclination to stick to the Syrian church's beliefs was enhanced to a great degree by the national feelings of the faithful that they had to differentiate themselves from the Byzantine, the foreigners" (1958:206).

The political and military struggle inside the church paved the road for the birth of Islam. Some historians even claim that these wars created an impression that Islam was just another new Christian heresy.

Records show that the treatment Arab-Muslims gave their Christian associates varied. While in the beginning it was quite friendly and warm, it increasingly turned less friendly and in some cases it became clearly tyrannical. The obvious reason for these ups and downs is that, like any other religion, Islam is based on holy books and traditions that are interpreted by human beings under the influence of different interests.

While Christian Arabs survived in many countries under Islam rule, they did not thrive in the Arab peninsula – the original homeland of all Arabs, both Muslims and Christians. The reason for this is simple: the second Muslim caliph, Omar Ibn al Khattab, issued an order for the deportation of Christians from the Arabian peninsula based on the teaching of the prophet in a *hadith*: "There is no place for two faiths on the Arabs' (semi) island" (Al A'ayeb 1997:144-149). Thus the command in a explicit and direct *hadith*: "Expel both Jews and Christians from the Arabs' island" (Ibn Hanbal 1953:201).

Some historians cast doubt on the authenticity of this *hadith* and their reasons are quite compelling. Al Masa'oudi, a most respected Muslim historian from the golden age of the Muslim empire, wrote in the tenth century that the prophet signed treaties and agreements with Jewish and Christian communities. He could have expelled any of these communities at any time, especially at the later stages of his life when he had become sole master of the young Muslim state he had established. He could have forced them to accept the Muslim faith, but he refrained from doing that, except in one case when he accused one Jewish tribe of treason and conquered them without mercy. Another compelling fact that supports doubts about the authenticity of this *hadith* is this conjecture: Why would the first caliph Abu Bakr (al-Saddiq) disobey the prophet's command and not deport the Christians, especially when historians have no reason to doubt the sincerity of this pious and obedient follower of the prophet?

These doubts about the authenticity of this *hadith* make room for questions about the motives of this move in 13th year after the Hijra (or 635) – about the same year Omar's soldiers were fighting at the gates of Damascus – and what relation these events might have to the expulsion.

These doubts have been brushed aside by a Muslim historian's counterclaim that Najran Christians themselves asked the caliph to permit them to move to the southern parts of what is Iraq today, but others disclose what looks like reliable information to refute this claims. For example, we read that the leaders of these refugees asked the fourth caliph, Ali Ibn Abi Talib, some 15 years later to allow their return to Najran. Such an appeal by Christian leaders protesting their forced deportation by the second caliph and re-questing permission to return back home discloses their feeling that an ill-disposed act and an injustice had been done to them earlier. They hoped for a better treatment from Ali, the prophet's own cousin, son-in-law and most favored follower. Ali refused their plea saying, "Omar (Ibn al Khattab) had been righteous" (Abu Yousef 1396 H:80).

Ali's failure to acquiesce to their appeal must have been influenced by his own weak position and his attempts to rule the expanding Muslim empire amidst the fierce challenges he was facing from his rivals, the Umayyad dynasty, who subsequently won that war – killing Ali in the most famous struggle for power in Islam's history (661). The transfer of the Christians from the Arabian peninsula, especially those of Najran tribes, who kept to the letter their treaty with the Muslim prophet, is worth mentioning since many Muslim tribes turned their back on Islam after the death of the prophet, and the caliph had to reconquer these tribes and force them into submission in the Redda Wars.

The Via Dolorosa of the Arab Christians under Muslim rule knew many fluctuations during 1,400 years. The most tolerant treatment came during the early stages, under most caliphs of the Umayyad dynasty and some of the Abbasid. To generalize, we might describe the Christians' life as reasonable during the sunny days and grim when Muslim rule was corrupt and the Muslims themselves were in trouble.

A consistently unfriendly treatment was to come later, with the advance of new Muslim converts from non-Arab backgrounds such as the Persians, Afghans, Kurds, Turks, Mongols, et al. These nations were conquered in central Asia, and step-by-step they replaced the Arabs as the soldiers of the Muslim empire. In turn, they refused to allow any special privileges to non-Muslim Arabs and in fact were annoyed to discover some Arabs who refused their new faith. Historians such as Albert Hourani (1972-1973) claim it is easy to list Muslim caliphs by their tolerant policy on parallel lines with the level of liberty that Christians experienced in relation to Arab-Muslims.

Beyond this, there is another complicating element. Some of the Christian communities under Muslim rule were trying to keep friendly relations with church authorities either in Byzantine, the Vatican or Moscow. Since these capitals often maintained hostile relations with the Muslim world, the Muslim rulers felt justified in doubting the local Christian's allegiance and loyalty. Thus the rulers kept the local Christians under surveillance and far from any influence on the life of Muslim community. One example is that Christians were not allowed to be food merchants so they could not threaten the Muslims' food supply. Nor were they permitted to ride horses or train in military cavalry games.

Another compelling question comes to mind. Since Christians were forced out of the Arabian peninsula, why didn't they survive under Muslim rule in North Africa as Christians did in Egypt, Iraq, Syria, Lebanon, Palestine, Israel and Jordan? What was so different in the North African countries of Morocco, Algiers, Tunisia and Libya? Why was the homeland of St. Augustine deserted by the flourishing communities that had resided in these lands for hundreds of years before Muslim rule? What made Egyptian Copts, Lebanese Maronites, Syrian Arabs, Iraqi Assyrians and Chaldeans survive while Christians in North Africa disappeared?

The simple and clear answer is that North African Christianity was not a native and deep-rooted community but one of Punic settlers from Lebanon or Europe, or a mixture of both. Most of the faithful were members of foreign urban communities, while Egyptian Copts at the time of the Muslim invasion were entirely Egyptian natives – including their church leadership and its rank and file. They were entirely Egyptian, speaking their own language and proud of their Egyptian-Christian heritage – with a long history in rural and urban segments of the Egyptian community.

For a detached observer, the fact that all of the North African region is entirely "clean" of native Christian presence is easier to comprehend than in the case of those countries in which the adamant Christians are still there. It is difficult to understand why the coercive Muslim rule failed to conquer these Christians and make them convert to the Muslim faith. The non-Arab Muslims seem to have been more annoyed by the simple fact that after generations of established Islam, they encountered Arabs who persisted in refusing Muhammad as prophet and that these Christians were willing to pay the price for their adamant defiance for most of the last 2,000 years.

Little wonder that historians seem unanimous in claiming the most ruthless treatment for Christians as *Dhimmis* was to come from the *Mawalis,* those Christians and Jews converted to Islam who were eager to prove both to the Muslims and themselves they were zealous in their new faith (Hitti 1958:300).

Anyone trying to understand the basic hurdles for Muslim and Christian coexistence should dwell on some basic facts:

1 – Islam's theologians do not claim their religion is a new and independent revelation from Judaism and Christianity. On the contrary, they posit that Islam is a renewal of the Abrahamic religion and Abraham, according to Islam, was a Hanafi, a member of a "natural" monotheistic religion. Moses and Jesus (*Iessa*) came to the people with holy revelations, but their teachings were not kept and preserved by their followers – the Jews and Christians – in their totality as a complete message. So Mohammed came as the last seal, to introduce the Koran as the last and perfect message. Ibn

Khaldun, the great Muslim historian, recites a *hadith* attributed to the prophet of Islam: "Every baby is born on the *Fitra* (nature) believing in one Creator, God. The parents turn the child into a Jew, Christian or Zoroastrian" (Ibn Khaldun 1964:215).

2 – Islam is the *Fitra* (natural) religion and so was Abraham's faith. So Abraham, Adam and all the other biblical characters were Muslims. St. John the Damascene (676-749), who lived in the early days of the Umayyad dynasty in Damascus, described Islam as another monotheistic heresy. The saint was intimately acquainted with Islam and Muslims of his day because he lived in the caliph's palace as the son of the minister of finance and grew up in the company of young princes and scholars. Later in life he opted for an ascetic life, joining the Mar Saba monastery in Bethlehem, becoming a great Christian theologian famed for defending the Holy Cross and the icons of saints in a famous discussion with Muslim scholars – who had accused Christians of idol worship because they displayed icons in their churches. St. John's riposte was to ridicule those who consider the black stone (of the pre-Islam idols' house of Quraysh the Ka'aba) as holy and challenged the Muslims' reverence toward the Ka'aba while they rejected the images of the holy saints which were meant to cause veneration and remind the faithful of the saints' contributions.

Still Islam demands that the faithful revere Jesus Christ, the only prophet born from the spirit of God, Allah, and from his unique mother, the blessed virgin Merriam. Philip Hitti considers the claim that Islam began as a Judeo-Christian sect (as per the Lebanese scholar Fr. Yousef Haddad [1982]) sheer exaggeration, but he notes the historic evidence that Muhammad grew up in a monotheistic community and was, according to him, related to Umayyeh Ibn Al Salt (c. 624) a spiritual leader in an obscure, primitive cult of monotheists called in Arabic history *Haneefs* (1958:152).

On the other hand, it is a well-established historical fact that Waraqah Ben Nawfal, the uncle of Mohammed's first wife, was a Christian cleric or a Hebrew-Christian bishop. Historians all agree that many faithful members and groups from the Church of Circumcision arrived in Mecca during the period Islam was born and that persecuted Monophysite, Nestorians of Syria, Iraq and Egypt were welcomed by the new conquerors and immediately integrated into the establishment of the new state (Hitti 1958:257-261).

The Muslim classic historian Al Masa'oudi adds some details about the affinity of Islam with Christianity. A certain monk called Nestor met and encouraged young Muhammad to believe in his holy message. "At the time Muhammad was 25 years old, he went for a commercial trip [to Damascus] on behalf of a lady called Khadijeh, daughter of Khwailed, accompanied by her servant Mysara. This monk, Nestor, noticed a special cloud hanging over him, which revealed that he was destined to become a prophet. When Mysara arrived in Mecca, he told Khadijeh and she sent messengers to Muhammad to propose to him to marry her" (op cit 197).

The first Muslims were certainly eager in the early stages of Islam to establish the best possible links with the Christians – including Islam's founders. One can also learn about the affinity of Islam with both Judaism and Christianity by observing the treatment Muslim rulers gave their Christian (and Jewish) subjects. The Koran records that the prophet learned about the Persian victory against the Christian "Rum" (Greeks) in 616 and was saddened. The Holy Koran revealed to him that the Christians were to win soon and cause joy in the ranks of the believers (Sorat Al Rum 2:5).

Historians tell us that at one point Muhammad sent a group of his followers to seek refuge across the Red Sea in Christian Ethiopia, and the emperor of that land granted them the needed refuge. Some of the Muslim texts seem quite similar (not identical) to that of the Christian (and Jewish) texts of the history, but it is surprising to find parallel lines to Christian visions as well.

Philip Hitti cites the famous vision of heaven written by the greatest Syrian scholar, Saint Efram le Syria (c 373), which is quite similar to Islam's description of the promised heavens. The Syrian sage advises his listeners not to drink wine and promises them, if they oblige, to find rivers of wine in Paradise. If they obey the rules of chastity, angels with pure breasts shall welcome them (op cit 143-144). Islam's vision of paradise is a similar evergreen garden of ripe fruits and milk rivers filled with the most enchanting virgins and angels.

It appears to me from my historical research that the first Muslim governors of the Fertile Crescent countries (Palestine, Lebanon, Syria and Iraq of our days) were quite liberal and prudent in dealing with their non-Muslim subjects – and certainly far more liberal than other ancient conquerors. For the most part Muslim conquerors usually welcomed the defeated population to embrace Islam on an equal footing with other Muslims, but also allowed them to keep the faith of their ancestors for a price. The Muslims had their reasons for adopting such a tolerant policy: they were fighters, merchants and nomad-herds people, not farmers and had little desire to take up this "despicable" trade.

A most striking example of how Islam looked down on farming is found in an episode mentioned in al Muqaddamah of Ibn Khaldun. In Medina, the prophet noticed tilling tools in the house of one of his allies (Ansar) and was quite annoyed. "These [tools] do not enter a house unless accompanied by humiliation." The reason for such a strange attitude is not irrational. The first Muslims, including the founder, were traders, fighters and merchants and thus these trades are hailed and praised in Muslim tradition. But Muslim fighters were discouraged from indulging in farming since such activity was seen as an inevitable bad influence on a soldier who would be reluctant to abandon his fields for war campaigns (op cit 703).

Soon after the occupation of Syria, the Caliph Omar ordered his followers not to divide the spoils in newly occupied territories – towns, villages and estates. He directed his generals to depart from the traditional practice for the spoils of war and not to interfere or interrupt the life of the local Christian farmers who paid the head tax (al jizya) "and [by doing this] feed the Muslims. And their children will feed the Muslims' children as long as they survive and they shall be the slaves of the Muslims as long Islam dominates" (Hamid Allah 1987:484).

Thus both Christians and Jews were allowed to practice their rituals provided that they paid the head tax and behaved in a humble way. This tax, according to early Muslim principles, was supposed to compensate the Muslims for the fact they were defending the non-Muslims residing in the Muslim state while the Christians and Jews were exempted from military duty.

One case is cited where the Muslim commander of Homs in north Syria refunded this tax to the local Christians before withdrawing his forces from that city in face of a Byzantine counterattack because he was unable to deliver his part of the deal and confer on them the security they had paid for (Farsakh 1994:59). This was certainly a rare case. In most cases, the *jizya* was meant to collect as much money as possible from the able "protected population" (non-Muslims) and humiliate them for refusing to accept the Muslim faith and surrender to Allah's will. This humiliation stemmed directly from a koranic order (*Sorat Al Tawbah* 9:29).

The Homs incident shows one side of how Islam was interpreted, but there are other aspects to Islam justice. One story says the prophet ordered his followers "to stone three people riding together on the back of a [miserable] donkey," to prove how merciful the prophet of Islam was in the treatment of animals. So Muslim history is far from being pacifist. After all, the prophet himself took part in military battles and led his followers in wars. At one point he even gave orders to execute two opponents – one of them because he wrote poetry praising his enemies and ridiculing him (Al Karim 1993:447).

The divided Eastern Christians did not unite to face the threat of Islam. On the contrary, many welcomed the new masters. There was, however, an exception to this rule. The Marada in the mountains of northwest Syria fought back and established "a copper fortress" separating the Muslim and Byzantine territories in Asia Minor. For two long generations they became permanent nuisances for the Muslim caliphs. In the seventh century some of the Muslim kings of Damascus, like Mua'awiya and Abd al Malek, paid a tribute to the Marada to maintain peace on their mutual borders and to be free to defend the eastern frontiers of their kingdom (Hitti, op cit 268-269).

Most Christians of the Eastern churches were on the other side. The Assyrians and Chaldeans felt relieved by the Arab Muslim rule. "After some disturbing periods of persecution under the Persians, [the local subjects] were hoping that this new power may turn more humane and merciful. [They based these hopes mainly on] linguistic nearness between the Syrian language and Arabic—since both languages are daughters of Aramaic. Add to this the simple fact that Islam was a monotheist religion, based on a similar narrative to the Biblical familiar chronology, unlike the Zoroastrian religion of Persia" (Abuna 1991:146).

Local church leaders, however, did not surrender to the new predicament without a struggle. To save their Christian community in its new situation of total isolation from Rome and Byzantine's spiritual authority, they decided to take the necessary initiative and act on their own. Monks like Theodore Abu Qura (750-825) from St. Saba monastery near Jerusalem translated Christian theology from the Greek and Aramaic originals into the Arabic language. In the period before the Crusades, many others wrote and translated texts into Arabic. These works are to be found today mainly in faraway academic libraries in St. Petersburg, Strasbourg or St. Catherine's monastery in the Sinai (Heyer 1995:100-101).

During this period, the mood in the Syrian community was definitely anti-Greek—possibly as a result of some inner controversy between Christians who blamed the others for their support of the Muslim invasion. The most blunt anti-Greek condemnation in an ancient Christian text on this subject is found in the patriarchal message of Michael, known as Michel le Syrian, the leader of the Syrian church in the twelfth century:

> Because God is the greatest avenger, able to do everything and he only replaces the kingdom of evil as he wishes and bestows grace to whomever he wishes. He raises the meek in place of the arrogant; and because he saw the crimes committed by the Greeks in plundering our churches and monasteries and torturing us mercilessly he brought the children of Ishmael to liberate us from the Greek heavy yoke, their evil, hate, persecution and atrocities against us (Rabatt 1986:26).

This is not the only witness to the Greek treatment of the Eastern Church. Hitti (143-144) quotes another Syrian church leader who depicts the Muslim rule as "sent by the Lord to rule the Universe at this point in time. They live in our midst and take no negative attitude against Christianity. On the contrary, they revere our faith and respect our clergy and saints and donate tributes to churches and monasteries."

Few dispute the claim that Muhammad had come under some Christian influence, most likely from Hebrew Christians. The most accepted Muslim biography of Muhammad, *Seirat Ibn Hisham*, recounts that Waraqah Ben Nawfal, cousin to Khadejeh—Muhammad's first wife, "was a Christian, fluent in the scripture" (Al Kheyami 1990:51). Besides being his first wife, Khadejeh was also the employer and benefactor of the founder of Islam. "Islam was established by Khadejeh's funds" (ibid 67).

Dr. Salwa Balhaj Saleh Al A'ayeb, a contemporary Tunisian Muslim scholar, confesses in her analysis of the division of these Christian churches that she is unable to comprehend why they did not join forces, except in rare cases, to fight against the Muslims. She feels that: "Christianity failed as a religious faith to mold those from Arab roots who embraced it into a crystallized entity, before or after Islam" (1997:226). In fact, some Christians embraced Islam and freed themselves from paying the head tax and shared in plundering the occupied towns, collecting what was seen as the fighters' legal right—the bounty from those that resisted them and who refused to surrender.

During the conquest, if a man fought on horseback he was entitled to more booty because the division of the spoils allocated one share for a fighter and two for the horse (Rabbat 1986:28). Still, some Arab tribes were so dedicated to their Christian faith they were ready to pay the full price, as did the Najran, Tanoukh, Gassan and Taghlib who paid the special tax and submitted to the discriminatory treatment. One exception to this was the large tribe of Taghlib, who refused to pay the *jizya*. Instead, they contributed to the Muslim victories and won the right not to pay the tax on the condition they would pay twice as much as Muslims paid in another tax, the *sdaqah*. Caliph Omar added another reason why the Muslims ought to exempt the Gassan tribe from paying the head tax saying: "Don't humiliate the Arabs" (Azzam 1964:238).

To understand the significance of the head tax on the Christian and Jewish subjects for the budget of the Muslim state, in the later stages when the expansion and the Jihad wars came to a lull, a great historian states, "Whenever the *Dhimmis* used to embrace Islam in big numbers, the financial affairs of the state and the state itself, were shocked in a surprising way" (Triton 1931:10).

In a famous instance, the Muslim governor of Egypt wrote to the caliph in Damascus about the decline of the state revenue because Egyptians were embracing Islam in growing figures. The governor then asked for a special permit to keep imposing the tax on new converts as well. This particular caliph, Omar Ben Abd al Aziz, known as the most pious caliph of the Umayyad dynasty, was outraged and refused the proposal: "Mohammed was sent [by Allah] to lead and show the right way, not to be a tax collector" (Azzam op cit:126).

The history of the Christian Arab clans, especially those from the Gassan royal dynasty of the clan Jafna, whose capital was called Harta (Aramaic for camp; *al Hira* in Arabic), was well known from the first Christian century and the early Muslim days. Under the command of their king, Jabla ibn al Ayham, and his children, Kalb and Taghlib, these Syrian Christians not only fought on the side of the Muslims, as mentioned, but Mansour Serjius, father of St. John the Damascene, became minister of finance at the caliph's palace. Another member of his family, Serjon Ben Mansour, and other Christian Syrians served as "script" for the Caliphs Marwan, Abd al Malik, Yazid and Mua'awiya.

That these Christians welcomed the Muslim occupation does not justify any serious doubts about the authenticity of their Christianity or their Arabness. They were just as Arab as the Quraysh, the strong tribe dominating Mecca of which the prophet was a descendant. Some of this tribe were Christians, like the aforementioned Qess (Reverend) Waraqah Ben Nawfal, uncle to Khadi jeh, Mohammed's first wife, and head of the Hebrew-Christian community in Mecca.

Fr. Haddad has done extensive comparisons of the text of St. Matthew's gospel ("the Gospel of the Hebrews") with the Koran and has concluded there were influences of the Hebrew Christians on Muslim dogma. He believes Muhammad was tutored by and fell under the influence of this uncle, the Hebrew-Christian cleric (Haddad 1982). Muslim scholars tend to find such suggestions insulting and try to refute them (Saleh 1965:44-45).

We must recognize that one's belonging to a particular nation or race should not be seen as a great privilege or, on the contrary, a cause for shame. However, for many Arabs this issue is a cause for heated arguments. Through the ages, myriad Arab scholars have attempted seriously to answer these frivolous questions: Who is an Arab? Are the Arabs one or many nations? At times we read an Arab polemicist claiming that the Pharaohs, the Phoenicians, the Canaanites, the Philistines, or the Jebusites were Arabs. Obviously, those who claim this want to manipulate history in order to achieve some political gain or counter the Zionist-Jewish claims over Palestine that the Jews came there first to live and have been longer in that land, so have historic claims to priority in Palestine.

There are also those who mix the Muslim religion with Arabism and those who use language as a yardstick for the right to claim such an "honor." The facts are simple. The Muslim holy book was written in Arabic and some Muslim theologians claim Arabic is the official language in heaven. Arabs and Muslims were rulers of a great empire stretching over three continents for many centuries. Some *hadith* attributed to the founder of Islam spoke of the Arabs' special features and superior qualities, and these teachings stimulate much pride and deep desire in many Muslim groups to belong to this special nation (Ibn Khaldun op cit:394). Black African states like Somalia and Mauritania have succeeded in this and are accepted as full members in the Arab League. The prime minister of Eritrea, Assassi Aforqi, does not rule out submitting an application on behalf of his country to join this regional organization of Arab states (*Al A'rabi* 5/22/1999).

We are left with several kinds of Arabs. Some are called Arab *Baida* (extinct) and are found only in folk tales or history books. Others are *A'rab A'areba* (genuine Arabs) who claim a centuries-long family lineage in an Arab tribe. Then there are the *A'rab Mostaa'ribah* (the *Arabasides*, the new Arabs) who were integrated into the Arab community after shedding other cultural features (such as a special way of life, loyalty and allegiance, dress, language, music or food). A new brand of Arabs consists of those who aspire to become Arab in order to achieve special Muslim status or to cash in on the Arab oil bonanza.

All of these folk call themselves Arabs, are referred to as Arabs and are considered as such by the Arab League—and are therefore entitled (especially when they are Muslims) to boast of being members of the same nation as the messenger of Allah, the last, the seal of the prophets. "That the shari'ah (Muslim law) is their Allah's binding law and that his commands and rulings illuminate their path between the nations while the others failed to notice it" (Ibn Khaldun, ibid:789). To confirm this claim some quote a *hadith* attributed to the Muslim prophet in which he said: "What makes a person Arab is that he uses the Arabic tongue."

Other scholars recite contradicting *hadith*. Ibn Khaldun reminds us that al Zohari, one of the *hadith* tellers and fuqaha (learned) said that fuqaha tediously tried to differentiate between the *hadith* verses and to distinguish the valid from the fake or the extinct *hadith*—but in vain (Amin 1983:58-59). This issue of the authenticity and truth of the *hadith* is one of the most disturbing problems for Muslim scholars, but can also become the most promising hope for an alternative Muslim school to face the current wave of fundamentalism. One can find in these *hadith* quite different and sometimes contradicting approaches.

If one turns the issue into a numerical illustration, it may become clearer. Abdullah Al Bukhari, one of the main authorities in collecting Mohammed's *hadith*, accumulated some 600,000 *hadith*. After checking and verifying, he dropped the figures to 7,397 reliable ones, but these complete—true (*sahih* in Arabic) *hadith* included many repetitions and thus the real figure is just 2,763, or one out of more than 200 "apocryphal" *hadith* (Amim 1983:58-59).

This short treatment of the ongoing debate of how to define an Arab and of how Muslims view the authenticity of *hadith* is meant simply to indicate that many Arabs are kept busy discussing these issues. There have been many attempts to come up with a generally accepted consensus, but no one can claim that all of the above groups are Arabs, or that just some of them are Arabs.

One should pause for a moment and ask the question: Is this issue of any substantial significance? Philip Hitti, the Lebanese-American historian, found that Arabs, more than any other group of people, emphasize and are deeply interested in this practice of defining their ancestral roots. Thus in the process, they elevated their "ethnic belonging" to a scientific level.

Some Arabs indulge in this practice to prove their family line, hoping that this search will lead to the "discovery" and recognition of their noble origin, or their legitimacy as royalty or nobility. The king of Egypt, Fuad (whose son, King Farouk lost his throne in a military coup d'état in 1952), busily looked for his royal family line, despite the known fact that his grandfather Mohammed Ali, came to Egypt at the turn of the 19th century as an officer of an Albanian contingent to fight against the French occupation. King Fuad decided to promote himself from being the King of Egypt (and Sudan) to the caliph of all Muslims. Even though the facts contradicted his majestic wishes, he was looking for some theological authority to declare him as related to the Muslims' prophet and therefore entitled to that title and post, as it was vacant at that time. By this move, he hoped to block the way of Hashimites and Saudis to the throne of Islam's caliph (Assaf 1967:272).

In fact the Hashimite monarchs (of Iraq and Jordan) were active in building a force that supports their aspiration to ascend to this throne, in the footsteps of the Sharif Hussein, the deposed governor of Mecca and Medina. Hussein made an abortive attempt to establish a new dynasty of caliphs when he declared himself the Muslim caliph on March 11, 1924 (Assaf 1967:272). Quite a few supported him but many more of the Muslim allies of Great Britain were antagonized, including the Indian Muslims, Saudia Arabia, Egypt and Palestine.

On the 13th of May 1926 an international pan-Islamic congress was convened in Cairo by the Egyptian government hoping to rally their support for Fuad in his pursuit for the title of Muslim's caliph. About the same time a rival congress met in Mecca in Saudia, but its fate was not better than the Egyptian and Hashimite initiatives. These moves and the 80 years that transpired since the post was abolished prove that in the modern Muslim world many aspire to the title – but in vain (Qatar 1982:115-122).

The Hashimite declaration came just one week after Ataturk (Mustafa Kamal), the founder of the secular Turkish Republic, abolished the role of the Muslim's caliph in Turkey, declaring this de facto royal system void on March 3, 1924. Sharif Hussein Ben Ali, the Sheik of the Hashimites (who claim to be descendants of the prophet's Quraysh tribe and of Hashim, the prophet's uncle) declared himself heir to the post. But no power with appropriate muscle was willing to force this old man from that post.

This was not the only instance in history where an ambitious Arab tried to improve status by digging for a "better" family lineage in order to achieve a political goal or position of power. Some contemporary Maronite Catholics in Lebanon claim to be descendants of the Marada who fought against the Muslim invasion in Syria while some radical Syrian nationalists, both Muslims and Christians, refuse to be called Arabs, insisting they are members of the Syrian nation and thus heirs to the Assyrians/Aramaic/Phoenician cultures – hoping thereby to unite the Syrian nation as a geo-political entity (Al Kattar 1982:115-122). These claims are based on the lines laid by Anton Sa'adeh and his political legacy – which in turn rests on the claim that the Syrians are a unique race, separate from the other Arabic-speaking nations (Saa'adeh 1937).

Many realistic people, from all Arab religious denominations, acknowledge the fact that the current population of Syria, Iraq and Egypt is a blend of massive accumulations of great nations and cultures that have forged the ancient history of these lands. None of these nations ever "evaporated," but rather, as is to be expected, integrated and assimilated with the newest group who had conquered them. Since the Muslim Arab invasion came later in history and focused on a religious call and a universal holy text (in Arabic), this enabled the Arabs to win the entire region.

Thus one can say that the modern population of Lebanon, Jordan and Iraq is a mixture of all peoples and cultures that were integrated before Islam and since its rule. Dr. Butrus Butrus-Ghali, the world's best-known Egyptian Christian Copt and the U.N. general secretary, has said that being an Arab is an ideology. Those who can claim to be "pure" Arabs by origin comprise perhaps a sixth of the 60 million Arabs who are descendants of Copts, Assyrians, Nobi, Aramaic and Phoenician nations (Sima'an n.d.:46).

Hisham Djait, a historian from the University of Tunis, defines an Arab in a novel way, claiming that the three consistent elements in the Arab identity throughout the ages are ethnic origin, language and the nomadic way of life. Zaki Al Arsuzi, a respected ideologist of the Arab Baa'th Party (currently ruling Syria), sees Bedouins as the ideal character of the Arabs and calls pre-Islamic days the golden era of Arab nationalism (1972: 236-237). To prove a "pure" ethnic origin is not possible in most cases, as was shown above; language is a positive and objective criterion. But why should Arabs be considered nomads? The Arab linguist Ibn al Manthour (Ben Makram, 1232-1311) offered a coherent explanation some 750 years ago when he wrote in his famous dictionary, *Lisan Al A'rab*, that the term "*Arab*" is identical to what we call "nomads" or "Bado" in contemporary Arabic (first published in 1882).

The Lebanese Butrus Al Bustani (known by Arabs in the modern liberal age as "the teacher"), was the author of one of the first and best modern Arabic dictionaries (*Moheet al Moheet* 1870). He agreed with Ibn al Manthur that "Arab" and "Nabat" are two terms used to describe a way of life. Sedentary tribes, those who began to live permanently in one place and practice farming and agricultural production were called Nabat. The nomads – desert shepherds who roamed from one oasis to another looking for water and green meadows to feed their cattle – were called Arabs. To demonstrate the usage of these terms Al Bustani says, "The people of Oman are

Arabs that became Nabat and those of Bahrain are Nabat that became Arab."

The interchangeable usage of the terms "Bedouin," "nomads," and "Arab" is quite ancient and still in vogue. One encounters this usage listening to villagers in Galilee today or reading modern Egyptian literature, like that of the famous novelist Abd al Rah man al Sharqawi who in describing life in a village calls the Bedouins who camp near villagers "Arabs," as did Abd Al Rahman A Jabarti, the Egyptian historian who lived in Egypt at the turn of the 19th century and the Lebanese-American writer Khalil Gibran during the early 20th century (Jabarti 1997:80; Gibran 1994:45).

The Nabateans were linguistically Arab, Aramaic in their writings and Greek-Roman in their architecture. As such, their culture was basically a Hellenic one in appearance, but an Arab one in substance and culture. The Nabats were the ones who introduced the alphabet to the nomadic clans in the Arabian peninsula and the first Arabic text extant was written in Nabatean in 321 and found in al Namarneh (Hitti 1958:427). One of the oldest texts witnessing to the existence of the Nabats is found in the Act of the Apostles which tells us Saul-Paul was arrested in Damascus during the reign of Al Hareth (Aretas), one of the Nabatean kings (2 Co 11:32).

Later on, especially under the Abbasid dynasty in Baghdad, the term Nabat was used pejoratively to indicate a non-Arab or one whose Arabic language was not "pure" (Hitti 1958:534). This usage remains current today, for Arabic poetry in "broken" language is termed "Nabat". It should be noted that since poetry is considered virtually a sanctified art in the Arab culture, it is necessary to abide by and accept assiduously all the ancient rules and regulations ascribed to the art in order to be utterly "pure" of diversions and renovations. Only in the last 50 years have a few modern poets dared challenge this universal consensus – which has opened a hole, though not a big one – for new winds to blow in the arena of ancient poetry that dominates Arab cultural life.

Since the Nabats lived in territory bordering the Roman Empire's frontiers, with the Syrian peoples on one side and the Arabian desert on the other, this brought them under the influence of

Byzantine religion, language and architecture—alienating them from their nomad desert kin and making them look suspect.

It is interesting how this treatment of the old Nabat society can be compared to some current attempts to cast doubts on how "genuine" a culture is. Today there are those who question the national loyalty of members of the Lebanese/Syrian/Palestinian Christian community or those Muslim graduates of European institutes of education who speak French and English and interject foreign words in their spoken Arabic. Often called Levantine (of the Levant), they are suspected of being shallow with only a cursory knowledge of the Arabic language while imitating aliens and taking external appearances too seriously (Sharabi 1987:35).

One may conclude from this exploration of the term "Arab" that no definition is universally accepted—all are met with doubt and ambiguities. This certainly happened during the early stages of modern Arab national activity. The first Arab Congress held in Paris in June 1913 was called "The Arab-Syrian Congress" and the term "Arab-Syrian" was used repeated throughout the eleven resolutions drawn up during this meeting (Hurewitz 1956:268).

The countries of the Arabian peninsula, Egypt and other North African countries were excluded from the meeting. Najeeb A'azouri, the organizer of this congress, was a Syrian-Christian who worked on the staff of the corrupt Turkish governor of Jerusalem (1898-1904) and personally witnessed the Ottomans' anti-Arab practices, which included resorting to any and all means in pursuit of personal wealth—including facilitating sales of Arab farms to Zionist settlers. A'azouri exposed some of these nefarious practices in the Egyptian press in 1904 and the next year published a book in France calling for an Arab national revival (A'azouri Paris 1905).

The conservative view claims that "pure" Arabs are those born from an Arab family with direct links to an Arab tribe. Such people claim—either proudly or humbly—that they are genuine Arabs. A few theorize that to be Arab both nationality and religion are part of the parcel. In this camp we find Abd al Rahman Azzam Pasha, the first secretary-general of the Arab League (the regional political organization that leaders of Arab states established in 1945 to facilitate more coöperation and amicable relations). This Egyptian diplomat and scholar, appointed to head the organization, wrote in most decisive terms in *The Eternal Message*,

There is no room to differentiate between Islam and Arab. The Mohammedans Call does not recognize the national and racial principles, as they are known today. The homeland of a Muslim has no physical borders. The homeland spreads and stretches with the Faith, because it is really a moral issue. A Muslim is brother to other Muslims, any place they live, in an adjacent country or on the other side of the globe (1964:1556).

He failed to notice that one of the founding members of the League, the Republic of Lebanon, was not Muslim and that prominent members of the important delegations from Egypt and Syria were Christians like Makram Obeyed, the Egyptian minister of finance and Faris Khouri, the Syrian prime minister (Goren 1958:377; Said n.d.:414-415).

Today, 55 years after the Arab League was established, its membership includes the African state of Somalia where, according to the *Encyclopedia Britannica*, the Arab population forms only 1.2% of the total population. Another member state is Mauritania, where 70% of the population is black African. Eritrea, which has nine official languages (none of them Arabic), may join soon (Al Ahram Al A'rabi May 1999). Israel, the state of the Jewish people, is also entitled to join the Arab League since at least 20% of Israeli citizens are Arabs and about half of the population speak Arabic. Some Israeli politicians believe this is not such a ridiculous idea as it may seem at first, especially if Israel wants to normalize its relations with the rest of the Middle East.

Professor Ismael al-Farouqi, a Moslem teacher at Temple University in Philadelphia, wrote many books promoting another view. In his first book on the subject he wrote:

Arabs include, unlike any other people on earth, millions of non-Arabic speaking persons living in territories adjoining the Arabic speaking lands, but stretching from Siberia to the Philippines, the Danube River to Equatorial and Eastern Africa, who represent comparatively higher or lower degrees of Arabness. But Arabs they all are, since their consciousness is determined by the values of Uruba, but represents those determinants to itself as elements of and in terms couched exclusively by Arab consciousness (Al Farouqi 1961:9).

There seems to be no easy way to settle this debate. It depends to a great degree on what the definition of an Arab is, to what level tribal groups are valued and to what extent religion is accepted as the dominant cultural factor and the driving force in the life of people. Many European visitors to the Middle East are puzzled to discover that for many people in this region the world is divided into Muslim and Christian camps. The NATO air attacks against Yugoslavia during the spring and summer of 1999 were incomprehensible to many Arabs. How could Christian nations attack another Christian nation in order to rescue the Muslims in Kosovo? There must have been a secret, undisclosed plot or conspiracy behind the scene. This is not what they expected from Bill Clinton, Tony Blair and the rest of the "Christian" NATO leaders.

The Arab commentators' failure to understand must be worse today, a century after the first anti-Turkish, Arab clandestine underground carried slogans demanding an "anti-centralist" administration system for the Ottoman Empire – or at least a limited Arab autonomy, if not a national independence. This was to happen only after 700 years of foreign, non-Arab Muslim rule by the Mameluks, Kurds, Seljuks and Turks.

The Muslim masses felt that under Muslim rulers, whether they were Arab or not, despots or benevolent, they were at home, secure and proud in the long lasting, strong Muslim state and that they were living evidence that Allah is keeping a pledge to stand by the Muslim believers and to secure their military superiority by supporting them in the battlefield.

3

Crusaders

"There never was a good war or a bad peace" – Benjamin Franklin

The first real challenge to Muslim rule in Palestine and Syria, after the Muslim occupation in the seventh century, came from Europe in the shape of the Crusades, which began in the last decade of the eleventh century (1095). These invasions by European knights were on the quest of rescuing the Holy Tomb, the Church of the Holy Sepulcher (which Christians in the East call *"al Qiyameh"*–the Resurrection) and the local Christians from Muslim hands. The Europeans united together–clergy, kings, knights and soldiers–as a multitude under the banner of the Cross and with papal blessing. Before reaching Palestine or before conquering the holy places, they seldom noticed the local Christian population and, on the whole, the local Christians were pleased to be ignored.

In those instances when Crusaders did take note of the native Christians, neither side was pleased, for the colonizers, although kindred in the faith, never accepted the natives as equals, who were barely freer to worship in their own way than the other locals–Muslims or Jews (Prawer 1988:95-96).

The friendship between local Christians and Latin European Christians was always fragile (Parkes 1970:248). Still, local Christian communities could not be overlooked, for during this period they made up the majority of the native population of the Holy Land, as they had during the period after the Muslim occupation (Heyer 1995:133). Crusader historians who accompanied the knights of the first Crusade seemed unenthusiastic about reporting their existence back home.

Raymond D'Aguillers did mention the 60,000 Syrian Christians who dominated the Lebanese mountains and the adjacent regions for many years and told some anecdotes about the persecution that they had suffered for 400 years under Muslim rule. He acknowledged the military advice received from their kind fellow Christians as to the best road the Crusaders should follow from Tripoli down to Jerusalem (D'Aguillers 1990:83).

Another Crusader historian, Peter Tudebode, scarcely mentions these Christians, although when describing the Crusaders' siege against the walls of Antioch, he recounts how Syrian women peering out through the small crevices in the wall encouraged the Christian knights against the Turks (Tudebode 1998:166). Although the native Christian men – Armenians, Syrians and Greeks – who fought on the Turk side, he reported, "coerced or willingly, attacking us by their spears" (ibid 142, 231, 255); when they saw the Turks running from the battlefield the Armenians and Syrians blocked their way and killed whomever they could lay hands on (ibid 259).

The Muslims, generally speaking, had refrained from forcing Christians to convert to Islam. Antioch, the great city of God, was a major flourishing center at the time the Crusaders came to liberate it from Muslim rule. This metropolitan city contained a plethora of Christian institutes – some 1200 churches, 360 monasteries and 1,350 bishops under its authority (D'Aguillers 1990:312). Major traumatic changes were yet to affect the local population, the majority of whom were Christian (Parkes op cit 95).

The appearance of the Crusaders in the region had been shocking. Although many certainly welcomed these foreign kindred in Christ, others were unhappy when the Crusaders retracted their initial pledges to the Byzantine emperor that in the towns they liberated they would reinstate the Greek clergy. So the native Christians were to face not only being treated with status inferior to these invading Christians, but they were expected to live subjugated to the foreigner's rule.

The Crusaders' presence caused even more problems for their Christian native kindred under Muslim rule in neighboring lands, who now were suspected of being disloyal to their Muslim lords. This made it an attractive option for these Christians to migrate to nearby Crusader territories in the Holy Land (Prawer op cit:70-73). These troubled relations did not come to an end with the defeat of the Crusaders. On the contrary, when the Crusaders' flags were lowered, the local Christians paid dearly in the ill feelings their kindred in faith had left behind, which made them endure much suffering at the hands of their Muslim neighbors. Many Christians had to convert to Islam because of the pressures, and so Christians lost their majority in the local population.

Still Christians survived in many places in spite of some 200 years of war and conflict under Crusader rule. Especially this was true in areas that had witnessed the life of our Savior – these are approximately the same areas inhabited today by Christians – Jerusalem, Bethlehem, Nazareth, Lydda, Ramleh, Gaza, Acre, Al Baa'neh, Mia'elya, Jish, Tiberias, Sebastia, Mt. Tabor.

To this list Prawer adds the names of other places that were inhabited by Christians during the Crusaders' reign – such as Beit Horon, Tira, Beit Lehem (in Galilee), Manot (north of Acre), Safad and Beit Jubreen (whose population is not currently Christian, but in most of these places there remains a strong Christian community to this day).

In the early days of the Muslim state under the Umayyad dynasty, Muslims and Christians lived in a fragile harmony. The Muslims were governors and soldiers. For the first three centuries of the Muslim state, Christians made up the majority of those who created the state wealth and population: academics, doctors, translators, farmers, merchants, skilled artisans and administrators. On the eve of the first millennium and the first Crusade, Christianity was basically the faith of an oppressed majority of the native population of Syria. The Christian presence was quite massive, especially in the rural areas.

There was never a sudden basic change of population. Christian enclaves survived, especially near the holy shrines. Jerusalem was a Christian town at the end of the tenth century. In Bethlehem, Nazareth and adjacent villages a strong Christian presence survived, as it did in the rural areas between Jerusalem and Bethlehem and on the road to Ramallah. That they had survived, after some 400 years of Muslim rule and a continuous process of Islamization, has surprised some historians. After the Crusades, Prawer notes, "The Islamization process was done, now, far more quickly in towns in which the Muslim authority was more present, their pressure more efficient and the reward for those who accepted the new religion more generous." In the towns rather than in villages, the anti-Christian (and anti-Jewish) official and social pressures were more apparent and humiliating (Hitti 1959:222; Prawer 1988:70 and Heyer 1995:131).

During the Crusades the local Christians had been caught in a difficult dilemma. Most European Crusaders did not treat them as partners and each side questioned the other's loyalty. The Muslims, who had welcomed the Muslim-Kurdish liberation from European rule, were sure their Christian neighbors were eager to see the Crusaders rule, but the Crusaders were not convinced that these Holy Land Christians were not heretics.

In 1095 Pope Urban II had a made a clarion call at Claremont for Crusaders willing to venture forth to liberate the Holy Tomb and their Christian kindred in the East. When the leaders of the first Crusade had conquered Antioch (September 11, 1098) they apprised the Holy See of their victory, but asked for the pope's advice about a new problem: "We are able to crush the pagans and Turks," but then found they were "unable to win the Minim [the heretics] such as the Greek, Armenians, Syrians and Jacobites." They begged the pope to join them at Antioch so he could sit on the first throne of Saint Peter of "whom you are his heir. So you may lead us, your children, and make us follow the right way and all heretics, be whoever they be, will vanish and be annihilated by the strength of your authority and our heroism" (Prawer 1988:164).

It is an overstatement to claim that a state of enmity toward the local churches dominated the entire Crusader camp. Certainly the Maronites, who allied themselves with the Crusaders and acted as their guides to the land, did not complain of harsh treatment. This they had experienced before the Crusades when they had taken up arms and resisted the Muslim invasion – a stance that became more tragic when they were betrayed and "sold" by their Byzantine kin some 300 years earlier. Still the Crusaders found them eager allies in their religious pursuits and eventually the Maronites were integrated into the Catholic church just before the fall of Acre – the last Crusader fortress. In 1291 the Maronite church leaders asked the French king, Louis IX, to guarantee their well-being. For the Maronites the fall of the Crusaders was a real calamity, but alas for them, this was to be neither the first nor the last betrayal they would experience at the hands of their allies.

The Maronites claim to be the descendants of the brave Marada – that Eastern Christian group who fought for some 60 years in the seventh century on the side of the Byzantine Greeks against the Umayyad caliphs in Damascus. At the end of the seventh century the Byzantine king, Justinian Rinotmetus, "sold" them to the Muslim caliph for a price: 1000 golden dinars every week. The contemporary Maronite historian Fr. Yousef Mahfouz has detailed the many failed attempts of the Muslims to occupy the Lebanese mountains – until the Marada-Maronites were betrayed (Mahfouz 1998:77-78).

Now, at the end of the second millennium the Maronites still are in the area. Down through the centuries they have fought many battles and paid a heavy price. In some conflicts they have been incited and "used" by European allies; in others they have rashly tried to extend their homeland beyond their military capacity to dominate. They have done poorly in choosing allies. The Greek let them down, as did the French and more recently the Israelis.

Such disappointments also came to the Copts – who trusted Napoleon in Egypt, the Assyrians with the British in Iraq and the

Armenians in the 20th century with the Russians (which we will discuss at length in "National Churches").

The depth of these tragedies becomes apparent when reading about some of the illusions Eastern Christians had in the early stages of the Crusades. The Armenian Patriarch Matai from Edissa was convinced that the Crusaders were a materialization of the vision of St. Nurses, the *Katholikio* that Armenians had venerated since 363. He had said: "God is about to send Franks to fight the Persians, to break the Christians' chains, to let free the holy city of Jerusalem from the infidels' captivity and to win back the Holy Sepulcher, which was to embrace the corpse of the Lord." The Jacobite Patriarch Michel the Syrian described his dreams: "The Franks who crossed the sea gathered and promised the Lord [that] if they stand at the gates of Jerusalem, they will live in peace with all Christian sects and will give churches and monasteries to all nations that believe in Jesus Christ" (Prawer 1975:229).

These Eastern Christians, tragically humiliated and eager for salvation at the hands of their kindred, were disappointed with the Crusaders who were unprepared to call them fellow Christians and showed curt animosity to their poor kin who had been expecting help. It was out of this indifference toward the native Christians that they could write in Antioch the above-mentioned anti-Christian letter to be sent to the pope in Rome. For the Crusaders the native Christians were never accepted as equals nor did it bother them that they harmed these Christians twice–by waging and losing that war.

Pope Innocent III, like his predecessor, blessed and urged faithful Christians to share in the Crusades, but soon he was forced to excommunicate the Venetian knights for diverting the Crusades from their original target. The terrors of this fourth Crusade–and the Crusaders' indiscriminate cruelty–caused the final schism in 1472 and prompted the Greeks to coin the famous slogan: "Rather the sultan's turban than the pope's tiara." In describing this catastrophe to Cardinal Peter of Capote, Pope Innocent III said: "How will the Greek [Orthodox] Church be brought back to unity and her devotion to the Holy See renewed? The Latins have given an example only of perversity and works of darkness. It is natural that [the Greeks] should look down at them as curs. These soldiers of Christ are drenched in Christian blood" (Attwater 1951:131-132).

These problems were the result of negligence, ignorance or sheer arrogance – attitudes we still witness today in the third millennium. Currently, Greek clergy maintain such a tyrannical policy that Orthodox church congregations in Palestine and Jordan seem on the verge of extinction. For the past 400 to 500 years the Greeks have had the most tragic influence on the Arab parishes, controlling the churches and all of their spiritual and economic assets, while refraining from helping deal with the problems of their Arab parishioners. Few Greek clergy attempt to master the language of their community, but they still dominate the church and insist on their "historic rights" to do that. Recently the Greek consul general in Jerusalem, Petros Banayotpoulus, gave an interview to the Arab Jerusalem daily, *Al Quds,* stating that the Orthodox patriarchate in Jerusalem maintains "a special autonomy, independent nature and Greek cultural traditions. These traditions instruct that Greeks only are to hold the senior posts" (April 3, 2001).

Like the Arab Christians, for millennia the Greeks were treated oppressively under the Ottoman Turkish rule, impoverished and unable to support themselves, let alone their Syrian Christian Arabs. In fact, for centuries they had been a burden to the Arab faithful – economically, politically and culturally. Still the Greek clergy remained aloof, most of them unable to read or speak Arabic. And they did not teach Greek to the locals, even though they read their masses in Greek which was an unintelligible language to the vast majority of churchgoers. As far back as 1810 the Swiss traveler John Lewis Burkhardt reported that the Orthodox Christian community in the southern Jordanian town of Karak told him they were unable to understand what their priest said in church.

With such clerical aloofness, it is no wonder that the faithful in the Greek Orthodox church have dwindled from the early days of the 19th century when they comprised some 90% of all native Christians to less than 50% of the Christians today in Israel-Palestine-Jordan. In Israel they have lost their status as the largest church to their Catholic offshoot, the Greek-Melkite Catholics.

The Roman Catholic presence has long existed in the Holy Land. Before the Crusades and the schism, the Orthodox were considered a branch of the universal Christian church like the Latins. After 1217, some European Christians maintained a live witness around the Holy Land shrines because of the success of St. Francis of Assisi (1182-1226) who won the approval of the king of Egypt, Al Kamel Al Ayyobi, a descendant of Saladin. St. Francis was granted a permit to return to the Holy sites, along with his disciples, to live side-by-side with Orthodox native Christians in Jerusalem and most countries in the Middle East.

In 1631 a second European group arrived in the Holy Land — the Carmelites. At the same time the Reformation was causing radical changes in the church (the first order of monks in the modern times inside the Catholic native church was established in 1695 – the Baladiati Maronite order). The Al Mukhaliseen Order (Greek-Catholic) was to follow in 1711 to herald the rebirth of a dry branch of the native holy churches of the Lord's homeland.

If we want to fully appreciate this miracle, we ought to look at the conditions in which this was to happen.

4

Dark Ages

"Dawn rises only after total darkness." – Arab proverb

The harsh treatment to which Muslims were subjected under the Crusaders offered them ample excuse to react with anti-Christian feelings after the Crusaders' defeat. During the Crusades 200 years of war and bloodshed, there had been an ebb and flow of the Crusaders' territories depending on the success of various attacks and counterattacks. None of this contributed positively to the native Christian's situation; they were an obvious target for those seeking revenge for Crusaders' insults.

The Christian population began a rapid decline and soon were a minor population whose voice no longer was heard by the new Muslim overlords who ignored their wishes with impunity. These governors were not Arabs, but migrants from Central Asia attracted by the caliphates' wealth. Some of these warrior nomads had volunteered in the caliph's army, others arrived as invaders, but most were enslaved ex-soldiers captured by Muslim victors. Rising from the ranks, these aliens found it easy to ignore historical cultural and national affinities between Muslim and Christian Arabs.

One can trace the climax of the dark ages of Muslim maltreatment of the local Christian population to the Crusader period and the time immediately preceding and following the end of the Crusades. The Fatimid Caliph, al Hakim, burnt the Holy Sepulcher Church in Jerusalem (1009) and Sultan Baybars, the Mameluk, demolished Nazareth in 1260. This maltreatment became more grievous during the 14th and 15th centuries when barbarian soldiers ruled the Muslim empire. They exploited the local population mercilessly and for the native Christians this was the ultimate deterioration of their status. It was also the lowest point in the Muslims' maltreatment to Christians – a process that had been going on since the third century of Muslim rule when many Christians embraced Islam and their community lost its majority status within the general population of the Muslim empire (Heyer 1995:130).

Yet in spite of all the hardships, the local Christian community survived in significant numbers. During the Crusades, Europeans had refrained from any contact with these "heretics," yet these Christians survived. A populous community lived on the frontiers of the Fertile Crescent near the Arabian Desert. Some 40,000 native Orthodox Christians lived during these dark years in the areas of Petra, Karak and on the far side of the Dead Sea.

The end of the Crusades was in many ways a turning point in the history of the Holy Land and its neighboring countries. The Arab-Muslim golden age had ended with the last caliphs of the Abbasid dynasty. They were corrupt and busily pursued pleasures of the flesh. They hired mercenaries to rule and represent their authority until finally the institution, including the title, of caliph was abolished by the Mongol invasion which captured and brought destruction to Baghdad in 1258. The Mameluks reëestablished the Muslim empire under their own rule in Cairo in 1261. For awhile these non-Arab Muslims kept a figurehead Arab dynasty as titular monarchs, but later on they abolished the whole institute of caliphs.

The Mameluks (which in Arabic means "owned") was a class of non-Arab slaves or mercenaries who joined the Muslim armies and later reached high command and finally declared themselves sultans, kings and masters of the empire. They divided the empire among themselves for 200 years until finally the warring tribes of the Ottoman Turks swept over Asia Minor. On May 29, 1453, the Ottomans conquered the Byzantine capital Constantinople (Istanbul of today) and by 1516 won their main battle to conquer Syria and Palestine. Within less than a decade the entire Middle East, including Syria, Lebanon, Palestine, Jordan, Iraq, Saudia, Yemen and Egypt, became Ottoman colonies. This occupation lasted another 400 long years. Under the Turks, Middle Eastern history reached its nadir during these darkest of ages. Almost no literature of any significance was produced during this period and little is recorded about what was happening to the local Christian communities as they suffered under these cruel despots.

What information is extant is derived, in most cases, from European travelers. Some of these were clergy, others were curious adventurers or fact collectors. Still, few of them recorded plausible information or any solid and reliable facts about the native Christians they met in the East. But how could we expect these travelers from the dark ages, who could not speak Arabic and who interacted with few native Christians, to be able to convey any reasonable message about the populace or their conditions?

Nevertheless, the literature from that period does describe the countryside as well as do most travel reports in popular newspapers today. Granted, much of the writing reflects the author's subjective point of view and most of the writers, being unable to understand the language spoken by the native Christians, demonstrated little interest in their life. That the local Christians were not Roman Catholics was enough reason for both the Crusaders and these travelers to ignore or look down on them. Yet their ancient notes and impressions are entertaining and disclose the complexities of the native Christians' relationship with Europe.

In the last few hundred years, many monks and missionaries have arrived in the Holy Land on pilgrimages or in an attempt to establish a solid Christian presence in the land of our Savior. Among these Western Christians were many celebrated writers and statespeople like the British Lord Robert Cursor (1810-1873), the

French François René Châteaubriand (1768-1848) and the American Mark Twain (1835-1910). They found some local Christians on whom they could rely and with whom they had common ground. In most cases, this contact was not clearly beneficial to either side.

The reality is that these local Christians were Christians before Europe knew about Christianity, before Middle Eastern Christians had heard of a continent called Europe and before America was "discovered" by Christopher Columbus. Most European guests seem to have often ignored – or failed to grasp – these basic facts.

Was the encounter between the missionaries – who stayed around longer than the travelers – and the native Christians helpful to any community? The answer here is mixed. The missionaries, as such, began to arrive in the Holy Land in the 17th century. Besides coming armed with the Gospel, many of these Europeans were loaded down with feelings of superiority; they tended to look down on both native Muslims and Christians in most unfavorable terms. The information they had garnered from travelers – both lay persons and clergy who had traveled in the Holy Land – tended to poison these missioners with prejudice, which only added arrogance to their ignorance.

In addition, these European missionaries were burdened with incipient colonialism and were so blinded to the community's needs that they taught English, French, Italian history and the geography of Italy, France or Great Britain to young children in Lebanon and the Galilee mountains, while failing to teach these pupils anything about their own native community. The internalized message was to encourage the locals to think of Russia, England, the United States, Spain or Italy as a superior homeland. Some missionaries created problems by dividing the Arab communities along religious lines, causing irreparable damage to the fragile coexistence that had developed between Christian children and their Muslim neighbors.

While the European efforts affected the outlook of their naïve charges in the Middle East, their reporting back home caused considerable more damage to those who accepted "information" from them. The locals in the Holy Land could balance what they were being taught with information derived from talking to their families and neighbors, but the European readers had no sounding board on which to bounce ideas written by those like the Dominican monk, Felix Fabri, who advised all to avoid Jews, Muslims and Eastern Christians. This well-intentioned monk caused irreparable harm to the potential relationship between the East and the West.

Fabri visited Jerusalem early in the 15th century and wrote in his *Evagatorium* that Jews, Muslims and Eastern Christians were to be avoided since they could not be trusted. He claimed: "The Eastern Christians are more lacking in moral sense than the Ishmaelite and the Jews. They cheat the pilgrims any time it is possible" (Eish Shalom 1965:345). How could this Swiss monk (a son of a noble family) arrive at such a sweeping generalization and compelling verdict? What made him an expert on the culture? And where was the morality of his sweeping judgment?

Fr. Panatela de Aveiro, a Portuguese Franciscan monk who visited the Holy Land in the 16th century, was even more un-Christlike in his remarks. To him, Jerusalem resembled "a golden vase inhabited by snakes" and the local Christians were divided among themselves and "united only in enmity to the Roman Catholic Church, full of sins and superstitions" (ibid 291-292).

Andrew A. Bonar and Robert Murray M'chenye, two Scottish Protestant missionaries who arrived in Palestine during the 19th century, "discovered" that the Greek Christians and the Roman Catholics were anti-Jewish and anti-Christ, while the Jews appreciated the Protestants and the English (ibid 501).

The most widely circulated travel book about the Holy Land, first printed over a hundred years ago, was by Mark Twain who accompanied some American "innocents abroad" and published a book about this trip under that title. After visiting Turkish colonies, Twain reflected in harsh words: "If ever an oppressed race existed, it is this one we see fettered around us under the inhuman tyranny of the Ottoman Empire." He suggested a solution to this problem of tyranny: "I wish Europe would let Russia annihilate Turkey a little – not much, but enough to make it difficult to find the place again without a divining-rod or a diving bell" (366).

Just a few years after the 1860 massacre of the Christian community in Lebanon and Damascus, Twain visited that city and we discover his phobia was not only anti-Turkish, but also anti-Syrian. For him "the Damascenes are the ugliest, wickedest villains we have seen." He concluded the Syrians "hate the very sight of a foreign Christian [so] that they want no intercourse whatever with him" (367, 376 & 383). This was said about a country where at least a quarter of the population was Christian and where some 5,000 people had been killed in a massacre three or four years earlier, simply because they were Christians.

It is interesting to note that what saved the rest of the Christian community from death at the hands of an incited brutal crowd was Abd Al Qader al Jazaeri (1808-1883), the Algerian Muslim prince and national hero who, after fighting the French occupation of his country for ten years, was captured and exiled to Syria. This gallant warrior was incapable of watching a brutal mob kill peaceful Christians, and so organized his men in rescue teams to defend Syrian Christians from a savage crowd of ignorant Muslims who had heard about the Druze (and Muslim) anti-Christian massacres in Lebanon and felt the time was ripe to rid themselves of these Christians in order to pillage their homes.

These disturbances came to an end only when European fleets landed on the Lebanese coast threatening the Ottomans that, unless they acted against the mob leaders, they would have to face the consequences. So, obviously Twain was unaware of even recent events of what had happened in the country he was visiting. He did mention visiting the mausoleum of the 5,000 Christians murdered in Damascus and noted that thousands more were killed in Lebanon and left unburied because the Muslims "do not defile their hands burying infidel dogs."

Strangely, Twain was outraged about the dead Christians while ignoring those surviving. In the end, he hated the Ottomans, Syrians, Muslims and the land of Syria. "The last 24 hours in Damascus we suffered a violent attack of Cholera – or Cholera Morbus. It was a dangerous recreation, but is pleasanter than traveling in Syria" (422-423). His vituperative comments spread abroad. Having

The Narrow Gate Churches

heard someone say an Arab knight would scorn gold for his horse, Twain refused to believe an Arab might feel affinity with his horse. He claimed Christian Arabs see nothing amiss in "a picture of Joseph on the donkey and Mary walking beside him," – which is a vicious lie. Especially Christian Arabs have treated women with the utmost respect so by drawing this caricature, Twain defamed the community, while demonstrating his own prejudice – to say nothing of his imagination.

Twain also discounted references to the beauty of the Nazarene women: "The pilgrims brought their verdicts with them. They expect the Nazarene women to look tall and graceful like Mary." But Nazarene women *are* tall and graceful and anyone visiting the town can tell how mistaken Twain was.

Bertha Spafford, an American living in Jerusalem at the time of Twain's visit, recounts anecdotes reflecting the manners of this obviously provincial author. She says Twain described his companions as "brutes" because he was served a salad made of wild plants and delicious herbs from the fields of Galilee (Spafford-Vester 1950:161).

John Lloyd Stephens, another American traveler, like Twain was biased and anti-Arab. Stephens ignored local Christians in his reports, and the only Christian who came into his sights was a lonely Egyptian Copt who lived in Hebron with Muslims and Jews and looked to the American traveler, "more Jewish than most Jews." It turns out this Copt was flattering the American guest shamelessly for he was under the impression that American travelers could recommend him to the authorities for a lucrative and safe job working as the American vice-consul in Hebron (Stephens 1991:321). The local Christians in Bethlehem whom Stephens observed left him with the impression (from the way they were dressed and treated their beards and moustaches) that they did not look like Christians (ibid 336).

While visiting Nazareth early in the 19th century, Stephens noticed other native Christians, but he wrote nothing about them, despite having hired a Nazarene to guide him on his trip to Tiberias. He tells us about encountering and listening to Jews in Hebron, Safad and Tiberias and about lobbying in Beirut for a Jew for whom he wanted to get some help from the Austrian consul.

In Safad, Stephens was annoyed when he heard his Jewish host call him a Nazarene. He misunderstood his host's remark and denied he was Nazarene, believing the fault was due to an interpreter's mistake. Most probably no one was mistaken except the American who did not know that Christians are usually referred to as "*Notsreem,*" followers of Jesus the Nazarene, (not *massiheyeen* which is the term for Christians in Hebrew). In current Hebrew and Arabic these terms are often used synonymously and are appropriate, but for some Christian and Muslim scholars they are used to differentiate between the Eastern Nazarenes and "European" Christians (Al Nashashibi 1932:73-74).

It is worth mentioning that the Koran does not use the term *Massiheyyin,* referring only to the *Nassara* (Nazareens or followers of the man from Nazareth) in warm, friendly superlatives. Religious Jews, who reject Jesus Christ as the messiah, call him *Yesho* of Nazareth, a perversion of *Yeshowaa'* (the correct name for Jesus in Hebrew). In Hebrew, the letters of *Yesho* stand for *Yemah Shemo Wazekhro* (meaning – erase his name and memory).

This enmity to the Christian faith persists 2,000 years after the birth of Christ. *Ha Aretz*, Israel's elite liberal newspaper, published a report about what young Israelis study in government schools. Most of them teach nothing about Christ in their history classes but when they do, he is taught in one class and for an hour only in the sixth grade. In the Jewish religious schools, Christ's name is never mentioned and students are forbidden to enter a Catholic church because Catholics display icons. They may, however, visit a Protestant one since no idols are worshiped there (12/23/1999).

Stephens traveled in the Holy Land in 1835 and 1836, the period in which the Egyptian warrior Ibrahim Pasha took over Syria from the Ottomans and made an attempt to establish a modern Arab empire. Ibrahim was the son of Muhammad Ali, the founder of modern Egypt and the first Muslim governor in the Holy Land to introduce a political system based on egalitarian treatment for all citizens. Yet little in Stephens' book indicates he understood a revolution was taking place around him.

After an encounter on the road from Tyre to Acre with a young man walking to Acre to take up his duties as a forced laborer in one of Ali's military industries, Stephens recorded that the man's "paltry wage" would be three loaves of bread daily. When Stephens heard about the anti-Egyptian rebellion in Mount Hebron he concluded, "I had seen misery in Italy, Greece, Turkey, Russia and gallant but conquered Poland, but I saw it refined and perfected under the iron despotism of Ali" (1991:454).

James Finn, a 19th century British consul in Jerusalem (1806-1872) felt it his duty to help the Jews, and to that end he initiated industrial and farming projects in Irtas and Talbeya, near Jerusalem, to supply the Jews with additional income. He wrote, "The Christians of the East have their prejudice against the Jews, based on a superstition that causes them not to bargain with them" (Eish Shalom op cit 648). This anecdotal conclusion could certainly not be extrapolated universally. At that time my grandfather, a Catholic peasant, was sharing a herd of cows with a religious Jew from Safad – and my grandfather was not a unique Christian.

Reports of travelers from this era are full of contradictions. In 1870 a Jewish traveler in this pre-Zionist time decided to negotiate the purchase of some Arab land for a Jewish settlement. Shimshon Berman of Krakau in Galicia offered to buy land from the Abu Shusha Arabs, north of Arab Migdal (near the Sea of Galilee). He was astonished to hear the answer: "We prefer to be slaves of the Jews and not masters of ourselves" (Yaa'ri 1976:604).

Such Arabs, I might add, found favor in the eyes of Colonel Richard Meinertzhagen, the British senior intelligence officer in General Edmond Allenby's expedition – the "last Crusader" to occupy Palestine in 1917. His diaries are filled with praise for the Zionists and their plans, while the local Christians of Palestine are unnoted except for one Christian Arab who lectured in London, although no mention is made of his Christian faith (1973: 118).

One of the most balanced reports came from the Swiss traveler John Lewis Burkhardt who visited Syria, Palestine, Jordan and Egypt. Among his honest impressions was one (incomprehensible to him) observation he made in August 1811 when he spent two weeks in the southern Jordanian town al Karak. He could not understand why his hosts said people in the village would despise any member of the community who would sell butter from their cows' milk, insisting they must instead keep such bounty for their guests (Burkhardt 1870:225).

Even today there is nothing odd for us in this custom. In my village people tended to look down on families who set aside their cream to sell to foreigners. Since our normal diet was poor in protein, except for that from milk products from cows, goats and sheep, any household that sold milk, eggs or butter was suspected of being stingy and/or harming their children's health by depriving them of essential nourishing food. According to Burkhardt, his hosts explained that butter is a food Arab Christians save exclusively to make guests feel welcome. We still have a traditional greeting in our community for guests: "Our new bed, our best food, any thing that pleases you, our most welcome guest."

This springs from our Arab (not exclusively Christian) tradition of sparing no time or resource for the sake of our guest – a sentiment deeply carved into our national heritage. Thus arose the legend of our mythical wealthy hero Hatem al Taie who ordered his slaves to light beacons in the chilly desert nights in order to attract straying potential guests, promising them that whoever brought him a guest, he would set free. Later on, having lost his fortune by feeding and pleasing his guests, he asked his mother to sell him as a slave in order to provide for the needs of his guests.

This basic necessity, which desert nomads feel and which makes them eager to play the role of hosts, understandably derives from their environment. There is a primal need for shelter for any who stray in the desert heat; that need if not met can be fatal. Since the tribe of someone who dies in the desert can blame those on whose territory the death took place, appropriate hospitality became the ultimate law of the desert – and it remains to this day.

Beyond this, an Arab who welcomes foreigners into the home is hoping for a reciprocal treatment by these guests. Thus a generous reception of guests serves as a public relations exercise. Also, the honor of being the tribe's host was the sheikh's and leaders', so stature in the community was derived from such generosity. Of course, to these material reasons some additional spiritual ones can be added: the urge to do good and feel better, the desire to widen the circle of one's friends, the wish to enjoy the company of others and learn from their experience and the desire to entertain and be entertained by the company of others during the long days and nights in the deserts of Arabia.

Burkhardt showed a lot of interest and curiosity, but very little empathy, with the Syrian Christians. Even his compliments regarding the Lebanese prince Bashir al Shihabi had a barb: "He is an amiable man and if any Levantine can be called the friend of an European nation, he is certainly the friend of the English."

Some Europeans who came to the East not quite as laden down with prejudice. One clearly pro-Arab visitor was Edward Dicey (1832-1911), an English writer who covered wars for the *Daily Telegraph* and edited the *Daily News* and *the Observer*. In 1870 he traveled to the Holy Land and returned to England with an expectation for the future. Unfortunately his prophecies did not come true. He found the Jews in Palestine so poor, corrupt and entirely dependent on charity from their co-religionists in other countries that he felt they had no future. Dicey could not conceive the rapid acceleration of national storms that would compel so many Jews to immigrate to Palestine and turn it into a Jewish state.

Dicey, convinced the future lay in Syrian-Christian hands, said:

"They are not an attractive people, in appearance or in character; out of my experience and the experience of other travelers, I would prefer the Arab Muslims. But I already noticed that, in individuals, as in peoples, the pleasant manners are not what assure success in our world. The little bravery, vigour and sense of progress that might be found these days in Palestine are confined to the ranks of the *Raa'ya*, [the subjects] not that of the Muslims" (1870:255).

A missionary who shared such feelings was Miss Frances E. Newton who arrived, like most other missionaries, with one goal: to convert as many Greek Orthodox Christians as possible to the Church of England's brand of Protestantism. Unlike most of the others, she fell in love with the local Christians – their food, dress, manners and culture, as well as their political struggle to achieve independence. She loved Nazareth: "Few can realize until they have been there the charm of this little town tucked away in a basin high up in Galilee hills." Along there:

> "legions marched and princes swept with their retinues and all sorts of travelers from all countries went to and fro. The Roman ranks, the Roman eagles. The noblemen litters and equipages cannot have been strange to the boys of Nazareth. Moreover the scandals of the herods buzzed up and down this road; peddlers carried them and the peripatetic rabbis would moralize upon them. ... A vision of all kingdoms of the world was as possible from this village as from the Mount of Temptation. But the chief lesson, which Nazareth teaches us, is the possibility of a pure home and a spotless youth in the face of the evil world."

Her last remark is a quote from another admirer of Nazareth – George Adam Smith (Newton 1948:19). Miss Newton was so much in love with the Nazareth of a century ago that she even was able to compliment the Ottoman rule. She describes Nazareth thus:

> Nazareth at the time I lived there was a prosperous thriving little market town with its blacksmiths' *souk* (Arabic for market place) or street and its grocers, jewelers and saddlers souks. Peasants from scores of villages resorted to its shops for the supply of their needs ... being a town with sacred association for Christians. There are many large and foreign buildings in Nazareth, such as churches, convents and hospices etc., which stand in vivid contrast to the humbler homes of the Nazarenes. A conspicuous landmark on the hillside as you enter the town is the fine hospital built by the Edinburgh Medical Mission. This building crowns the magnificent medical work done in the early days by Dr. Vartan and his wife" (ibid 30-31)

Newton then compares the Ottoman rule in 1900 with the British rule at a later date in Palestine: "In those years, under the Turks, we were safer than now [in the 1940s] under the British mandate. A *Franji* [French, European] hat was then a sure shield for protection against thieves and highway robbers" (ibid 23).

Miss Newton blamed the policy of her country and the 1937 recommendation of the Royal Commission (published in 1938) and accused the British government of exploiting religion to extend its rule in the country, like its apparent concern about maintaining the holy lake of Tiberias known as the Sea of Galilee and the River Jordan. The British Royal Commission had concluded that "Christian religious sensibilities would be seriously offended if the maximum level of the Sea of Galilee were such as to submerge the sites closely associated with that religion, or if the minimum level were such as seriously to impair the natural beauty of the lake shores" (ibid 150). (Unfortunately Christian sensibilities are no longer much consideration, for the lake is less than half full these days and the river is dry most of the year, except for some polluted agricultural drainage and salty mineral water from natural springs.)

Another distinguished British visitor to the Holy Land in the later part of the 19th century was Colonel Sir Charles W. Wilson who also showed kind feelings towards the local Christians. About the Nazarene women he wrote that, "We cannot fail to notice both the bright costumes and the healthy, intelligent and often beautiful faces and figures of the woman of Nazareth, owing, doubtless, in some degree, as in the case of their Bethlehemite sisters, to the admixture of Crusading blood in their veins. But this cannot be the sole cause, as in the sixth century they are spoken of as noted for their beauty, which was attributed to the blessing of the Virgin" (1975:47). Wilson found that of the 6,000 Nazarene residents, two-thirds were Christians.

John Lamond's small volume *Modern Palestine or the Need for a New Crusade* published in 1893, agrees with Colonel Wilson's pleasant impressions from meeting Nazarene Christians (1897:160-174). Lamond takes much pride in being European and feels that it is because the Continent opened its gates to Christ and thus progressed, while Asia blocked its own way to progress when it refused Christ (ibid 202-203).

Unfortunately, we are unable to report what Arab Muslim travelers wrote about Christian lands simply because Arab travelers, throughout the ages, seldom made their way into Christian lands. Few Muslim travelers visited the Crusaders' kingdom of Jerusalem during the 200 years of its existence, yet from the few travelers that visited we learn, as the Muslim diplomat Osama Ben

Munqez said when he visited the Crusaders' territories, that in his estimation – "these beasts' [the European infidels] only quality is their bravery" (Hitti 1958:761).

Another Muslim pilgrim who came on a *Haj* to Mecca, toured the Middle East and wrote a book to tell about life in the region, including the Crusaders' kingdoms in 1189-1191. With his religious bias, and with no attempt to conceal his feelings, and using every opportunity to curse these infidels and pray for their destruction, still he was honest enough to admit that many Muslims were able to live under the Christian government in peace and enjoy life to such an extent that their Muslim faith was endangered. He was saddened to hear from these Muslims that they preferred life under the Crusaders (Ibn Jubair nd:210-213). The Muslim subjects of the Crusaders' kingdoms were able to pray in some of their mosques and the Muslim population managed to survive and circulate as a defeated community within the Crusaders' territories.

Significant Arab Muslim travel to European countries began in the early 19th century when they went as political delegates, merchants or students – and left detailed accounts of their impressions. The Egyptian historian Abed al Rahman al Jabarti wrote about the Mameluk delegation to London headed by al Alfi Pasha to convince the British to support the restoration of Mameluk rule in Egypt after the French invasion of their country. This historian reports that after their October 1803 visit to London they "returned to Egypt after their approach, transfigured by what they saw of the British country's architecture, orderly government and the affluence and justice in their midst, despite their being infidels, to such an extent that there are no poor in their community, no beggars, or people in need" (Choueiri 1991:16).

Rifa'at al Tahtahwi (1801-1873), another well-known Egyptian Muslim sheikh, accompanied the first group of young students given the opportunity to study in France from 1826 to 1831. He was on an official religious mission to make sure these young students did not deviate from orthodox Islam while they studied at the French universities. Al Tahtahwi himself was "corrupted," falling in love with Paris and becoming a true Francophile. He praised the French way of life, finding it superior to that of Egypt – as did most other Muslim visitors to Europe in the 19th century. In fact the superiority of Europe's economic, political and social systems caused much frustration for the pious Muslims. How could these infidels be superior to Muslims and why? Al Tahtahwi concluded loudly and clearly: "The truth deserves to be said and followed," but he added that he "does not like whatever contradicts the Mohammedans law [shari'ah]" (op cit 19-27).

This Muslim conundrum is apparent also in a report a Moroccan emissary wrote to his king after visiting Great Britain and the court of Saint James in 1860. Abu al Jamal Muhammad al Fasi found the British far superior in so many ways, but after describing his observations, he found it necessary to add the caveat about these infidels "who deceived" or "manipulated" their fortunes. In other instances he simply cursed them ("may they be destroyed") or hoped (privately) that the British, to whom he brought a message of friendship from his king, would suffer "misery." The British fleet included 1,200 vessels, he writes and immediately adds "praise to Allah that determined them to be infidels and doomed them to be born blind and by his firm will, those who are blind in this world shall be blind also in the second" (ibid 63-68).

Another Egyptian traveler recounted his impressions from a lengthy trip through Italy, France, Spain and Portugal on his way to participate in an international conference of a group he was vague about their identity. Ahmed Zaki Pasha, delegated by his government to attend an Oriental scholars' gathering, spent six months during 1892 and 1893 traveling and writing back home to the Egyptian public about the wonders of modern life in Europe. A clearly fascinated admirer, he describes the Europeans and their civilization in flattering and complimentary detail. The rare critical remarks in the large volume of his collected letters, "*al Safar ela al Moatamar*" [The Journey to the Conference] (1893:122) are directed against the inquisition in Spain after the fall of Muslim rule in 1492. Still, the Egyptian admits being enchanted by the Spaniards' charm and tradition – he also felt their civilized treatment of visitors was linked to a Muslim influence on Spanish culture.

The rare Arabs who wrote memoirs about their visits to Europe during the Middle Ages are in good company with the few Arabs who published books describing life in Palestine before the 20th century. The celebrated Lebanese writer Michael Noa'imeh (1889-1970) went from Beskanta, his hometown in the Lebanese mountains, to study at the Russian seminary in Nazareth from 1902 through 1906. In the last years of his life he published a multi-volume autobiography under the name *Saba'oun* (Noa'aimeh 1959) – or "Seventy." He describes much about the physical and mental conditions in the Holy Land during the early days of the 20th century and the story in the Lebanese mountains that drove ambitious and brave young men like himself to emigrate and leave their young families behind.

Noa'imeh describes the colonializing European missionary schools that indoctrinated the young to regard the sovereigns from their European countries as theirs as well. Thus Noa'imeh, in a Greek-Orthodox school run by Russian monks, spent much of his time there dreaming of going to Russia. All subjects were taught in the Russian language and although Arabic was a subject, it was taught like a foreign language.

Rev. Asa'ad Mansour authored a comprehensive book on the history of Nazareth describing this same period. It was published in 1924 in Cairo. His family lived in Shafa Amro, and Mansour was an Anglican vicar in Nazareth and a devoted student of history so his observations give us good background information about life in Nazareth during the last decades of the 19th and the early years of the 20th centuries. Entitled *Tarikh al Nassera* (History of Nazareth) it is not the only book published on this topic, but it is by far the most comprehensive (Mansour 1924).

Mansour confirms the information gleaned from other sources describing the modern revival of the Christian communities in the Holy Land. These communities had suffered unbearable harassment during the Fatimid, Mameluk and Turkish periods – a treatment that had driven many Christians to convert to Islam, while it led others to look for shelter in the faraway mountains of Lebanon, in the Houran in Syria and at Ajloun and Karak in Jordan.

5

Early Renaissance

"The people that walked in darkness have seen a great light" (Isaiah 9:2).

The ideals of the French Revolution reached the Middle East before Napoleon arrived, attempting to conquer Egypt and block the British road to India. Long after Napoleon was banished, these ideals lingered on. First carried to the Middle East by Christian missionaries and Egyptian Muslim soldiers, these concepts, especially that of equality, were drastic and contributed to creating havoc in the traditional society—including the dreadful massacres of 1860 in Lebanon and Syria.

Another consequence of these ideals came a century later and took a political shape. Najeeb A'azouri convened in Paris (June 18-24, 1913) the first Arab congress, whose aim was to ease the suffering and oppression of Arabs under Ottoman rule. Young educated Arabs, mainly Christians, met on invitation from A'azouri, a Syrian Christian who lived in France.

The First Congress of Arab Nationalists produced eleven modest resolutions—the central issue being: "It is important to guarantee the Ottoman Arabs the right to exercise their political rights by making effective their participation in the central administration of the Empire." No one was demanding Arab independence from Turks, only that they be given a voice and allowed to share in the Turkish administration of Arab provinces and that Arabic be learned in government schools along with the Turkish language.

The congress also asked the Ottoman imperial government to establish a *mutasrriflek* (an autonomous area) of Lebanon in order to improve its financial situation (Hurewitz 1956:63). It is also worth mentioning that this Syrian-Arab Congress "affirmed favoring the reformist and decentralizing demands of the Armenian Ottomans."

To this congress came 24 delegations of different political groups, mostly from Syria and Lebanon, with three delegates from America and two from Iraq (Mesopotamia). A'azori, the initiator of the congress, caused a stir when he published his book *Reveil de Nation Arabe* in which he called Arabs to awake from their long sleep and warned them of the Zionist danger and intention to renew the Jewish Kingdom (1905). Unfortunately, his call was not heeded.

The educated circles in the Arab provinces of the Ottoman Empire and Egypt (which was under the more relaxed regime of British occupation) were to witness some heated political debates. The famous Muslim cleric Mohammed Abdo and his partner Jamal ad Din al Afghani called for a modernizing reform in Muslim thought to make it more compatible to the contemporary world, while insisting that Islamic rules should be the basis for this Arab renaissance. Contrary opinions were voiced by nationalists such as Anton Farah (1874-1922) who believed the time had come for a separation of religion from the state.

This Lebanese journalist in debating with Muhammad Abdo insisted only a secular regime could unite the nation while Abdo maintained such a "secular idea was imported from the West by those under the influence of the missionaries" and so he concluded that even though European missionaries had offered some help, in the end they had caused political injury as well (Hourani 1970:278-279).

The Syrian Abd Al Rahman al Kawakibi was another prominent Muslim who believed in Arab non-religious nationalism. He issued a famous call to non-Muslim Arabs (directed mostly to Christian Arabs) urging them to join the Arab national movement and to forget the oppression and persecution of their ancestors. He pointed out how the Australians and Americans, working with non-religious national ideals and political solidarity, were leading in science and modern systems. Kawakibi urged that historical disputes be settled and forgotten and that Arabs – Muslims and Christians – stand together to support and console each other on this earth, "and leave religion to suffice in ruling the other world" (Hourani ibid 253-259).

Letters which Khalil Sakakini, a famous Christian Arab intellectual from Jerusalem, sent to his son and family members were published posthumously. This popular book articulated his feeling that although he acknowledged that Arab Christians were among the world's scientific, industrial and economic elite – still "despite that, I can't be unaware of my national identity. I would, certainly, rather belong to a nation, even if it was in an inferior state, than be naked without any national identity ... Even if I was member of a advanced people, such as the American, French, or the English, I would volunteer to serve the Arab people, to awaken them to overtake other races and nations" (1955:62-63).

At the end of the 20th century the Arab-Lebanese-French writer Amin Maalouf addressed the identity issue. After discussing the rapid change in the political and demographic maps of the world, he arrived at a liberal concept on how to determine the identity of people – taking into consideration the many subjective and objective components involved. He admits that personally he can't choose between being just Lebanese, since he was born there, or French, since he found refuge there and embarked on writing his novels in the French language. But, he claims that he feels that his Christian faith, his Greek-Catholic heritage and his long family tradition in dealing with Muslims and Arabic cultural life give to his identity its genuine flavor (1999).

During the 19th century, the Arab countries in the Middle East and North Africa came under the military occupation of the European colonial powers of Britain, France, Spain and Italy. The new rulers pursued their own economic and political interests, but these colonial regimes (by the basic fact that they were foreign "heathens") set a new mark for the local population to shoot at. They could now blame the colonial officials for any problem, real or imaginary, and consequently galvanize a new spirit in the Arab population.

Certainly there was much needless imperialism. I remember as a young child during the 1940s how British soldiers would check our donkeys at the gates of our market town, Safad, to see if our farmers were properly treating the wounds of their animals. Any donkey with a poorly treated laceration gave the soldiers an excuse to beat its rider. These same "merciful" soldiers drove their military vehicles dragging behind them the corpses of Arab rebels and then forced the population of my village to pass by these mutilated corpses to identify them. Any poor peasants who made the mistake of claiming any of the dead or who expressed readiness to take responsibility for their burial were punished by having their house blown up. Apparently this was meant to deter any from offering succor to rebels fighting against the British (and the Jews).

So it is understandable why people in my country accuse the British of mistreating the Arabs and imposing a colonial regime on us. However, I also remember that the British rule introduced into our rural area the first mother-and-baby care clinic and that in my school (like hundreds others throughout Palestine) the Mandatory authorities offered free education to all comers and provided all pupils with free textbooks and small blackboards on which we solved mathematics problems.

This system was unlike the traditional *Kuttab*, a standard facility next to the main mosques in the more advanced Muslim communities where parents had to pay the local *imam* to teach their children to recite by heart their holy book, the Koran. Christian children attended the church's *Madraseh* where, again, they learned to memorize the Lord's Prayer, the Nicene Creed, the Psalms and some basic prayers and hymns included in high mass liturgy. By contrast, the official Mandatory elementary schools in towns and villages taught Arabic, English, mathematics, history, geography and religion – and in the process introduced new values and methods of government by which our people were able to join the enlightened world community.

The school system was not the only thing the British introduced when they took over the rule of the Holy Land after the First World War and began to move rural Palestine down the path towards modernization. The era of the Arab Renaissance had begun during the last years of the 18th and first years of the 19th centuries. Some scholars attribute this movement to the French during the time they invaded Egypt under Napoleon, but I find little of merit to support this overly generous claim for the famous French warrior who waged two full years of war and bloodshed in the region at the end of the 19th century.

Despite the fact that the French invaders were accompanied by a huge scientific mission, it is hard to perceive this operation as the opening needed to till the soil for a cultural revolution in that short period full of hate and hardships. Of course, Napoleon's military encounter with the East and the French Revolution's concepts of equality, fraternity and justice in a non-religious state (introduced later in both Egypt and Syria by the Egyptian Ibrahim Pasha) were strong influences. Add to these the massive appearance of European and American Christian missions in the Middle East and we must admit that compelling pressures for change were blowing in with these new winds coming from the West.

Mount Lebanon, the only enclave in which native Christians survived as a majority up to the 19th century, paid a heavy toll for translating these ideals into real daily life. Their attempts to align with the French were costly but they won autonomy in the aftermath of the most infamous 1860 massacre which in the end produced massive European military and diplomatic pressure on the Ottoman sultan, forcing him to grant this special status to the Lebanese. Thus this area became a relatively free and secure haven where groups of Arab intellectuals could gather and foment a genuine revival movement calling for freedom for all Syrians which would grant them the power to build a national Arab state.

Now, a century-and-a-half later, this movement, in which Christian Arabs played the major role, can look back on all the triumphs that have emerged. The Arab countries of the Middle East had long been entirely under the rule of the oppressive Ottoman Empire where Muslim Arabs were treated as second-class citizens in a world that had little enough respect even for its first-class citizens. The Christians were simply *Raa'aya* (subjects). This status was a modified replacement of the *Dhimmis* of the older days, but they were not exempted from the military service. They, like the Muslims, were drafted, but then encouraged to pay *Badal* (substitute) or serve the fighting soldiers *Sukhra* (unpaid).

The French expedition to Egypt (1798-1799) provided a short intermezzo. Napoleon lived in Egypt and Palestine for less than two years—too short a period to expect the introduction of much lasting effect. Napoleon tried to win the allegiance of the populace—Egyptian or Palestinian—by claiming to be a devout Muslim, acting under the Muslim (Ottoman) caliph's requests and positing that the aim of the French occupation was merely to drive Egypt back to the faithful Muslim flock under the sovereignty of the "commander of the believers," and away from the Mameluk despots (Hurewitz op cit 63).

This proclamation was written in a Koranic-style and was delivered to Egypt on July 2, 1798, but it convinced very few. Some who took it seriously thought it was the proper time to put this claim to a test and organized an anti-Copt pogrom in order to rid themselves of local Christians and to test the French reaction.

The French did not allow any massacres. On the contrary, they encouraged local Christians to look to the French as allies and some Copts trusted them and fought under their command in special units. When the French decided to leave, the Copt units' officer accompanied them, hoping to change the mind of the French occupiers (which we will discuss later).

The French invasion of Egypt and their encounter with the Copts, (and the Syrian Christians), shook the feeble coexistence between Muslims and Christians and endangered the Palestinian Christians who were unlucky enough to be caught in the middle when they were en route to Acre. The local Muslims decided the Christian/French army was headed to Jerusalem, so the Muslim authorities arrested the entire Christian population of Jerusalem, sequestering them inside their churches, including the Holy Sepulcher, for 72 days (Al A'aref 1960:271). It was only when the French army withdrew its units and returned to Egypt without attempting to conquer Jerusalem that the local Christians were released.

In the Arabic language, the term "Greek" carries two meanings: that of the population of Greece (and Asia Minor before it became Turkey) and the name of our mother church – the Rum or the Greek-Orthodox church. The reason is obvious. The Eastern Byzantine church used the Greek language in its rituals and consequently the church was called "Greek" just as the Roman Catholics, who used Latin in their worship rituals, came to be known by the Arabic-speaking population as "Latino."

Like the Arabs, the Greeks suffered under the Ottoman empire for hundreds of years and when, in 1821, the Greek patriots came to the conclusion that they were going to throw out these foreigners from their land, the Ottoman governor in Jerusalem incited a Muslim mob in that city to attack the Greek Orthodox population there. (At that time the Greek Orthodox community made up over 90% of the Christians in town.)

Only when a higher and more prudent authority from Damascus interfered did the onslaught and pillage come to an end. But this happened only after new regulations were promulgated (to raise the taxes imposed on the Christian population of Jerusalem from 60,000 Qursh to 100,000). Actions were also taken to disarm the Christians, collecting any weapons from them, and forcing them to wear only black clothes.

A similar anti-Christian pogrom was repeated two years later when rumors flew that a large Greek fleet was headed for Beirut, endangering the Muslim state. A few days later this news proved to be exaggerated at best so the Christian community of Jerusalem went back to its "normal" life. Aref al Aref, a Palestinian-Muslim contemporary historian, blames the initiative of these pogroms on a "wicked born Jew" by the name of Suleman Efindi, who was newly converted to Islam and had risen to power (Al A'aref 1960:358). The authenticity of this story – from a Palestinian historian – may be questioned since it dovetails into the Palestinians' attempts (during the anti-Zionist struggle) to cement a national unity of Muslims and Christians against Jews.

Still, despite the short time that the French occupied Egypt, there was cultural fallout which left a permanent impression on the land – including the first official gazette in an Arab country, the first printing press and a legal systems based on modern ideas. Thus, although the French occupation was short, the seeds of change sown were never to leave the Middle East. Ibrahim Pasha, Mohammed Ali's son and the Egyptian commander of the Egyptian invasion to Syria, carried and planted the ideas of egalitarianism between Muslims and non-Muslims in Syria and Palestine.

Ibrahim Pasha's expedition against Ottoman provinces in Syria and Palestine (1831-1832) was the first attempt of Egypt in modern times to regain its historic leading role in the Middle East. Under his command, aided by a group of professional French and British officers, such as General O.J.A. Save (known in Arabic as Suleman Pasha al-Fransawi) and General Prissic, he occupied Palestine and Syria (Kalbouni 1992:88; Al Bishri 1980:18-27). He received much support from the Egyptian Copts who also backed Egypt's new dynasty.

The Egyptians defeated the Ottoman army at Cony, endangering Istanbul. This forced the Ottomans to agree to cede their rule over Syria and at this point the Egyptians introduced the revolutionary concepts of equality for all citizens – the first time in a society where Muslims made up the vast majority of the population. Perusing the Egyptian edicts of the time, one grasps the petty control that had been enforced on the native Christians before the arrival of the Egyptians. Rescinded were the restrictions that declared non-Muslims could not wear red shoes or ride a horse. Hitherto they could only ride on the back of a donkey or a mule provided they used a wooden saddle only, "like women do" and always be ready to dismount to pay their respect to any Muslim they might meet on the road.

The Ottomans had not been the first to introduce humiliating restrictions on Christians. Similar restrictions had been imposed in the first century of the Muslim state. According to a ninth century

Muslim historians, a caliph ordered his governor in the newly occupied Egypt to, "seal with tin the necks of non-Muslims, to cut short the hair on their foreheads and prohibit them from riding on a horse's back. They are not to ride an animal on a saddle, but with their two legs on the same side of the mule or donkey they ride, the way women do. The *jizya* [head tax] must be collected, but not from women or from those who are too young to shave (their beards). The *Dhimmis* should not imitate the dress of Muslims or wear similar shoes" (Al Sayouti 1967:145).

Unfortunately, the Egyptian rule in Palestine lasted only nine short years. The European powers forced Ibrahim Pasha to withdraw to Egypt and let Syria, including Palestine, fall back into the long black night of the Ottoman Empire.

The Christians in Syria, Lebanon and Palestine did not wait for Napoleon's occupation of Egypt to renew contact with Europe. Lebanese Maronites had maintained friendly relations with Rome and the rest of Europe since the Crusades. Maronite clerics went to Europe to study in Catholic institutions and a special Maronite school was established in Rome in the 16th century. In 1610 graduates of this school in Rome established the first printing press in the Middle East – at the Maronite monastery of Dair Quzhayya. Soon the region's first books were printed – religious and literary – helping to usher in the cultural revolution.

The first Muslim printing in the world was introduced in 1727 in the aftermath of a revolutionary *fatwa* from the imperial mufti, Abdallah Efindi. That printing press, built in Istanbul, printed first in Turkish and later in Arabic (Rifa'ai 1967:117). This historic fact may explain the cultural gap between the Christian and Muslim Arabs (and Turks) in the last centuries. Christians established almost all of the Arab presses. Even the distinguished Egyptian newspaper *al Ahram* was only one of many Egyptian newspapers established by Syrian-Lebanese Christians in the 19th century.

Early in the 20th century a new regime came to rule the Ottoman Empire. A junta of colonels organized as a party of "Young Turkey" took power hoping to modernize the empire. One of the measures they introduced was a policy aimed at turning Arabs into

Turks by imposing the Turkish language as the only official language in government offices and schools. Educated Christian and Muslim Arabs discovered their mutual interest in resisting this threat to their national culture and founded some national Arab clubs and cultural groups. They were hoping for a reform in the imperial administration with the aim of establishing a state of decentralization (*la markaziya* in Arabic). This movement paved the road for the eruption of the first Arab revolts in modern times, and here Christians played a decisive role from the beginning and were a driving force in adopting this national approach.

A clash was almost inevitable between the Young Turks, with their attempts to force the peoples of the Ottoman sultanate to accept the Turkish culture, and the Arab elite who were willing to revolt against the Ottoman sultan – or the "Muslim Caliph" as he was called (Farsakh 1994:173). This uprising had been brewing (mainly in Lebanon) since the early decades of the 19th century, but only came out in the open after the Young Turks' military coup in 1908 and materialized in the form of an alliance between Great Britain and the Hashimite dynasty. These new allies fought side-by-side under the flying Union Jack against the Ottoman sultan in his capacity as Muslim caliph in the first Muslim jihad in history. This sultan declared the World War I a jihad or holy war with his German allies against the British "infidels" and their Arab allies.

In the small Muslim Museum next to al Aqsa Mosque in Jerusalem visitors can read both declarations of holy jihad by the Ottoman sultan and his enemy, the Sharif of Mecca, Hussein Ben Ali. These contradicting declarations could have demonstrated a new phase in Arab history – the triumph of an end of manipulating religion for sheer political ends and the birth of a secular movement. Alas, that was not the case.

After World War I the trend of mild secular Arab nationalism played a major role in Arab politics in the new independent Arab states. The short-lived Arab kingdom that was established in Damascus at the end of World War I was declared to be Arab and was meant to secure equal rights for Muslims, Christians and Jews (Al Arnaout 2000:18-19; Zurayk 1986:114). But this rapprochement vanished after World War II and this retreat came in the face of the military ambitious – and undisciplined – officers on the one side and the fanatic religious groups on the other.

The fact that Arabs still live in ambiguity about the legitimacy of the political regimes in most Arab states, or the basis on which these states stand – religious or secular – bears witness to a simple fact: that the national concept is still fragile. All Arab states consider Islam as the official religion of the state. The liberation from 400 years of continuous rule of the ignorant and corrupt Ottoman sultans freed the Arabs of the Middle East to try to build their own national institutions. But the skeleton of these new states could not stand the heavy burden of their grand expectations and they all collapsed under the military pressure.

The military juntas, in most cases, tried to gain legitimacy by promoting pro-Palestinian, anti-Zionist slogans and pledging to prepare military forces to take revenge. In order to plant these objectives in the consciousness of the masses they used religious terms and symbols. The "secular" liberal age – that period which started to take shape with Muhammad Ali declaring Egypt as an independent state in the 1820s and up to the Arab failure to prevent the establishment of Israel in Palestine – soon came to its abrupt end, cutting off the rare opportunities where relative freedom and openness between different religious groups in the modern Arab communities had prevailed. The Arabs usually refer to this short period as the Renaissance Age.

Muslims claim that Islam behaved in humane and just ways in their treatment of the *Dhimmis*. Many scholars on the Christian and Jewish side agree (Goitein 1964:62-88), drawing such conclusions by comparing the Muslims' treatment of the *Dhimmis* with the behavior of other conquerors during the same period. Of course, some of this might be simple propaganda generated by the hope that if students are taught to commend the past relations between Muslims and Christians, they will be encouraged to emulate such tolerance in their own time. Of course any generalization is risky and we can agree with Dr. Constantine Zurieq, a famous ideologue of the current Arab national movement, who writes: "Tolerance was typical to the treatment of Christians in the advancing, rising, open Muslim communities but this tolerance was limited and even diminishing at the era of withdrawal, division and troubles–or when non-Arabs came to rule the Muslim state.

The treatment of the non-Muslims was influenced, naturally, by the personal character of the various caliphs and their advisors and by the improving or deteriorating relationship the Muslim state was experiencing with foreign states, especially with the European Christian powers. On the whole, "Muslim states favored [Christians] which had no connections with Byzantine" (Parkes 1970:71). One fact was constant throughout Muslim history–the Christian community enjoyed the special status of *Ahl al Kitab* (people that own a holy book) and thus were entitled to be treated as *Dhimmis* (the protected). Christians paid a special head tax but were exempted from military service–nor were they allowed to bear witness in court against or for a Muslim. In those cases when a Christian was killed in a squabble with Muslims, the victim's family was entitled to receive some compensation, but it was an inferior sum compared to that of a Muslim in similar circumstances. As a group, Christians were recognized as religiously autonomous *Millet*–enjoying cultural autonomy inside their own ghetto.

Discriminatory laws against Christians and Jews were always on the books, but fortunately they were applied leniently. At times the Arab military aristocracy applied discriminatory regulations to both local Muslims and Christians. This happened in Egypt during the reign of the Abbasid Caliph Al-Mahdi (775-785) with unrest that went on for 40 years (782-832) climaxing in a general uprising of all Egyptians–Muslim and Copts–in the year 831 against oppressive policies. This revolt lasted nine months and was crushed only after a military onslaught against the rebels was led by Caliph Maamoun himself.

Basically we can conclude that throughout Muslim history, the status of the *Dhimmis* was grim but not often precarious and was fluid, especially during the rule of the Abbasyids in Baghdad (Farsakh 1994:73-74). Also this was true during the reign of the Shiite caliphs of the Fatimid dynasty that dominated Egypt and Syria for some 200 years between 969-1172.

The most notorious of these caliphs, Al Hakim Beamr Allah (996-1021), brutally demolished all churches – including the Holy Sepulcher in Jerusalem – forcing Christians to convert to Islam. The Jews, on the other hand, were treated quite leniently by him and became so enthusiastic about this caliph during his first years on the throne, they almost declared him holy. Finally he changed his policies towards both Jews and Christians, and during the latter part of his reign he reversed himself, liberalized his policies and permitted Christians and Jews who had been forced to convert, to go back to the faith of their ancestors and allowed them to rebuild their churches (Goitein op cit 83-85).

The Ottoman rule in Syria which lasted for some 400 years was so despotic that the entire population fell into poverty and ignorance. Thus in 1931 the Bedouin Arabs of Beir Shiva in southern Palestine were almost entirely illiterate, as were the majority of farmers. Even urban Muslims were illiterate, but the Negev nomads were in the worst shape. According to the British census conducted that year, only 53 persons (out of a total population of 47,981) claimed to be literate (including one female) (Mills 1931:334) which meant that 99% of this nomad society was illiterate – even after 15 years of British rule during which time they had opened some free governmental educational institutes in the Holy Land.

In the urban and rural areas of Jerusalem, Samaria and Galilee, Christian institutions functioned and contributed to the education of the entire population, so the picture was better: a quarter of school-aged Muslim boys studied while only one of every 20 girls attended; at the same time two-thirds of Christian males and almost half of the Christian women were literate.

At the beginning of the liberal 19th century, Christian Arabs made up some 10% of the general population of Palestine – between 12,000 and 15,000 – most of them Greek Orthodox (Colbi nd:43). Much of this community lived near the holy sites, in almost the same towns and villages their ancestors had lived in all the way back to the first centuries after the birth of our Lord – as has been confirmed both by church history and the latest archaeological discoveries (Briandt op cit 13).

Our ancestors were Jews and Arabs, but they also intermarried with those who came from other nations to the Holy Land and accepted Jesus as Lord and Savior. There were probably no Muslims in this lineage, for until 1841 the Muslim government had no choice but to kill any Muslims who refuted their faith for any reason. The Muslim holy texts command believers to impose a total and eternal submission to Islam on those who ever "made their faith public." The crime of leaving the Muslim faith, *al Redda*, is the worst a person can commit according to the shari'ah (Muslim law). Thus it is easy to draw the inference that none of the ancestors of native Christians today came from the ranks of the Muslims. In a Muslim state, Islam is a one-way street.

Obviously, this Muslim policy caused many problems for the European missionary groups so this issue was frequently raised and discussed with Ottoman authorities under the rubric of human rights and freedom of religion. Sir Henry Bulwer, the British ambassador to the sultan's court, "won" an answer to his memorandum to the sultan (18 July 1864):

> The Turkish Government will not allow any attempts, public or private, to assail the Mussulman religion. They will not allow the missionaries or their agents to speak publicly against Mohammedanism. All attempts to convince Mussulmans that their religion is not of God must be regarded by the Turkish authorities as an insult to the national faith. They will not allow the sale or distribution "in public or private" of any controversial works" (Al Tibawi 1961:166).

Until today, even in the most "liberal" states such as Egypt, any Muslim-born persons who accept Jesus Christ as Lord and Savior may be held in jail until they repent or discover a solution to this "major problem." According to the shari'ah, the punishment of those who commit apostasy is clear. Such persons should be stoned to death and any spouse should be divorced. Sheikh Abd Al Latif Fayed, editor of the official High Council of Muslim Affairs monthly *Al Manbar Al Islam* in his defense of the verdict in the case of a Muslim scholar who challenged some interpretations of the old texts, wrote that since this legal code has not been fully adopted (in Egypt) as a valid civil law, a person born into a Muslim family should be isolated away from any contact with students or any other person outside the religious community to make certain they will be susceptible to enticement or seduction. (July 1995).The Egyptian government may also use emergency legislation to detain citizens without pressing specific charges on the ground that converts threaten social peace and inter-communal relations.

Thus we can conclude that most of the current Christian population in the Middle East are ethnically Arabs (though some are of Jewish origin) or have roots in one or more of the ancient peoples who accepted Jesus Christ before the birth of Islam and who remained faithful to Christ. The fact that they are a blend of many origins does not make them less Arab than their Muslim neighbors, who are a similar blend of Arab, Kurd, Turk, Selcuk, Persian, Greek and other ancient nations – Semites or Arian. At a certain time in history, the ancestors of today's Muslims decided to desert their Christian (or other) faiths and embrace Islam. These new Muslims were forced to know some Arabic because all Muslims must recite their prayers in the Arabic language. They lived, in most cases, under a Muslim government in which the Arabic language had an esteemed status and this was another incentive for a non-Arab Muslim to aspire to be accepted as one.

The Arab Muslim empire began its downfall 150 years after it was established. The first move in that direction took place when the Abbasid Caliph Al Maua'tasim (798-842) decided to hire the first non-Arab warriors to replace Arabs (Al Masa'oudi 1958:41, Farsakh op city 67). These shepherds from central Asia came first to offer their services in the ranks of the Muslim armies as soldiers of fortune, but soon their outstanding officers began seeking influence, interfering in the government and dictating policy to their liking. As mentioned, in the final stages, the Mameluks divided the empire between them and turned the caliph into a mere puppet to give themselves legitimacy in the eyes of the populace. Unfortunately these were bloodthirsty despots and the traditionally acknowledged human liberties in Muslim lands under the first "righteous" caliphs became scarce. Tyranny became absolute.

Thus began the Arab diaspora with many of the elite heading toward the flourishing colonies on the western flank of their empire in Andalusia or Spain. For much of the second millennium, the Arabs in the Middle East were under the heavy yoke of their non-Arab Muslim warring dynasties – the Seljuks, Turks, Kurds, and others. Only in the 19th century was there to be a change in the power structures. After 400 long years of stagnation under the Ottoman Turks, people in this part of the world perceived the coming of the European colonial powers as a progressive step. Today all Arab peoples live in Arab-run independent states. The Palestinians, who won a right to their national land in the Oslo agreements of 1993, are also included in this number.

In the early days of this movement towards independence, the Arabic language was in a state of miserable confusion. Almost no printed books were available in the language aside from old traditional religious texts and a few collections of old stories in local spoken dialects. Such decadence invited other old languages and local dialects to fill communication needs and to create cultural barriers between the Arab countries. The golden ages of Arab culture had crumbled into a dark, damp cellar. Today, however, millions of Arab university graduates are busying themselves in every field of human knowledge, in hundreds of educational institutes worldwide and Arabic is a modern, living language used for daily life, cultural expression and for scientific purposes by all Arabs, including all native Christian clergy of the Middle East.

The Maronites, the Assyrians, the Copts and those Armenians who live in the Holy Land use their own historic languages, but in most cases they depend on Arabic for school and commerce and even liturgical rituals. The renaissance of Arab culture was made possible by the revival of the Arabic language during the second half of the 19th century which in turn made it possible for all Christian churches to gather together with a common language.

Of course there were still problems to be surmounted if Christians were to survive as a viable community in the Holy Land.

6

The Lost St. Augustine Church

"How the mighty are fallen" (2 Sam 1:19).

It seems reasonable to accept the fact that Christians survived during the last 1,400 years in the Holy Land under the Muslim Empire because of the early Islamic tolerance towards others of monotheistic faiths. The Muslims were wise enough to permit conquered Syrian Christian farmers freedom to continue with their normal life and worship – and were satisfied with exacting special taxes from them. But this leaves us with disturbing questions: What happened to all those flourishing churches in North Africa? Except for those in Egypt, why did they vanish entirely? What made the Egyptian church an exception? What happened to Saint Augustine's church?

Enough historical evidence exists to explain why no Christians lived in the Arabian Peninsula for most of the last 1,400 years (except for the British and American soldiers who were posted there for military reasons or those involved in the petroleum industry). Christians had been driven from this region after the first decade of Islam's triumph due to the controversial orders of the second caliph, Omar, who claimed that Mohammed, Islam's prophet, ordered it.

But then why were Jews permitted to live inside Islam's Holy Land until 1948? And why were Jews able to continue enjoying relatively warm havens in Morocco, Algiers, Tunisia and Libya until the establishment of Jewish Israel – with its subsequent results of creating the catastrophe of Palestine and the mainly Muslim Palestinian people? Did Muslims consider Jews more deserving than Christians? Was this tolerance shown the Jews because of or despite their religion? The Muslims' holy book *Al Koran* orders Muslims to prefer and befriend Christians. Why did they then act in such contradictory manners?

I began asking these questions over 40 years ago after an accidental meeting in Florence with the only Christian-born North African intellectual I had met: Jean Amroushe. At this point – August 1960 – this Algerian-French poet was ardently occupied by his personal dilemma. This son of an Algerian family, educated in France, wanted only one thing – to bring peace and freedom to his people in Algeria. To my disappointment and subsequent annoyance, he was uninterested in the Christians' history or even in discussing the topic of North African Christianity under Muslim rule.

The classic explanation for why the North African church disappeared is that the Islamization of the native tribes, the Berbers, was a consequence of the Muslim conquest. They were neither forcibly converted nor systematically missionized by their conquerors. Rather, Islam became an ideology through which the Berbers justified their rebellion against their caliph and lent their support to rulers who rejected the caliphical authority.

This theory is less than convincing, for why was this way of embracing Islam not adopted in the neighboring country of Egypt or on the slopes of Mount Lebanon? A more plausible explanation, to my thinking, is to note the basic differences between Arab, Assyrian, Maronite and Coptic Christians. These all were natives of the respective lands they lived in. On the other hand, the dominating leadership of North African Christians was not an integral part of the indigenous population – the Berber tribe – but rather Punic Roman citizens who settled in Carthage after they fled defeated from their Phoenician settlements (in the Tunisian, Libyan and Algerian seacoasts of our days).

These Punics of a foreign race were relatively new settlers when the Muslims conquered these lands. Once again most of them decided to pull up stakes and not live under Muslim rule. Abandoning these colonies, they sailed across the sea back to Europe – their original homeland. This is basically parallel to what happened in the mid-20th century when French settlers packed their suitcases and returned to France immediately after Tunis won its independence peacefully (1956) and later in Algiers after their long struggle for independence (1962).

Interestingly enough, in most cases North Africa's native population not only embraced Islam, they also accepted an Arab-Muslim identity as well. Possibly the Berbers, as nomad shepherds and warriors, could relate to the Arabs and soon many Berbers became distinguished leaders of Muslim expeditions – including the most famous Muslim conqueror of Spain, Tariq Ben Zeyad (whose name was placed on the Arabic form of Mount Gibraltar – Mount Tariq).

Later something similar occurred in Turkey in a much more protracted process. The Greek Christian community in Asia Minor fought adamantly – on their own – against Muslim armies for over 800 years (636–1452). Military help from European Christians did not appear because Rome demanded one strident condition: the return of Byzantine to "union" with the Roman Catholic church. Byzantine refused the dictate and fought bravely until their defeat and surrender to Ottoman-Muslims in May 1453. At this point most Greek Christians, like the Latin Catholics in North Africa, had little choice other than to leave behind Greek territories in Asia – after 2,500 years of settlement in those lands.

The last Greeks left Turkey in 1924 in compliance with the infamous "transfer" agreement between Greece and Turkey some 500 years before. This "exchange of population" was the result of an interior struggle Greeks had between king and prime minister over the future policy. They reluctantly signed the Lausanne

Treaty on July 24, 1923, and the result was the evacuation of 1.3 million Christians from Turkey to Greece.

This briefly explains how the vast majority of North African society joined Islam and became "Arab" – which until recently was a term used interchangeably. But now growing cultural movements in Morocco, Algiers, Tunis and Libya are demanding recognition of their separate national rights (*Al Quds* 8/6/2001). The North African tribes lived as desert nomads with interests revolving around tribal and regional issues, unlike the Persians who had a national life before the birth of Islam. Thus after the military defeat of the North Africans, when they embraced Islam (and Arabic as the ritual language) they saved and preserved their own national-cultural language and heritage.

The history of the Catholic church in North Africa traces the decline of the Christian community after the Muslim invasion. In the fifth century, before the birth of Islam, 535 bishops presided over dioceses in North Africa. In the year 650 in Algiers alone there were 220 bishops. Within a few years this number had been reduced to 40 bishops and by 1053, on the eve of the Crusades, only five bishops were left in North Africa. In 1975, after the French occupation was removed and Morocco, Algiers and Tunisia became independent states, only some 60,000 Catholics lived in these countries, most of whom were originally French citizens. This community was served by 330 priests, monks and nuns (*All Massarah* July 1975). Fr. Jean Corbon, a French-born priest who served a parish of Greek Catholic Arabs in the Middle East for decades, said, "No doubt the churches in Asia Minor and the Maghreb countries vanished because of their failure to take root in the land of those countries" (Corbon 1980:22).

This theory seems quite valid, at least for the Turkish chapter in this tragedy: Asia Minor, Byzantine (the site of so rich a history of apostolic activities) and the land of Antioch ("the great city of God"), evangelized by Paul and Barnabas where Christians were first called by that name, became a place where Christianity lives virtually underground. Antioch today is a desolate town called

Yalvac and Great Ephesus a hill of rubble with a small Turkish town called Selcuk nearby.

Even in the 19th century the Christian community had a significant presence in Turkey. In Istanbul, 80% of the population were Christians. Today, the total number of Christians from all cultural backgrounds comes to under 100,000 people – .015% of the total Turkish population. Of course, an integral part of this decline was a result of the genocide of the Armenians – the first nation on earth to embrace the Christian faith. A wave of bloodshed at the hands of Kurd tribes at the end of the 19th century (with the Ottoman sultan's blessing) was followed shortly thereafter by the Ottoman-Turks themselves killing 1.5 million innocent civilians up through 1915.

Many of the survivors of these massacres found refuge in Syria and Lebanon and their offspring still make up a noticeable community of the Syrian Christians – especially in the northern town of Aleppo – as well as in Lebanon. Some 10,000 Armenians survivors arrived in Jerusalem by the end of World War I and by 1920 this community had doubled, but unfortunately their industrious presence did not last long. Those who could, emigrated elsewhere at the first occasion to escape the violence between the Arabs and the Jews in Palestine. Another exodus of the remaining Armenians left Jerusalem in the aftermath of 1948 war; more fled after the 1967 war and the severe conditions that dominated the city during the struggle that has continued ever since. Today fewer than 2,000 Armenians live in Jerusalem.

This pattern of small Christian communities hastily vanishing seems to be the alarming rule. There were 200,000 Tunis Christians in that country when the French rule ended in 1956. By 1995 this population had dropped to 10,000 Christians with a further dwindling expected throughout this century. This same story can be told of the Greeks and Greek-Catholics in Egypt and Sudan.

During the last century Egypt and cosmopolitan Alexandria, in particular, were home to many Greeks and other European expatriates. Since the Free Officers coup in 1952 the members of these communities have abandoned Egypt in the face of heated national and religious prejudice. For example, the Arab Greek-Catholic community: it originated with Syrian and Lebanese traders, publishers, writers and artists who for over a century had found such safe haven and welcome in Egypt that by 1940 some 40,000 Greek Catholics resided mainly in urban Egypt. By the end of the 20th century this population was reduced to 9,000 people in both Egypt and Sudan (Hakim 1988:71).

The common denominator for the disappearance of these Christian communities in Jerusalem, Tunis and Egypt seems to center on their being transplanted foreigners. The Tunisian Christians were mainly from France; the Greek-Catholics were Lebanese and Syrians, and the Armenians were fleeing the massacres in their homeland. Mostly, they lived separately from the main population and usually did not share the low economic standards nor bleak future faced by the majority of Egyptians since they were better educated and mostly middle-class. They did not share the Egyptians' unique pride in living by the Nile ("sea") in *um al Donya* ("mother of the universe"), as the Egyptian call their homeland.

National Christian churches tend to be the norm in the Middle East where most of the faithful are divided on linguistic lines. Religious belief was always impacted by the local heritage and became an integral part of it but little effort was made at amalgamation. Mostly the efforts were for propagation – so the kings and highest clerics of Byzantine were united in trying to force the Greek language and worldview on the entire population.

To this day most Arab Christians in the Middle East chant their hymns in Greek, even though most of the prayers and hymns of the Greek-Orthodox and Greek-Melkite Catholics have been translated into the Arabic language so the faithful could understand what is said in church. The Greek Orthodox patriarchate in Damascus, reigning over a diocese that includes Syria and Lebanon, won independence from the Greek hierarchy a century ago; this diocese has been entirely Arabized. Unfortunately the Jerusalem patriarchate, whose diocese includes Israel, Palestine and Jordan, is still struggling for independence and most of their Greek clergy are not fluent in Arabic.

In 1725 the Greek Melkite Catholics split from the Greek Orthodox and the agreement they signed with the Vatican granted them autonomy from the Holy See as far as running their own internal affairs. They use Arabic as the main language in the liturgy, but add a few Greek hymns as a cultural relic of their church tradition. Other local Catholics and Maronites use two Aramaic-Syrian dialects, while the Assyrian-Nestorians, or the Christian Church of the East (mainly in Iraq), jealously preserve their own old dialect, as do the Copts of Egypt.

It seems obvious that the national tongue is a decisive factor in determining what church a Christian belongs to. The failure of Byzantine to force the Greek language and culture on the empire was probably why the division in the church occurred, rather than the theological controversy expounded at the Chalcedon Council of 451. It was 1,520 years after this tragic schism in the church at Chalcedon before the Roman Catholic pope met in 1971 with the head of the Church of the East in Rome and these two heads of the divided church agreed the catastrophe that befell the church "was not justifiable, since it was based on a wrong understanding of some cultural terms only" (*Al Hikma* no. 4:1999). Several years later Pope John-Paul II reiterated during a visit to Athens (May 5, 2001) that part of the blame for the schism between Catholic and Orthodox churches was due to linguistic misunderstandings.

There were other non-theological reasons behind this schism. Byzantine was too weak militarily to impose its political hegemony in the region. Christians under Persian rule had to distance themselves from any alien influence since Byzantine was considered an enemy to the Persian Empire; thus any relationship between Persian subjects and the Byzantine enemy was seen as a threat by ruling monarchy, making these subjects automatically suspect. A graphic illustration of this had happened in Persia after Constantine issued his famous decree to stop oppressing Christians. In response, an anti-Christian edict was issued by King Shahbur of Persia demanding that Christian subjects be persecuted since "they live in our land but share the views of Caesar our enemy" (Waterfield 1973:19-20).

So hostilities continued between the states–who saw the religious community eroding their loyalty base. And the churches, faced with the danger of extinction, had to maneuver to survive– by demonstrating basic allegiance to the government and proving their loyalty to the national powers. Thus the rather docile, solemn, but consistent Copts in Egypt managed to persevere; as did the vibrant, hard-working and industrious Maronites in Lebanon and the Orthodox natives from Syria and Palestine, who assimilated in many areas, but who preserved their distinctive entity.

The differences between these churches and the style they were to follow was deeply influenced by the unique predicaments of each community–a topic we shall explore further.

7

Egypt's Twins: Muslims and Copts

"On that day Israel will be the third with Egypt and Assyria, a blessing in the midst of the earth" (Is 19:24).

Egyptian-Christians, or Copts, like their Egyptian Muslim neighbors, have known much suffering during their history. They can claim the title of being a nation that ruled a great empire in ancient history, but has lived under foreign domination for most of the last 2,000 years. The majority of Egypt's Muslim and non-Muslim governors for the past 1,400 years have been Turks, Mameluks, British and Albanians – but not Egyptians. The first Egyptian officers were enlisted in 1822, some 16 years after Muhammad Ali, an Albanian officer, seized power and established a royal dynasty that ruled Egypt for the next 150 years. The last king from this line was deposed in 1952 in a coup d'état led by the first Egyptian Arab to rule the country (Al Bishri 1980:18).

The founders of the Christian community in Egypt were subjected to harsh persecution and oppression by the Roman Empire when they became Christians under the apostolic influence of Saint Marcus (Mark), the evangelist. Cruel massacres and mass martyrdoms reached their peak in 284 at the hands of the Roman emperor Gaius Diocletianus (245-305). But the Copt church heralded this holocaust as a landmark in their history and consider this date as the starting point of their church calendar.

Strangely enough, even though Byzantine embraced Christianity as its official religion, this did not bring much peace between Constantinople or Rome and Alexandria. The Chalcedon Council opened old wounds and the Copts insisted on adopting the dogma of one divine nature for Christ, while Byzantine and Antioch declared this a heresy. The leaders of both churches exchanged mutual excommunications.

This heated controversy ended in separation and internal conflict for hundreds of years until finally the birth of Islam and the Muslim occupation of Egypt put a stop to the ecclesiastical dissension. Arab historians tend to emphasize that the first Muslim occupation was in response to an invitation from the Coptic hierarchy extended to Omar Ibn al A'ass because the Egyptian Copts wanted to rid themselves of Roman oppression (Badawi 1980:34-35).

Sadeq Aziz, a Coptic writer, agreed with this assessment and published his view in the aftermath of the sectarian unrest that shocked Egypt in the last days of President Anwar al Sadat in 1980. Aziz wrote that Benjamin, the Coptic patriarch (pope of the Saint Marcus Church, according to his official title), ordered the faithful to welcome the Ishmaelite soldiers (Badawi ibid 113). The official Coptic version of these long-ago events utterly contradicts this picture. Egypt at the time was under Roman occupation, and the Byzantine establishment was forcefully acting to impose its hegemony, including their belief that the Egyptian church should adopt the Nicene Creed and the Chalcedon Council resolutions.

Bishop Yuhana of the Nikiu diocese near the city of Damanhor (which includes within its borders the famous Wadi Natrun monasteries where 70,000 monks lived at the time) was an eyewitness to the Muslim occupation and left a firsthand account of the event—a book of some 120 chapters recording Egypt's history from the creation up to the Muslim invasion. The last chapter is dedicated to the Muslim invasion and entirely contradicts the Muslim claim they were invited to come to the rescue or even that any monks welcomed the Muslim soldiers. This text, originally written in Coptic, was translated into Arabic, Greek and the Ethiopian languages. The original text plus the Arabic and Greek translations were lost, but one copy of the Ethiopian translation was found in an Ethiopian church and translated into German by H.M. Zotenberg (1834–1914), with an introduction in French. The English translation was done by R.H. Charles in 1916.

The Copt bishop-historian describes some of the military operations that took place between the Muslim-Arab invaders ("the Ismaa'ilites") and the Greeks (whom he called "the enemies of Christ"). He prays that God will inflict his punishment upon the Muslims for the atrocities they committed against the Copts, invoking God to deal out to them the same punishment inflicted against the pharaohs. On the other hand the bishop does not conceal his happiness at the fall of the Roman-Greeks and considers it a heavenly revenge on the "unclean, dirty enemies of Christ and the enemies of the right faith–the Orthodoxy."

He attributes the failure of the Roman soldiers to corruption in their ranks and the conflicts that divided them, creating disharmony inside their confused military units. A policy of "divide and conquer" had been used by Emperor Justinian to secure his reign and weaken any potential military adversaries. Thus after the Byzantine victory against Persia, the emperor ordered his military units only be deployed in defensive posts along the seacoast.

Even still, according to this text, Egypt did not welcome the Muslim Arabs. On the contrary, the Copts joined the Romans in fighting back and resisting the Muslim invasion forcing the Muslim commander Omar Ibn al A'ass to engage in a long year of fierce fighting against united Roman and native Copt forces before capturing the Egyptian ports on the Mediterranean Sea. In the process the Muslims perpetrated cruel atrocities against the local population to halt the resistance and bring the country to its knees. Soldiers set towns and harvests on fire, uprooted trees and caused widespread hunger to those who stood in their way. But immediately after his triumph the Muslim commander paid his respects to the heads of the Egyptian-Coptic church–and announced that their clergy would be exempt from the heavy taxes that he ordered collected from the towns and villages that had fought against him –triple the amount they had paid in previous years.

Another Copt historian, Rev. Dawod Aziz, paints such a gloomy picture of this period that one is left questioning his analysis and obvious exaggeration. He claims the Coptic community in Egypt diminished under the Muslims from some 35 million to a few hundred thousands (Aziz 1980:35). But Gamal Badawi, a late 20th century Egyptian Muslim writer, has a different take on this issue: Amro Ibn al A'as made it very difficult for Copts to convert to Islam because he wanted them to go on paying the *Jizya* tax, for he was most interested in assuring a proper revenue for his coffers. This *Jizya* tax was traditionally imposed on non-Muslim monotheists such as Christians and Jews–a "privilege" that was sometimes an option for other non-Muslims (Badawi op cit:36-37).

Iris Habib al Masri, also a Coptic historian, quotes various sources, European and Coptic, who ridicule the Muslim version of the flowers with which their soldiers were welcomed in Egypt. She finds the tale about a Copt patriarch named al-Muqawqas who signed an agreement with the Muslim commander to be a total fabrication. The Coptic church never had a patriarch with such a name and she thinks the person referred to might have been a Greek bishop called Bishop Cyrus who had been dispatched to Egypt by the Byzantine church a few years before the Muslim invasion in order to try to dominate and control the Coptic church. He was never successful in his goal nor accepted by the Egyptian clergy as a leader of the Coptic church (Al Masri 1978:278-279).

In any case, the Coptic church survived these assaults with an impressive vitality for 1,400 years under various Muslim dynasties and religious sects. The theory of German historian Otto Meinardus of how the Copts managed to do this with such strength after extended adversity was that the preservation of firm Christian family ethics overcame social pressures and hardships. He concluded that the Coptic minority survived because the Coptic family and homelife sustained the group's identity (1970:281).

In many ways the Coptic church embodied the Egyptian society, amalgamating the virtues of a genuine Christian with the pre-Christian Egyptian culture, pride and heritage—thus preserving much of this ethos down to our present day. The Christian churches of neighboring North Africa who took the opposite routes arrived at a dead end—and have vanished all together.

Perhaps the fact that Egypt was already under foreign rule (Persian, Roman and Greek) before the Muslim conquest, prepared the Copts for the frugal life of an oppressed society. This millennium-long tradition of having alien rule explains why Copts tend to delight in repeating a story about the Egyptian Patriarch Anba Butrus VII, who was visited by the Russian imperial ambassador early in the 19th century. Arriving at the patriarch's residence, the ambassador was met by an old monk in shabby dress. The Russian asked him to announce his arrival but the lowly monk explained there was no need because he was Anba Butrus.

The guest was impressed by the humble Egyptian monk's simplicity and modesty and informed the head of the Coptic church that the czar, Alexander I, the great emperor who had defeated Napoleon was willing to become the protector of the Copts of Egypt. The Egyptian prelate politely inquired about the czar's intentions, wondering what reward he might expect from the Copts. The Russian diplomat explained the czar's only interest was the well-being of his fellow Christians. The Copt graciously explained that although the czar had defeated Napoleon, still he was not "stronger than our Lord Jesus Christ" in whom the Copts had their tradition of trusting for protection and so they saw no reason to change that.

Interestingly enough, the Crusader knights did not consider Egypt as a target on their way to liberate the Holy Sepulcher until the fourth Crusade. Even though they were not welcomed in Egypt, still their presence was disquieting for the local Muslim community's suspicion of the Copts' loyalty rose up to meet both dangers—from the invaders and the potential Trojan horse. There is a cynical Arabic saying that says, "When you can't hit the horse that ran way, you can always take revenge by beating the saddle." Thus as it is always easier to take revenge on docile civilians, when the "Francs put the town Fustat, including its inhabitants, on fire ... Syroukh, the local governor took revenge against the Copts. But the merciful Lord did not allow Syroukh to live long and Saladin – his successor as the vizier of the last Fatimied Caliph – was a friend of the Copts" (Al Masri op cit 388-390).

Of course, Saladin might have been a friend of the Copts, but a decade later as commander of the Muslim power, he defeated the Crusaders at the Horns of Hittin near Nazareth. He did, however, remain generous to the local Copts, inviting them to visit Jerusalem and commanding they be allotted a church inside the Holy Sepulcher Cathedral.

In fact, Copts owned that church until 1970 when on the eve of Easter the Israeli police helped Ethiopian monks capture it. I was personally at the scene when the Copts' traditional procession marched from that church ("The Angel Gabrial or Dair as-Sultan Monastery") to the Holy Sepulcher. At that point some Ethiopian monks, with the help of the police, blocked their way of return and changed the locks on the spot so the Copts could not get back into their own church. When the Copts appealed to Israel's high court (and won a unanimous verdict in their favor) the Israeli government intervened, asking for a delay "to restore the status quo" (Benziman 1973:127). Then they simply overruled the court declaring this case was "a religious issue not to be decided in court."

Of course, three decades later it is obvious to everyone that this was purely a political act. At the time, Israel was trying to curry the favor of Ethiopia and had bad feelings towards Egypt. The circumstances later changed and Egypt was the first Arab state to sign a peace treaty with Israel, but for the Egyptian President Anwar al Sadat, the Coptic monastery was not a burning issue. Today, more than 30 years after the Copts lost their shrine and 20 years after the Egyptian-Israeli Peace Accords, the monastery is still in the hands of the Ethiopians. The Egyptian government is indifferent towards this issue, but the Coptic church still maintains a state of war with Israel – church authorities refuse to permit their faithful to visit Jerusalem on pilgrimages and those who defy this mandate are excommunicated.

An Israeli scholar on the Christian churches and their relations with the Israeli government, in speaking of this sordid intervention in the dispute between two Christian churches, admits "the problem remained unsolved" since both Ethiopia and Egypt are essential to Israeli interests (Tsimhoni 1993:96).

As to Saladin, the famous Kurd soldier who defeated the European Crusaders, Copt historians are generous in their praise. Saladin's personal secretary was a Copt and held an esteemed post in the Ayyobi Court (Al Masri ibid 74-76). Coptic historians also claimed that Saladin's sons, Aziz and Kamel, were friendly and tolerant to the Copts, who often managed to make positive contributions to the public life of their homeland and worked assiduously to manipulate systems and advance in the political life and influence of their community. Many Egyptian historians, Muslim and Christian, agree with Zaher Reyad's analysis: he claimed that Mohammed Ali, founder of the modern Egyptian state, was assisted during the first decade of the 19th century by Copts (Reyad 1979:22).

The Copts were in turmoil during the Napoleonic invasion. Some were overjoyed with hopes that these 37,000 French soldiers, supposedly Christian, were modern-day angels sent by God to save them from the dangers of growing "Muslim nationalism." But the French proved disillusioning. Napoleon, attempting to win the Muslims' fealty, declared himself and his army as self-appointed servants of the caliph who came with the Ottoman sultan's blessings to rescue Egypt from the wicked Mameluks and restore the Ottoman rule. Egyptian Muslims, rather suspicious by nature, decided to test the sincerity of Napoleon's conversion to Islam by proposing a massacre of the Copts. The French military governor refused to concur when he discovered the Copts were the only community he could trust (Meinardus op cit 14-15).

In his memoirs, Marshal Louis Alexander Berthier, chief of staff of the French Army of the East under Napoleon's command during the Egyptian expedition, seldom mentions the Christian population of Egypt and Syria. He does tell about some Christians from Damascus who informed the French about the movement of Turkish troops and about a village called Ramleh in which Christians formed the majority of the population and where they discovered biscuit stores to ease their hunger. He also recounts the story of some 400 local Christians who were killed and mutilated by the Acre governor, the infamous and cruel Ahmad Pasha al Jazzar, during Napoleon's siege of that town (Bertia 1999).

Many Copts volunteered to fight on the side of the French under their leader Moa'llem Yaa'cob (the teacher Jacob), who enlisted some 2,000 soldiers before the French pulled out of the Egyptian front three years after their initial landing in Alexandria. Zaher Reyad and Iris Habib al Masri, two contemporary Coptic historians, both praise Yaa'cob al-Mallawi's attempt to ally the Copts with the French colonial government by rallying this large military force in support of the endangered French. This Francophone Egyptian joined his allies when they returned to France in an effort to persuade the French to make Egypt a French protectorate and establish there a base for further colonial expansion in Africa (Reyad op cit 56). His hopes were dashed when the English defeated the French fleet at Abuqir (near Alexandria) and then proceeded to deliver Egypt back to the rule of their Ottoman allies through their Mameluk agents.

An ambitious Albanian soldier, Muhammad Ali, who arrived in Egypt intent on expelling the French, was so disappointed to find his enemies missing that he embarked on a new idea. In 1811 he rebelled against the Ottoman sultan, massacred his agents—the Mameluks—and declared himself ruler of Egypt. The Copts stood by him. This alliance was not in vain. Famous Austrian monk and traveler Maria-Joseph de Geramb, writing of his Holy Land tour (1881 to 1883) 40 years after the Egyptian attempt to "liberate" Syria from Ottoman rule, discovered that Mohammed Ali and his son Ibrahim were still considered the main source of hope for Christians and Jews (Eish Shalom 1965:444).

Mohammed Ali's dynasty ruled Egypt for 120 years—until 1952 when a military coup ended it. Through the years this royal dynasty had not been in total control. When European British soldiers conquered Egypt in 1882 they left the local government in place, but subject to British oversight. Egyptian Copts were willing to help the British, hoping this divide-and-rule policy might result in a Coptic autonomy in the southern region of Egypt around the town of Assyot.

When this controversial arrangement was published in the Egyptian press – which had been established late in the 19th century by Syrian-Lebanese Christians who had fled to Egypt to escape the tyranny of the Ottomans in their homelands – it caused a furor. Finally this "war of words" between Copts and Muslims over Coptic rights in Egypt, culminated in a general congress of the Coptic nation that met at Assyot in March 1911. Surprisingly, the majority of the Copts who addressed the congress did not call for a Coptic irredenta. Instead, most expressed dismay at the rising Muslim nationalism and the move to return Egypt to the Ottoman caliphate, an idea that had been propagated by the celebrated Muslim sheikh Jamal Ed Din Al Afghani (1839-1897). The reaction of the Muslim majority to the Coptic congress was mixed, still "they were cautious not to bring things to an explosion in the sectarian relations, on a Muslim-Christian line" (Badawi op cit 29).

This policy of restraint on both sides soon yielded its fruits. The Egyptian national unity, as a modern movement for both communities, was born and crystallized during the 1919 revolution against British rule in Egypt. Muslims and Christians marched together, demonstrating to the world a unity with their Egyptian flags embellished with a crucifix inside a crescent. Their slogan was "Faith for God, Homeland for All" (*Al Din lilah, wal wattan lil Jamiea*). After the marches they prayed together in churches and mosques as Muslim and Christian leaders declared allegiance to a homeland for all Egyptians based on universal egalitarian lines.

Thus the modern Egyptian national ethos was born on the banks of the Nile under anti-foreign slogans. One could hope that both the Copts and the Muslims were like the two wings of a bird, carrying Egypt into happier days of sovereignty where they would recover some of their glorious past.

At the forefront of Egypt's national movement stood the Coptic leaders Makram O'baid and Wissa Wassif alongside the Muslim Sa'ad Zaghlol. They worked together in the struggle against British occupation and received their reward when Egypt won its initial independence in 1922. Eight years later King Fuad made an attempt to limit the authority of the Egyptian parliament and ordered its speaker, the Copt Wisa Wassif, not to convene the assembly. Wassif, however, personally broke the locks the police had put on the gates and forced his way into the meeting hall, leading the other members with him. A year later, when Wassif was poisoned, a tumultuous crowd at his funeral decried the terrible deed.

The Egyptian struggle for human and civil rights and against those in the royal court who collaborated with foreigners became the rallying cry for those who shaped modern Egypt. Alas! This struggle for self-rule was stifled before it came to fruition, because there was a simultaneous rise of totalitarian and revolutionary ideas in Europe. Soon the revolutionary Communists, Marxists, Socialists and racist Fascists and pro-Nazi groups began to spread across the Mediterranean to Egypt and the Middle East.

Coinciding with the ferment of these various ideologies, the Egyptian king decided it was the proper time to declare himself the Muslims' caliph and establish a new populist Muslim political movement – the Ikhwan al Muslimin (the Muslim Brothers Movement). The ideologue of this movement, sheikh Hasan al Banna, soon let it be known that beyond setting the base for the organization, establishing 300 branches, they were ready to proceed to the action phase and "place our hopes in the royal majesty, may Allah support him" (Shukri 1993:193-215).

This action phase of the Muslim Brothers soon arrived with devastating consequences – dividing Egypt between Muslims and non-Muslims. The entire national heritage was threatened, and the threat proved to be more real than most Copts had originally feared. Egyptian voters, during the four Parliamentary election campaigns between 1924 and 1929 had granted the Copt candidates 15 to 23 seats. Now the Copts had to be satisfied with four seats in 1931, six seats in 1938, twelve in 1945 and only five in 1950 (the last elections before the military coup that ended Egypt's multi-parties political system for generations).

The British occupation, begun in 1882, officially ended in 1922 but the British presence, both politically and militarily, did not disappear for another 30 years. Even so, most of the blame for the corrupt regime was laid on the foreign influence. British troops became the main target for any shortcomings and hardships the Egyptians faced – and these were myriad. Rampant inflation, poorly paid labor and limited cultivable land caused much suffering, especially during the World War II period.

When the war ended, the hopes for a new world order proved illusory. The triumph of the U.K. and its democratic allies did not solve Egypt's problems. Instead thousands of Egyptian workers who had been feeding their families from the war industries lost their jobs, and unemployment skyrocketed. Then the humiliating defeat of the Egyptian soldiers in the 1948 war against Israel added more fuel to public anger.

The Arab states' ruling elites were divided in two camps. The Hashimite dynasty (that ruled Iraq and Jordan and has a following in Syria and Palestine) were opposed by an ad hoc coalition of Egyptian-Saudis and Palestinians. Each side accused the other of conspiracy and treason. How could a "tiny Jewish army of cowards," as the Arabs were fond of labeling them, manage to win against seven armies of Arab heroes? A simplistic answer that spread like wildfire said the Arabs were defeated because they were not following the word of Allah, who had promised Muslims success as long as they were faithful to Allah.

This remains the core ideology of the Muslim Brothers Movement, established in Egypt in 1928, which flourished in the fertile soil of despair and defeat. Their message promised a return to the "golden" days of the first four pious Muslim caliphs when justice was the rule. Then Allah's word had been the law and their glorious Muslim soldiers had swiftly and victoriously spread the boundaries of the Muslim empire.

These slogans attracted the support of many Egyptians during the royal period – but in 1950 the Muslim Brothers candidates failed to win a majority in the elections for parliament and in their defeat they turned their ire against Coptic churches – many of which were looted and torched (Shukri 1980:292). The Coptic did not take this without protest. Ibrahim Fahmi Hilal, a young lawyer, mobilized 92,000 young men in the Coptic Nation movement (*Al Umah al Qobtiyeh*) (Badawi op cit 64). Egypt came to the brink of civil war with much unrest, which culminated in massive demonstrations on February 25, 1952, in Cairo with much of the city torched and set on fire.

Using this state of emergency as a pretext, a few months later some army colonels calling themselves the "Free Officers" led a successful military coup on July 23 – and this same group rules Egypt today. Their first president was a popular figure, General Mohammed Nageeb, but he was an outsider that the unknown colonels used to legitimize their military junta. Soon after winning their first battle against the king, Nageeb was ousted and replaced by the "populist" leader Gamal Abd al Nasser (1954-1970) who became the most prominent 20th century figure in the Arab world.

Nasser's goals, outlined in his small book, *Falsafat al Thawra* (The Philosophy of the Revolution) (1960) were to struggle on three fronts – to unite the Arab states (Cairo is the permanent seat of the Arab League), to liberate and lead the African states and to make Egypt the dominant leader of the Muslim world (with its prestigious Muslim university Al Azhar). The Copts of Egypt were not entirely ignored in Nasser's grand plans, for they were offered a generous grant to build a major cathedral – which was still under construction at his death in 1970. He was succeeded by his vice-president Anwar al Sadat (1970-1981) who was assassinated and followed by his vice-president Hosni Mubarak.

None of these three were ever elected in a normal election against an opposition candidate. Most of them were "elected" by vast majorities of almost 99% of the vote. Because they had no opposition they felt they could enact or abolish any law as they saw fit. Unfortunately, none of these despots was benevolent enough to introduce a secular regime.

Military rule did not improve the situation in a nation divided on religious lines. Half of these officers were ex-members of the radical movement – the Muslim Brothers (Shukri 1976 300).The rest were generally not far afield in their cultural-political leanings.

Only a few officers of the Egyptian army at that time were on the left politically. Muhammad Hassanain Haykal, a famous Egyptian writer and Abd al Nasser's personal friend and confidant, has publicly admitted that Egypt's strong man for 18 years (1952-1970) had a clear anti-Coptic bias. So resentful was he that when his Syrian allies were led by a Christian ideologist, Michael A'flaq, he was willing to listen to him only when he was assured that A'flaq was not a Copt but a Syrian-Arab native. Regrettably, when the royal regime ended, the Copts lost their major assets as citizens – stability in public life and, like their Egyptian compatriots, the right to form political parties. They also suffered as a minority group with little access to decision-making circles for the new regime incorporated few Copts or even Muslims friendly to their cause.

The Free Officers were mostly drawn from the ranks of the less educated – including poor farmers who had flooded into Cairo and bloated nearby towns looking for work. Since many Christians, Greeks, Italians and Egyptian Copts were prominent members of Egypt's small affluent class, they became easy targets for the populist demagogic speakers to scapegoat while inciting people against the Christians, Jews, British, Zionists and foreigners in general. The British still maintained influence and had military forces deployed in the canal zone, a presence which the Egyptian military found onerous. Although the military regime spewed grand socialist clichés as well as secular slogans to allay the fears of the Christian minority, the Muslim Brothers provided their ideology and fueled the anti-European sentiments that soon forced many foreign-born to flee the country under Nasser reign.

Inconsistencies in the government's policy seem to be normative: The claim to implement a policy of equality coincided with the jailing of all "suspected" socialists. Simultaneously the military regime declared that Islam arose as a socialist theory. To "enhance" Arab national pride, Egyptian schools taught that the great Egyptian Pharaohs of the early history were Arabs. Still, the Free Officers had saved Egypt from the sectarian strife that had loomed in 1952. They also won a major battle nationalizing the Suez Canal and then built the Aswan Dam, both of which provided Egypt's basic need for electricity and expanded its arable land. On the home front they lost many battles. Because they were keen in their crusade against corruption in the political system, they outlawed political parties – whom they deemed responsible for this plague. This meant the only avenue left for Egyptians to find their identity was through religious organizations (Shukri ibid 200-201).

As part of his effort to strengthen Muslim "circles" Nasser forced all Egyptian students to study Muslim religious classes and pass special religious examinations before graduating from university. He turned Al Azhar, the ancient Egyptian institute established in 988 by a Fatimide Shiite caliph who hoped to convert Sunni Egyptians to his sect, into a full-fledged university and used it as a spearhead in his drive to win Muslim world support. Al Azhar soon became the Muslim authority on theological issues and a modern university in every aspect, even admitting women in 1962 – but it was closed to Christian students and teachers.

Soon Al Azhar was seen as a major impediment to the peaceful coëxistence of Muslims and Copts and even the moderate and fanatical Muslims. One Egyptian Marxist intellectual noted, "The graduates of Al Azhar reject science in any field except that of the production of explosives and are themselves quite often in the rank and file of the Muslim Brothers movement and other extremist groups." Along with its anti-European drive, in January 1958 the military regime closed down all church and other private Christian schools – a prohibition which lasted over eleven years (*Al Massarah* June 1969:442-445). Interestingly, the pan-Arab Nasser, using socialist rhetoric, allied himself with the Soviet Union in the international arena, and so he could not wholeheartedly embrace Muslim fundamentalist doctrines. But he wavered. On the one hand he oppressed fundamentalists, on the other he created and sustained the proper atmosphere for their growth. To keep them in their place, he resorted to a military force making Egypt a police state. All the gains of the 1919 liberal revolution were lost before Nasser's death and Sadat's ascension to power in 1970.

Anwar al Sadat came from the right wing of the Free Officers group. In his memoirs he admitted having admired the Nazis –

even attempting to join forces with General Rommel's Afrika Korps during his North Africa campaign in World War II. No one was surprised when he freed the religious political activists and called his regime one of "science and faith." He chose the title of the "Believer President," deeming it necessary to distance himself from his Pan-Arab and socialist rivals.

Mohammed Ottoman Ismael, a prominent activist in Sadat's Socialist Union Party, coined an ill-omened slogan for the regime: "Our enemies are three: the left, the Copts and the Jews." Another Egyptian intellectual, extremist Mustafa Mahmoud, also a staunch Sadat supporter, called for a return to Muslim law and tradition. He even accused the Greek philosopher Aristo (Third Century BC) of being behind the humiliation of the Egyptian army in the June 1967 war against Israel. This and other similar irrational ideas were quoted in Ghali Shukri's book, *The Secret File of Egyptian Culture*, published in Beirut (but not in Cairo) in 1975 (200-201).

Shukri was a Marxist and a Copt, so one ought to take what he writes cautiously, yet he is reliable and respectable thinker. During President Hosni Mobarak's reign, from the early 1980s until his death a decade later, Shukri was editor-in-chief of Egypt's leading cultural magazine – *al Qahira*. Shukri opposed Sadat and was quick to criticize him – once calling Sadat's decision to appoint Butrus Butrus-Ghali as Egypt's minister of foreign affairs a "most wicked and vicious act" since he perceived this appointment as being an attempt to turn the Muslim masses against the Copts and blame them for the policies of betraying the Palestinians and other Arab states. Sadat, who had failed three times to convince a Muslim senior diplomat to accept this post, concluded that a Copt intellectual could more aptly negotiate with Israeli Prime Minister Menahem Begin – and any failure or blame could be put on the Copts, thus reviving anti-Copt feelings for they would be perceived as unpatriotic, pro-Israel and anti-Arab (Shukri 1976:300).

For all this, Sadat was too much of a radical for Egypt and he failed, with his stormy temperament, to pacify the people. On the one hand he won almost universal fame in the West by his peace initiative with Israel, but internally he was unable to bring peace.

His gestures to pacify Muslim radical elements created a hostile mood in the country and he did not confront the Muslim fanatics nor initiate badly needed legal reforms. This failure was behind the growing resentment between Muslim fanatics and Christians.

Patriarch Shenoda III said in a long interview on the LBCI (July 1999) that he had written Sadat in 1977 telling him how Christians were being harassed. In his reply, the Egyptian president assured the Copts' leader "his children" do not cause any harm to others. Shenoda added, "Unfortunately Sadat, especially in his last years, was unable to tolerate any other point of view. If you did not accept his point of view, you were listed as an enemy." Many Egyptians protested Sadat's position and he responded by throwing top Copt and Muslim leaders into Egypt's infamous prisons. The charismatic Copt patriarch Shenoda III was detained and Sadat threatened to sack him entirely from his office.

Sadat's days were turbulent. Before his assassination, he felt he had no choice but to use police force to prevent sectarian strife. In the end this wave of hate engulfed him and he died at the hands of one of his "sons" – as he used to call the soldiers. The assassin was a Muslim fanatic opposed to peace and reconciliation with Jews, a by-product of the intense anti-European, anti-American and anti-Christian propaganda circulating in Egypt, accusing them of supporting Israel and humiliating Arabs and Muslims.

From afar one is unable to judge the atmosphere of Egypt's public opinion – since no research institute was allowed to exist. Occasionally the military junta was willing to conduct parliamentary elections. Most observers doubted the fairness of those in a one-party state with no free press and dominated by secret police. Still these elections demonstrated the Copts' minority status. The eight Egyptian parliaments elected under the military junta rule between 1964-1994 never included more than four Copts out of over 400 deputies, except in the 1987-1990 session when six Copts were elected. During Sadat's rule (1976-1979) the Egyptian Muslim majority blocked all Copt candidates so the parliament was entirely "clean" of them. The election of November 2000 returned only three Copts to parliament – less than 1% of its members.

8

Modern Egypt and Ancient Problems

*"Blessed be Egypt my people, and Assyria the work
of my hands, and Israel my heritage"* (Is 19:25).

Muslim clergy tend to claim the right to speak for the people
on all subjects, dominating both secular and sacred issues. They
base this on the assumption that Islam is a comprehensive system
for both *Donya Wa Akherah* (the present world and the hereafter).
Yet in only a few cases throughout Islam's history has the state
actually accepted the dominance of clerics. Usually it has been the
caliphs who have manipulated and used the clergy by employing
policies that accept some religious practices and traditions if and
when these are deemed convenient.

Sadat was a member of this school. His famous visit to Jerusalem brought him into direct confrontation with wide circles inside
the Muslim hierarchy, his previous allies, the fanatic anti-Commu-
nists and the anti-secular Muslims. A few months before his assassination, explaining his policy to the Egyptian parliament, he said,
"They insist on telling us there can be no separation between the
state and religion because Islam is both. Of course we accept that.
But we refuse politics in religion and religion in politics."

This risky stance was a weakness of Sadat's, but his achievements still are remarkable—the most obvious being the accord with Israel that helped forge a modern economy for Egypt. He also relaxed some control on the media and permitted opposition political parties to exist. Tolerance was never his best suit. Under Anwar al Sadat, Egyptian children were taught from official text books that Islam was the religion of nature (*Fitra*) and that normal babies are born Muslims, pure and willing to absorb anything, like the land which welcomes any plant, fruit or thorn, poison or medicine. Thus the human spirit accepts religion and knowledge and not those rotting ideas which "some tutors" introduce like those taught by "Christian parents to their children" (Qladeh 1999:171).

Such "scientific" textbooks are still compulsory in Egyptian schools today where the half-millennia of Egyptian history in which the country was entirely Christian is never mentioned. Still, some Copts hope the process of liberalization that began in 1981 immediately after Sadat's death may continue. Others feel such longings are futile since it appears Mubarak, like Sadat, will not properly address the "national unity" issue of Christian and Muslim Egyptians. Christians in Egypt today complain they are not treated as equal citizens. Their faith is ridiculed publicly by the state apparatus. They are not allowed to defend their beliefs on state-owned radio or television stations. Egyptian laws guarantee religious freedom for all, but even such mundane matters as building or repairing an old church require a presidential permit which may come in a week or in a decade or be ignored for a century.

Celebrated Egyptian Muslim writer Amina Said summarized this impasse in her weekly column in the weekly, *al Mussawar* (July 1991:3479), writing about Copt parishioners from a village near Alexandria who were assaulted by police for the crime of restoring the church's sewage system after waiting fruitless months for a permit. Madam Said concluded her article saying, "I am ashamed of being a citizen in a country that rules according to such a law."

It is shameful for Egypt to treat modern minority groups according to a decree enacted by the Turkish Ottoman Sultan Abd al Majid I (*hatti hamayoni*) in 1856 which was meant to set rules for the treatment of the *Dhimmis* group inside the Ottoman Empire as part of a general reform. At that time a few progressive ideas were included such as: "A state of complete satisfaction from all sides must be comprehensive to all citizens because they are equal in the eyes of the Sultan." Not until 1934 did the Egyptian government got around to introducing more detailed regulations facilitating this royal decree. Al A'azbi Pasha, minister of interior affairs, signed the so-called "liberal" regulations law that still govern Egypt's treatment of Christian communities with such draconian terms or questions to be met before a church may be built:

1 – The land must not be farmland and must be properly owned by those who ask for the permit.

2 – The land must be a "proper" distance from any Muslim mosque or cemetery.

3 – Is the land in a Muslim or Christian neighborhood and how do the neighbors react to the idea?

4 – If the planned church is to be built near Muslim houses, their consent must be asked.

5 – Is there another Christian church in the town?

6 – Are there churches in neighboring towns?

7 – How many Christians live in the neighborhood and does their number justify building a church?

8 – In cases where the church is to be built near a bridge, waterway or railway installations, a special permit is required.

9 – A thorough report of the neighborhood must be prepared including any public buildings and their precise distance from the planned church and submitted to the proper ministry.

10 – Those requesting such a permit must submit detailed architectural drawings signed by the head of the church and attested to by a qualified engineer.

These bureaucratic and discriminatory restrictions on building a church obviously carried the veiled message that it would be dangerous for Christian villagers to build a church near a railway, the Nile River or a bridge. Having to justify their need for a new church insures that the government gets to determine whether citizens are allowed to worship in any particular manner. Whereas the government claims such regulations are necessary to keep the peace by keeping a proper distance between those of different faiths, its underlining message is prejudicial treatment of some worshipers; as the Copts point out, such restrictions are not imposed on those Muslims who wish to build another mosque.

The Muslim traditions prohibiting new building of Christian churches and not allowing old ones to be restored are attributed to the second caliph, Omar Ibn al Khattab, a devout follower of Mohammed considered one of four *rashidon* (pious) caliphs which adds weight to his views. Fortunately for the Copts, not all Muslims agree that these regulations originated with Omar, since such prejudicial treatment has been going on for over 500 years *(Ahram Report* 1995:87). When asked about these restrictions and whether the Copts fear the future, Patriarch Shenoda III said he had been assured by high Egyptian officials these regulations would be reformed and he feels it is bureaucrats who are delaying the process of licensing building and repairing churches. He also points out that during the 20 years of Hosni Mubarak's presidency, all applications which have been processed through the ministry of interior and sent on to the president have been approved. During these years the Copts have been granted permits for 120 new church buildings, their college was re-licensed, many students enrolled and 2,500 students graduated.

Patriarch Shenoda sees trouble coming from the popular influence of radical anti-Christian groups. To illustrate this he told President Mubarak the church had wanted land to build a new church in an area of Cairo. After twelve appropriate purchases of suitable land, each time they applied for a building permit, they were told there was a nearby site designated for a new mosque. Finally the Copts decided to stop looking for a new site and instead converted an apartment into a church hall "to save the government that budget needed from building the thirteenth mosque" (LBC1 18 July 1999). Since all mosques in Egypt are built and maintained with public financing, Shenoda felt he was doing Mubarak a favor. Also any Egyptian can avoid paying taxes on a building by converting the ground floor into a mosque which is open to the public (Hanafi 1996:157-170). Any apartment on top of the mosque is then exempt from municipal taxes.

Shenoda has been publicly critical of President Mubarak. He

convened press conferences to deplore not only Serb atrocities against Bosnian Muslims in July 1992, but compared these to fanatic Muslim terrorist assaults in Egypt against the Copts in the town of Dairut. Rejecting the official theory that the assassinations were the result of blood feuds, Shenoda said, "It is clear in this case and there is no place for silence – 15 Christians were killed and people are afraid to leave the safety of their homes at night." He has also categorically denied as a vicious rumor the government newspapers' allegation that Christian vigilante groups were operating in revenge (*Al Montada* #34 1991:1).

The issue of building new churches is critical for Egyptian Copts. In the mid-1970s they had 1,442 active church buildings, but the interior ministry recognized only 500 as official churches for Christian worship and of these only 286 churches were Copt. According to *Al-jihaz al markazi leltaa'bea wal ehsaa*, the Egyptian bureau of statistics, between 1960 and 1970 some 127 new churches were erected: of these the Copts built 68 (*Al Ahram* 11/29/1972).

If we are willing to accept official figures (and few do) there was one Christian church for every 5,000 worshipers. The government admits to two or three million while the Copts estimate there are at least twice that many in the Christian community with "at least" 1,500 worshiping sites. Since many villages have no church and are prohibited from building one for economic or bureaucratic reasons, the Coptic church has invented a new paradigm: the mobile church. Buses are outfitted with all that is needed to turn a gathering into a high mass for the faithful and are driven by priests who travel to various villages on a scheduled timetable.

In 1980 the church reported mobile visits to 2,154 villages in the Nile valley thus serving some 70,000 families scattered over the land, but these bureaucratic machinations have produced tragic mistrust between the Coptic church and Egypt's establishment (*Ha Aretz* 3-17, 1/1982). The country's officialdom has tried to sweep the problematic Muslim – Christian relations under the carpet, belittling the Copts' complaints and claiming the fanatic Muslim extremist groups that attack Copts are simple criminals terrorizing the entire country, best left to security forces. But Copts counter these claims with detailed accounts in which police and other security agencies coöperate or look the other way when crimes against Copts are committed.

When Copts held a national convention in Alexandria in 1972, they forged a demand that the government defend its citizens' rights to live in peace and be free to worship in accordance to their faith; "otherwise martyrdom over the sacred religious beliefs shall be preferred to a life of humiliation." These remarks were widely disseminated in the world press especially among the American and Australian Coptic communities.

Within a week President Sadat responded by convening a meeting of the ruling political party of Egypt–the only one allowed to function at the time–which adopted a law with a "few carrots and a lot of clubs." After reiterating a firm prohibition of any political activity outside the government's party and letting Copts know they would not soon hold another "political" convention, they filled the rest of the reply with empty phrases and colorful rhetoric claiming an egalitarian society where all citizens, regardless of religion enjoyed a rule of law. Since a free press was prohibited, the only recourse for complaints in Egypt was to appeal to the president and the bureaucrats.

Many Egyptian Copts, like the late writer Musa Sabri, believed in Sadat's good intentions, but others did not. Certainly in my travels there I have yet to meet an Egyptian who believed the Egyptian bureaucracy could produce just treatment for any citizen, let alone minorities like the Copts. The official-parliamentarian inquiry, in the aftermath of the Alexandria convention, found "no infringement on the freedom of religion in Egypt" (Badawi op cit 75).

Still they were "liberal" enough to recommend reëxamining the regulations on building new churches–a recommendation immediately forgotten by all concerned. At the time President Sadat was digging his own grave by encouraging fundamentalist Muslims to play a role in Egypt's public life as a counter-pressure against the followers of Nasser's pan-Arabs and the Free Officers junta, especially the pro-Soviets. So neither Nasser, a socialist like Sadat, nor his successor Mubarak (who has launched a fierce war against the terrorist fanatic fundamentalists) did anything to revoke these regulations. The Egyptian establishment has never stood up to the conservative religious forces in order to support the freedom of non-Muslims to practice their religion.

Copts live today all over Egypt in urban and rural areas, attending the same schools, visiting the same worship centers (since mosques and churches are open to all) and going to the same universities except for the University of Al Azhar, the tenth century school founded for Muslim clergy. In fact, this religious institution developed during the last century into a university by introducing philosophical studies early in the 20th century and then by adding other faculties in the '60s when the Free Officers came into power.

The Copts were never allowed to establish similar institutions even though they were keen to have their parish priests educated at the university level. Over 200 years ago Patriarch Demitrious was able to get the Egyptian Wali, who succeeded Mohammed Ali, the founder of modern Egypt, to grant the Copts a helping hand in starting modern educational institutes including an industrial school in Bulaq, twelve schools in Cairo (one inside the Old City), another in Giza and two in Alexandria. These schools did not restrict themselves to religious teaching but added mathematics and foreign languages – French, English, and Italian (*Al Masri* op cit 137).

Foreign missionaries from the West, trying to establish a foothold in Egypt as they had in Palestine and Syria several centuries before, arrived in force at the beginning of the 19th century. These included Catholic and Protestant rival missions supported by Lebanese, Syrian and Palestinian Christian immigrants fleeing Ottoman tyranny in their homelands. The results of this "invasion" are still obvious in Egypt because of contributions made to the cultural life. *Al Ahram*, Egypt's first and most prominent newspaper for over 120 years, was founded in 1875 by two Lebanese brothers – Salim and Bishara Taqla. In 1893 Jorji Zeadan (1861-1914) established *Al Hilal*, the cultural monthly. These two publications have survived over a century in this troubled land. Egypt's literature, theater and cinema were equally impacted by this cultural invasion.

For many in the Christian Egyptian community, the appearance of new rival Christian churches was traumatic. Almost all the new converts for these churches left the Coptic confession. Although Catholic Copts never exceeded 210,000 in the country, by the end of the 20th century, Protestants from various other denominations totalled over 100,000 members (*Al Ahram Report* 1995 110; MECC Perspective#6-7 1986). These newly arrived Christians made a lasting impact on the educational system because the schools and institutions they founded were open to all students – Muslim or Christian. The Catholic church alone established 168 education institutions serving 125,000 pupils while the Evangelicals had 18 schools serving 16,000 students (*Al Ahram* Report 1995:110).

A telling statistic that could be extrapolated to the entire region and demonstrates the Christians' diminishing presence in the Holy Land pertains to an exceptional Protestant school in Sidon, the main Lebanese town in the south of that country. When Dr. Rona Mackay visited there in 1995 she found that of the 3,000 students in attendance, only 65 were Christian (1999:95).

Little outwardly distinguishes Egyptian Copts from their Muslim neighbors in features or dress. Most Egyptians are pleasant, soft-spoken and known for their sophisticated sense of humor. However Dr. Samira Bahr, in her study of "The Copts in Egypt's Political Life," found immense differences: Copts make up 10% of the population, yet hold 60% of the jobs in the financial market, 90% of the managerial posts in this area and 20% of the managerial class in the government. Since 1952 no Copts have been chosen to represent Egypt in any embassy around the globe nor manage any of Egypt's universities. At the government's medical school, 40% of the students are Copts, but Coptic teachers on these faculties have dropped in two decades from 40 to 4% (Bahr 1977:183).

Gamal Badawi discounts Dr. Bahr's claims of prejudicial treatment of Copts in governmental policy by pointing out that in 1973 the ministry of foreign affairs published a list of new appointments that included two appointees to ambassadorial posts with Copt names (out of 50) and 14 of the other 186 diplomats with Copt names while Dr. Butrus Butrus-Ghali was at the time deputy minister of foreign affairs. Beyond this, he found five Copt writers at top posts in the Egyptian press (Badawi 1980:93-96).

When Dr. Ghali was elected UN secretary-general, within Egypt he was not regarded as a "normal" citizen, according to his friend, the celebrated journalist Mohammed Hassanain Haykal. In a review of Ghali's book, *Egypt's Road to Jerusalem*, he laments that Ghali describes himself as "a Christian in a Muslim country, the son of an infamous family for being traitorous in Egypt's history, and husband to a Jewish lady" (1999:3-7).

Regrettably, in Egypt anti-Christian discrimination is practiced bluntly, in the open and legally. Muslims are not free to change their religion from that of their parents, but a Christian is legally bound to Islam in the case of "conversion" according to Al Redda religious laws. Thus should you be heard in public to declare you are a Muslim, you can never retract that position and must live as a Muslim or be stoned to death. Luckily for contemporary Copts, malefactors are no longer stoned, but they can still face police detention, prison and harassment. For Copts the problem is not embracing Islam, since few do that, but that many Copt minors, especially young girls, are seduced or forced to say the Muslim *Shahadatain* declaring the oneness of Allah-God and professing Muhammad as God's messenger. This makes them permanently full-fledged Muslims who can never return to their family's faith.

Since the 19th century, Muslims in Egypt who renounce Islam have not been killed for apostasy, but only arrested and questioned until they return to "the right path" of Islam. Sadat, to curry favor with extremist Muslims in Egypt, proposed in the mid-70s a parliamentary change to the constitution declaring the shari'ah as the sole source for Egyptian law (not merely as "a source" – as it had been prior to that). He asked the Sonni–Islam's most respected scholars from Al Azhar–to draft a detailed shari'ah law for approval. Before this could be adopted into law, the Copt clerics staged a public protest. Since many Egyptian Muslims were equally upset by these proposed changes, they supported this challenge.

Some of the horrifying proposals for the new penal code crafted by a committee of Al Azhar scholars said, among other things, that a woman who betrays her husband was to be stoned; anyone convicted of stealing the equivalent of 4.6 grams of gold was to have the right hand amputated on the first offense and the left leg amputated the second time. Fornication or homosexuality were crimes to be punished by stoning if the perpetrators were married or by 100 lashes if they were not. Anyone found with alcohol or drunk was to suffer 40 lashes (Abd Al Fattah 1984:141-174).

The Copts' outcry against these proposals, plus the support of Egyptian liberals and worldwide reaction, forced Sadat to abandon any efforts to adopt this code, yet currently there are Egyptian prisoners behind bars because someone testified they heard them repudiate their Muslim faith. Only Muslims can testify in Muslim courts when another Muslim is involved in the litigation. Interestingly, a Copt husband wanting a divorce can embrace Islam for a short while since Muslims are allowed to get a divorce and remarry. After successfully shedding their spouses, such husbands are often quietly embraced back into their own communities.

Although the official educational curriculum had long ignored Coptic history before the Arab invasion and the history of the Coptic church, when Copts prepared to celebrate the third millennium of their founding, the government realized they could benefit from the festivals and the influx of tourist-pilgrims to this event. Then they began to teach a bit of the Christian history of Egypt, even recalling publicly that the Holy Family had taken refuge in Egypt to escape Herod and that later in the Egyptian deserts the first great monasteries and hermitage movements were born. Finally Dr. Hussein Kamel Baha Ed Din, minister of education, announced he was about to introduce a revision in Egypt's educational system to reflect this new historical emphasis.

During the rule of the Free Officers, the Egyptian government restricted the rights of citizens to emigrate, claiming the young, able, educated and relatively affluent were seeking a new life and their departure would be detrimental to the society and the country that had given them free and expensive education. After the humiliating defeat in the 1967 war against Israel, this policy was modified in order to encourage potential opposition leaders to take their ideas elsewhere. The Egyptian regime also felt that since their economic growth was not keeping pace with the increase in population, they needed other solutions. An easy one was to encourage mass emigration of those who could not find employment. Of course, this ignored the fact that in the emigration process Egypt was losing its most educated and capable young people while keeping the poor and illiterate inhabitants. Some Egyptian intellectuals, like the popular Muslim writer Anis Mansour, crusaded for a movement of emigration from Egypt and wrote books praising ambitious young people, like *Those Who Emigrated* (1988).

Emigration was especially attractive to the Copts after two waves of violence had been launched against them. The first, in 1972 in Khnaqa, a poverty-stricken quarter of Cairo, began with articles and paid advertisements appearing in local and respected Egyptian dailies. The campaigners urged the Copts leave to "go away and rid you from filthy Cairo" (*Al Ahram* 30 May 1975). As a result, a totally counterproductive situation arose for the illiterates in Egypt were growing at the same pace emigration was occurring. Thus some 44 million Arab adults were illiterate in 1960 whereas by 1970 this number had grown to 50 million (Zurayk 1977:370). The second emigration surge happened in the aftermath of a similar incident in al Zawiya Al Hamra in July 1980. After the first violence in 1972 the government appointed a parliament committee to investigate the events, this time President Sadat rather nervously and harshly arrested the Copt leader (and some Muslim leaders, as well) declaring the nomination for patriarch abolished for four years and threatening to remove the current leader from office.

A year later a fanatic Muslim terrorist assassinated Sadat, thus bringing in a new era. President Hosni Mubarak, keen on enforcing law and order, declared war against on any terrorists who turned Egypt, a traditional tourist site, into a risky adventure. He managed sporadic success in curtailing the terror, but his bureaucracy, police and security forces were too undisciplined to treat the Copts as equal citizens. To exacerbate this discrimination policy, the Egyptian ministry of interior issued to all citizens identity cards which cited their religion, thus making it easier for the police and the terrorists to find their targets. This identification was deemed necessary since Egyptians tend to look alike and many Copts give their children Arab-neutral names.

Although no one knows precisely how many Egyptians emigrated during these difficult years, President Mubarak estimated the number at 2.5 million (*Al Ahram* 22 Nov 1985). A few days later the ministry for emigrants' affairs estimated the number to be 4.5 million and *Al Ahram* countered by claiming the figure was at least "double that of the official figure" (Abd Al Nabi 1989:15-25).

The impressive size of the Copt emigration can also be observed in the growth of the Coptic church in their diaspora. In the last three decades, from having twelve active parish churches serving them outside Egypt, there are now 166 churches serving Copts around the world. Their current leader, the pope of Alexandria, Patriarch Shenoda III, is a popular world figure who reminds all who ask of Egypt's great contributions to Christendom. He has personally ordained 62 bishops to serve the one million children in Cairo who attend weekly religious training classes. Throughout all the persecution they have suffered at the hands of Muslim extremists, the Copts have carefully maintained a Christian presence, never resorting to arms or counter extremism.

The basic problem faced by Copts today is that they live in a poor country with swelling unemployment. Poverty-stricken underemployed people whose hopelessness drives them into the ranks of fanatic-terrorists see Copts as easy prey for their frustrations. The Egyptian security forces that are not corrupt struggle to cope with unruly outlaws; the others aggravate a worsening situation. In the face of this the Copts, especially the young and educated, continue to flee the country in search of a safe environment.

During the 1400 years of the Muslim occupation of Egypt, the Copts have felt oppressed, both as Egyptians and as Christians. Whereas in the seventh century they had a population in Egypt of eight million, by the latter part of the 20th century their number had fallen to three million (Hitti 1958:848). For the most part they felt tolerated as *Dhimmis* but unappreciated. Few maintained hopes of being treated as equals by the Muslims, feeling patronized by a regime that refused to recognize them as equal citizens.

9

Lebanon and Syria

"The trees of the Lord are watered abundantly, the cedars of Lebanon which he planted" (Ps 104:16).

The Lebanese-Syrian Christians' predicament was different from that of the Copts in Egypt for many reasons and over a long period. Historically speaking the Copt-Egyptians were heirs of the pharaohs who conquered and dominated an empire during more than 3,000 years where they built one of the ancient world's great civilizations before falling to a foreign invader, Alexander the Great in 332 BC. They became part of the Roman-Byzantine empire until the seventh century with the Arab-Muslim occupation. The culture and language of Egypt were exclusively theirs.

In the fourth century all Egyptians adopted the Christian faith and were organized in one church, dominated by local clergy using one liturgy, praying in their national language and accepting the primacy of their patriarch.

During this period of time Syria (which included today's Lebanon, Palestine, Israel and Jordan) was never the seat of an empire. Mostly it was dominated by various forces of the region – Mesopotamia, Persia, Egypt, Rome, Greece (those who lived both in

Greece of our day and in Asia Minor – which encompasses today's Turkey) with one exception.

The first Arab-Muslim caliphs, the Umayyad dynasty, turned Damascus into their capital for 120 years in the seventh and eighth centuries. The peoples that populated Syria did not have a common language, nor did they claim the same origin. When Christianity became the dominant faith in the fourth century, they established many churches using a variety of ancient languages – including the Greek language of the Byzantine empire that ruled Syria at the time. The patriarch of the Syrian See was in Antioch (and still uses that title).

In regard to their relations to Islam and Arab rule, the Egyptians and Syrians were also quite different. Some non-conformist Christians of Syria (and Mesopotamia) were eager to join forces with Muslim-Arabs to rid themselves of Byzantine rule and either fought with the Muslims or welcomed them. Still the Muslims were unsure of the loyalty of these Syrian Christians, fearing they would feel solidarity with the Byzantine Christians across the border.

In Egypt this was not an issue as the Byzantines were quite distant. With the Greek patriarch residing in Antioch (close enough to dominate Syrian Christians), the Egyptian church was fairly independent – even though Copts tended to be confined to ghetto-like territories vis-à-vis their Muslim overlords.

The Maronite Christians of Syria took an opposing line. They allied themselves with the Byzantine state. Historians feel they succeeded in blocking Islam's expansion to the north between 635 and 690 (Hitti 1958:268-269). Despite Byzantine's shrinking power, some Christian presence – mainly that of the Maronites – was preserved in resisting the Muslim overlords and hoping some day to restore Christian political power in Syria.

From the seventh to the 15th century, although war between the Muslim governors of Syria and the Byzantine was waged during most of this period, enmity between them had few lulls. Byzantium regularly lost ground, but there were a few successful counterattacks like that of Emperor Nicephorus Phocas who reconquered Antioch in 964, establishing the reign that lasted 120 years.

In 1084 Antioch was occupied by the Turk-Seljuk sultan and kept under Muslim rule for 14 years – but then it was recaptured by European Crusaders who came across the Byzantine territories in 1098 and held on to power there for 180 years until it was conquered by the Sultan Baibars in 1268.

Unlike Egypt's Copts, who were at war with their Byzantine rulers at the time of the Muslim conquest, Syria and Lebanon accepted the Chalcedon Council's dogma and lived in relative peace with the Byzantine authorities, watching with admiration as the great city of Constantinople (Istanbul today) prospered. They were confident they could stop the Muslim conquest, as in fact they did for centuries.

So while Egypt was submissive and peaceful inside the Muslim state, Syria, Lebanon and Palestine were theaters of dramatic changes and bloodshed in the protracted Muslim-Christian wars. For hundreds of years Byzantine was a constant target of Muslim *Ghazo* (forays) who considered it a constant threat to themselves. In turn, Byzantine rulers hoping to restore Syria to Christian rule encouraged the Maronites to rebel against the caliphs from the Umayyad dynasty or, later, to join the Crusaders' expeditions.

Arabic Christians were sorely disappointed, for they had believed that by helping the Muslim Arabs they might win a share in the new state, but while at first they received some tolerant treatment, their assistance was soon forgotten and by the late stages of the Umayyad dynasty, most Christians were denied basic rights. Some Muslim caliphs were worse than others, especially during the Abbasid dynasty when new converts from Persia dominated the courts in Baghdad. The Abbasid Caliph Al-Mahdi (775-785) gave the Arab Christian tribe of Tanoukh near the town Qnsarin the choice of converting to Islam or death and then proceeded to martyr some 5,000 who persisted in their Christian faith (Hitti 1949:99).

The governors of Asia Minor never relinquished their hope of retaking Syria, even after they converted from Christian-Byzantine to Muslim-Ottoman. Eventually they conquered Syria and ruled it for 400 years under the Ottoman Turkish sultan (1514-1918). This came on the heels of an extended rule by non-Arab tribes under a variety of names – Mamluks, Mongols and Kurds. These warrior-shepherds arrived in the Middle East in the ninth century either as slaves or nomads looking for greener pastures. At first they were hired as mercenaries by the Abbasid Caliph al Maamoun in 833 – the first sign of the weakening of the Arab-Muslim state. This was a repetition of the Turkish Empire downfall that had started with the hiring of the Janissaries (*yenitsheri*, in Turkish) in the Ottoman Empire (Hitti ibid 185).

Eventually many of the Arab Muslim caliphs were little more than titular puppets in their palaces – posing as sovereigns while the real power lay with their ministers, advisors and soldiers. Eventually the charade was no longer kept up and power passed from one demagogue to another, everyone competing to see how they could introduce more novel means of oppression and exploitation of their impoverished population, especially non-Muslims, but including Muslims.

Most of these new governors were not Arabs but Afghan, Turk, Kurd, Seljuk, Mongols and Persians – non-Arab Muslims attracted to Baghdad by its rumored wealth. Their rule was interrupted for some 200 years by the Crusades. Although never in a position to occupy anything of Syria outside the coastal strips along the Mediterranean, the Crusaders managed to control 25% of the population (Sivan op cit 250).

This weakness of the Crusaders created problems for the Christian population inside Syria whose loyalty became suspect. Many were forced to move west and find refuge in the Crusaders' realm. Historians estimate that Christians made up at least half of the entire Syrian (and Egyptian) population in the first two centuries of the second millennium during the Crusaders' wars (Hitti op cit 222; Haddad 1970).

Unfortunately the Crusades did little to improve the lot of the local Christians, for their presence generated basic mistrust between the native Christians and the Muslims outside the Christian regions. Christian towns (such as Nazareth) were torched immediately after the Muslim occupation and many communities were driven to accept Islam in order to make peace with the new rulers. The Crusades, initiated to "save" the native Christians and the Holy Land, instead heightened anti-Christian attitudes among many Muslims and in the end made life more difficult for the local Christians (Sivan op cit 260).

An exception to this occurred with the Lebanese Maronites whose church leaders made their peace with the Holy See during the Crusades. Their patriarch traveled to the Crusaders' last post in Palestine – Acre – during the final stages of the Crusaders' occupation in order to ask help for Lebanon from King Louis IX for France's pledge. (This amazing treaty seems to be valid today, at least on the cultural level, 700 years later).

Thus it was that these Maronites, together with other local Christians plus some non-conformist Muslims – such as the Shiites and Druses – joined together and inhabited the high and easy-to-defend mountains, forging what became the modern Lebanese people. Not just a charming strip of land, their homeland is also the land of the ancient and proud Semites, the Phoenicians, who in ancient times introduced the first alphabet to the world. As the colonizers of Carthage, the Phoenicians were one of the greatest military forces in Middle Eastern history.

Under the command of Hannibal they invaded Europe, crossed the Alps on the back of their African elephants and threatened Rome. Their achievement in architecture and the arts brought King Solomon of Jerusalem to ask for their help in building the Temple. This industrious, seafaring nation established trade colonies on commercial routes they visited from North Africa to Iberia and as faraway as Wales.

This rich heritage came down to their heirs, the Lebanese, who sought to forge multiple alliances. It is no surprise the Muslim kingdoms of the Middle East allowed relatively free access and activity for American and European Christian missions (and politics), and that encounter made possible a European renaissance took root in Lebanon before it affected any other Middle Eastern country.

The local Christian community was open to new influences and thus Lebanon and Syria became the most advanced provinces in the Ottoman Empire, and Lebanon became a haven for the oppressed, Christians or not. The Maronites and other inhabitants of Lebanon did not always have luck with wise leaders. In the few cases where they did, they were the envy of their neighbors and a common Middle Eastern saying goes: "Lucky the person who owns even the little bit of Lebanese soil necessary for a goat to sleep in."

The glorious days of Lebanon began in 1590 and continued through the reign of Prince Faker Ed Din II, a twelve-year-old Druze who ascended the Shihabies throne. His predecessors were vassals of the Ottoman Sultan, but during his long reign and triumphant battles, he signed treaties with Italian towns, introduced the silk industry, built palaces and towers, forced law and order on the land and was secretly converted to Christianity. In 1635 the Ottoman government murdered him as a rebel, along with his two sons.

Anther time of prosperity occurred in Galilee – which included most of Lebanon – during the long reign of Daher al-A'omar, the only Palestinian Arab in history who attempted to create an independent state in this country. In 1737 he occupied Tiberias and Acre (the last Crusaders' fortress), still partly in ruins centuries after its fall in 1294, making necessary repairs to create his capital there. The Turks were obviously unhappy at this local sheik's success, but with help from some Russian allies, he withstood the Sultan's army until 1775 when he was assassinated by his own soldiers who had been bribed by the Ottomans.

Al-A'omar was, according to Arab historians, an enlightened despot, friendly to his Christian subjects. He urged Jews who had emigrated from Tiberias to return and build a synagogue for their community. He helped the Nazarenes, Greek Orthodox, Catholics and Maronites build churches and his original mandates are still found in the Nazarene churches' archives (Mansour 1924:72-73, Al A'aref 1961:280).

The 19th century ushered in a dramatic period for Lebanon and its Christian population. The first year of the century saw

Napoleon outside the walls of Acre facing a bloodthirsty tyrant inside the fortress – Ahmad Pasha al Jazzar who had terrorized the entire region. An Egyptian invasion under the command of Ibrahim Pasha was at first welcomed (and aided by Lebanese soldiers) but later he antagonized the Muslims because he gave equal treatment to Christians and Jews "contradicting Islam's doctrine," which led to a vicious rumor being circulated that this Egyptian was a Christian in disguise (Al Bishri 1980:27).

Although this story was never substantiated, he did surround himself with many top officers who were French and British. Later this Egyptian occupation army antagonized the Syrians by imposing high taxes to finance their administration and instituting compulsory military service to fill out the ranks of the army. In less than a decade, under European pressure, the Egyptians were forced to depart from Syria leaving a vacuum behind.

The Ottoman Turks' main concern had been to collect taxes and keep the populace in line, but for centuries a process of demographic changes had taken place in the Lebanese mountains that began to affect the local situation. The Maronite population, having increased substantially, began demanding a more prominent role in government. Squabbles between Druze and Christian groups started in 1840, but were not important enough to make the Ottoman governor pay attention. When trouble erupted again five years later, the Europeans intervened demanding that the Ottomans create administrative borders to prevent future clashes.

These boundaries did little to produce understanding or coöperation in this strife-torn area, and many felt the Ottomans were making feigned efforts at peace when in reality it was to their benefit that enmity between the different groups kept them from uniting and becoming powerful. Certainly the French, Russian and British consuls located in Beirut were too busy trying to establish their own power base among the various groups – the Maronites, Greek-Orthodox, Protestants and Druze – to care why so few Lebanese were able to live at peace with one another.

The autonomous Catholic Christians, the Maronites and the non-conformist Muslim-Druzes all yearned to be the dominant force in the land. When the superiority of the Druzes began to be threatened by the increased population of the Maronites, they became increasingly hostile until finally in 1860 savage clashes deteriorated into a massacre of the Christians. At that time Muslim Shiites and Sunnis joined forces with the Druze, under official Ottoman approval and support, and attacked the Maronites in four major areas–the Shouf Mountains, Hasbaya, Zahleh and Damascus–wreaking a terrible massacre.

This got the attention of the European powers, mainly the French, who set out to the rescue. The number of Christian victims–11,000 murdered, 4,000 starved to death and 100,000 forced from their homes–was the rather conservative claim of the British consul in Beirut, Colonel Churchill (Churchill 1862:219).

As the Brits were backing the Druze, the colonel had obvious motives for downplaying the Christian casualties since theirs was the winning side in the civil war while their French rivals were on the Maronite losing side. The Greek historian of the Orthodox church gives a more detailed account of the casualties: 17,000 men, 7,000 women and 10,000 children killed in 40 days, starting May 20, 1860. The only reason the Christians were not entirely annihilated was that France and other European forces interfered (Papadopoulos op cit 846-847).

Maronite sources claim even different figures. Father Yousef Mahfouz quotes "an eyewitness" who wrote that "in a period of 22 days 21,900 were slaughtered from all ages and genders; 360 villages were destroyed; 560 churches and 42 monasteries were set on fire. In Damascus some 6,000 were killed and 150,000 became refugees, 7,000 houses were burned to the ground and another 14,000 perished from hunger and distress" (Mahfouz 1984:107-108). Other historians come up with similar figures (Salibi 1967:142).

The pressure from the European powers on the Ottoman Sultan made the Turkish governor intervene, stopping the slaughter when it had spread south to Hasbaya, near Mt. Hermon. Then ten days after a cease-fire agreement was reached in Lebanon between the defeated Maronites and the victorious Druze, a bloodbath erupted in the east with again thousands of innocent Christians in Damascus – killed for no reason other than worshiping in church. All this in that glorious capital of the Umayyad Arab Empire where St. Paul's eyes were opened to the truth of Jesus Christ.

One of the few great Muslim righteous men who lived in that town during those dark days was the prince Abd al Qader Mohyi ad din al-Murabit al-Jazaeri (1808-1883), the North African rebel who had fought against the French occupation of his country for some time before being captured and exiled to Syria. This banished Muslim became a bright ray of light in these dark days of ignorance and brutal savagery, for he heroically saved many thousands of innocent Christians after three days of slaughtering and pillaging that took the lives of 5,500 Christians in Damascus (Salibi ibid 146, Lutski 1975:163).

Finally the European powers intervened and some 7,000 French soldiers landed in Beirut threatening the Ottoman Sultan who had no choice but to order the arrest of the leaders of the mob. Hundreds of Turk officers were hanged in Damascus' public squares after a short court-martial. The Turkish government made an attempt to apprehend the perpetuators of these Lebanese crimes and filled the prisons with suspects, mainly Druze, but also some Sunni and Shiite Muslims as well. However no Christian felt secure enough to come forward and testify against the criminals.

This massacre and the subsequent European intervention built pressure on the Sultan to grant Lebanon special status and autonomy under a Christian administrator, still subject to the Sultan, and then divide Lebanon's mountain area into two separate zones for the Druze and Christians. This plan, known as the Mutasarfiyah under Daoud Pasha the Austrian (1818-1873) produced a season of law and order. Subsequently an influx of American and European missionaries, educators, doctors and political-economic agents turned Lebanon into a thriving community. Soon this little strip of land had produced the hard-working pioneers of the Arab national revival, Arab political groupings, the first modern hospitals, universities, newspapers, theaters and writers, a modern dictionary and modern concepts of politics.

Because the territory was so small, there were limited opportunities for young people pursuing new careers. Some moved south to Egypt, contributing greatly to the modernization movement there – as well as in the rest of the Arab nations. These Lebanese cultural pioneers emigrated during the 19th and the 20th century to Egypt not only to find more personal freedom, but also because they were attracted by the multicultural nature of Alexandria, Port Said and Cairo and by the ambitious, enlightened Egyptian regime. Lebanese, Syrians and Palestinian Christians helped establish the most respected cultural institutions of Egypt: Salem Taqla and Jorji Zeadan in the field of publishing; Yousef Wahba and Bishara Wakim in theater; Bader Lama and Omar Sharif on the screen; Khalil Motran, Rose al Yousef and Mai Zeyadeh in literature.

This was the fruit of a semi-independent Lebanon between 1860-1914 which ended when the First World War broke out and the Ottoman tyrant returned in full force to annihilate Lebanese's last drop of enlightenment. Some 100,000 Lebanese civilians died of hunger under the Turkish atrocities of World War I and some estimate the Lebanese were divided in three – one-third perished of starvation, one-third emigrated and one-third survived the war (Mahfouz op cit 109). Although the news of the Lebanese suffering reached those in the diaspora causing the American Lebanese community to attempt in 1917 to organize a military unit to rescue those suffering in their homeland, they did not arrive before the war came to its end and so few ever came to the rescue (Jobran op cit 49).

After World War I, the League of Nations placed Lebanon and Syria under the French mandate whereas Palestine, Transjordan and Iraq were put under the British, paving the way for the Lebanese to forge an independent sovereign state. Ever since the Crusades the French had felt a special protectionism towards those in the Maronite church and now this attitude flourished.

The Lebanese patriarch, Elias Al-H'wayek, assigned new borders to Great Lebanon, forging four districts – Mount Lebanon, Beirut, Tripoli (including the fertile plains of Biqaa') in the east and Jabal A'amela in the south – despite the fact that the Christian population in most of these areas was in the minority. Thus was created the conditions necessary for the irredenta movements which the Lebanese have faced ever since.

In the early 1940s the Lebanese leaders–the Muslim Riyadh Sulh and the Maronite Bishara al Khouri–agreed between themselves on the division of the top governmental posts on sectarian lines: a Maronite president, a Sunni Muslim prime minister and a Shiite chair of parliament. The lesser posts were allotted on similar lines. This arrangement was embraced as almost "holy" by the conservative Lebanese and "profane" by the liberals, progressives and the radicals, who felt the universal ideas of equality, civil marriage, one vote per person and regional coöperation needed to be the standard.

The first group rejecting this agreement were the traditional Sunni Muslims who believed Lebanon was part of the Muslim political and cultural entity which encompassed neighboring Syria and Palestine and that Lebanese Christians should be treated as *Dhimmis* inside a united Muslim state.

The liberal Syrian Arab nationals–Muslims and Christians–also rejected the division of Lebanon as a separate entity, claiming rather that Syria was one country and Lebanon part of that. However, the still-fresh memory of Turkish atrocities and subsequent hardships caused a vast majority of Christian Lebanese and Muslims to endorse the national convention of 1943 between Khouri and Sulh.

Syria has never been willing to consider Lebanon a separate political entity. They never established a Syrian embassy there nor formally recognized the Lebanese state. This policy has persisted throughout all the changes in power in Damascus causing a great deal of unresolved conflict. The subsequent Lebanese irredenta attempts mostly came from the Sunni-Muslim minority under the aegis of the Syrians.

The first armed assault against the Lebanese Republic came in 1949 from a mainly Christian Lebanese political party, the Syrian-Social-National Party, which professed loyalty to a great Syrian state. The founder of this party, Anton Sa'adeh, agitated for decades inside various youth groups. This attempted military coup was secretly supported by the Syrian military government under Hosni al Zaa'im. Anton Sa'adeh (1904-1949), believed the united Syrian state should include Lebanon, Palestine, Jordan, Iraq and Cyprus – the fertile crescent – and be a secular state.

The coup failed and like his prototype, Mussolini, Sa'adeh was executed after a hasty court-martial along with some of his aides. His party, *Le Parti Populaire Syrian (PPS)*, established in 1932 by six students at the American University of Beirut, is still active with some success in Lebanon and Syria, especially among the educated.

Later a more dangerous attempt was made to dissolve the Lebanese state and annex it into the United Arab Republic (which in 1958 united Egypt and Syria for three years). This also failed but the forces that supported it have never given up but consistently call for Lebanon's unity with Syria as the first step in the direction of pan-Arab unity. During most of the 1975-1990 civil war in Lebanon these forces called their coalition "the national forces".

The armed Palestinian group, the P.L.O., were party to this alliance, as were most of the Sunni, Shiite and Druze Muslims. The Lebanese Forces were entirely Christians – and mainly Maronites. During the 14 years of hostilities many sides changed alliances (with Israel and/or Syria), shed much blood, destroyed their flourishing economy and structure – and then went back to the Saudi city of Al Taif and made a pact almost identical to the old Sulh-Khouri agreement, dividing the state along sectarian lines.

One of the most tragic outcomes of this catastrophe was that in 1989, after years of bloodshed, the Arab League – in which Lebanon was a founder state – finally convened a special Lebanese summit with top Arab diplomats in the Saudi city of al Taif in an attempt to solve the dispute. Their one goal was to force a ceasefire agreement between the warring factions.

Under heavy pressure from Saudi Arabia, Morocco and Syria, the Lebanese combatants agreed to return to the 1943 status quo, with a few microscopic modifications. The president would be elected from the Maronites and the prime minister would be a Sunni Muslim. The ratio between Christians and Muslims in parliament would henceforth be five Muslim and five Christians whereas the 1943 agreement had given the Christians an "eternal" advantage of five-to-four.

The original agreement had been a verbal understanding between Lebanese leaders; the Al Taif agreement was an officially signed treaty recognized internationally as a binding document. The blood of 150,000 Lebanese and 750,000 refugees, added to the massive damage to Lebanon's economy and reputation as a tourist resort and banking haven, had been entirely needless. Before the carnage ended some 500,000 Christians had lost their homes or were forced to look for a safe refuge. After the cease-fire was signed, another 100,000 managed to leave the country every year until only a million of the original three million Christians were left in Lebanon (*Boston Globe* 1/19/1999).

The demographic estimates of the Lebanese press during the 2000 millennium celebrations claimed that more than 1.2 million young Lebanese had left their ancestral homeland looking for new opportunities. Most of the refugees were Christian single males. As a result of this emigration, a vast majority of Lebanese young women failed to find spouses, a situation that has perverted the natural demographic balance.

In a recent assessment on Lebanese TV (LBCI 11/2001) of this vast exodus, a variety of experts concluded that although emigration after the Al-Taif agreement slowed while many Lebanese were enthusiastic and hopeful, after five years of disappointing economic growth plus corruption and ineptitude settling back into the system, many were encouraged to seek safer havens. Around 50,000 per annum left during 1990-1995, but this number escalated to almost 200,000 by 1999.

Many Muslims found refuge in Arab lands or in the ex-French colonies of Africa. Most Christians emigrated to Latin America, Australia, Canada or the U.S. joining relatives who had gone before. Many young men left their families behind in Lebanon for several years while they worked hard and lived frugally in order to build a nest egg and return to establish themselves back home or else managed to get their dependents to emigrate as well.

The census in Lebanon in 1932 showed that Christians made up 54% of the population. By 1943 they had dropped to 52% and ever since their percentage of the whole has been on a steady downward spiral until today it is estimated they constitute only a third of the populace.

Alas, this trend had begun in 19th century when many young, educated and ambitious Lebanese emigrated to seek their fortunes elsewhere. Some sailed to Alexandria, for Egypt was under a more liberal regime (compared with Ottoman tyranny). Others journeyed in increasing numbers to North and South America carrying with them their great heritage. In their new homes these Lebanese formed cultural and literary societies, established exiled presses in New York and contributed to modern Arab literature by establishing important literary schools – with Kahlil Gibran its most famous representative.

Today the number of ex-Lebanese and Syrian Christians living in foreign lands exceeds those who remain in their original homeland. Six million Syrians, Lebanese and Palestinians (and their descendants) live in Brazil alone (Radawi 1988:33), of these at least five million are Christians. Millions also live in Argentina and Chile with three million Arabs living in the U.S. (Haiek 1984:203). In the ex-French colonies of Africa there are some ten million Lebanese.

In 1969 Kablan Eisa Khouri, a Lebanese member of parliament traveled extensively visiting Lebanese communities abroad. He discovered that the Lebanese cultural forces outside of Lebanon included 1,000 members of parliament, 700 army generals, 150,000 military officers and soldiers, 15,000 medical practitioners, 22,000 lawyers, 14,000 engineers, 221 judges and 11,000 university teachers (*Al Massareh* 5/1969:389). Since he did not disclose his sources, some doubt their accuracy, but this did show how the cream of Lebanese society had contributed their efforts abroad instead of back home.

Dr. A'touf Mahmoud Yaseen, one of the few Arab scholars who has noted the social implications and economic consequences of this brain-drain, quotes warningly from UNESCO statistics: 10,000 doctors and engineers leave Lebanon, Syria, Egypt, Iraq,

Jordan and North Africa Arab states every year (Adiiseshia 1969:8, 12). She also quotes U.S. statistics that point out that 70% of all Arab students who come for advanced studies in America never return to their own countries and 90% of the Lebanese and 65% of the Syrian medical doctors and 61% of their engineers emigrated between the years 1956 to 1969 (Yaseen 1984).

This is a tragic loss for the Syrian/Lebanese society where in 1964 one general practitioner in Iraq served on average 4,760 persons; in Jordan, 5,300; in Syria 5,100; in Algiers 9,000; in Morocco 9,900; in Tunisia 9,400; in Egypt 2,380 and in Lebanon 1,320. On the other hand in Israel there was a doctor for every 420 persons and in the U.S. one for every 680 (U.S. Immigration Dept. 964:103-105). The same disastrous story can be told about nurses who are so essential to any medical treatment. The Syrian population is about equal to that of Australia, but there is one Syrian doctor for every 13 in Australia; yet 6,000 trained Syrian doctors left their country between 1964 and 1974 (Yaseen op cit 117,123).

Unfortunately, the vast majority of these emigrants were Christians. Dr Khalil Jahshan, president of the National Arab American Association (NAAA) estimated in 1998 that 80% of the Arabs in the U.S. were Christians. Two decades earlier, they had made up 90% of the community. As Christians, these Arabs had sought a land where they could practice their religion in peace and tranquillity (Naff 1988:26).

Thus the Greek-Orthodox church in Australia has grown mightily with many of the members immigrants from Syria or Lebanon. Since these newcomers prefer to worship in their native tongue using traditional liturgy, the local bishops have tried to accommodate their needs. Often the church becomes the central focal point in the émigré's life.

Does this mean that Christian Arabs are doomed to vanish from the Holy Land and the Middle East? Does the contribution of the Arab Christians to the common cultural life of the Arab world not entitle them to the right of being accepted on the same footing as Muslim citizens in these countries? Why do all Arab regimes reject a pluralistic culture in their own countries but insist this needs to be established in Lebanon? They want Lebanon to adopt a policy of equality, but do not treat them as equals. Instead they give militarily feeble Lebanon poisoned gifts, first the PLO and later the Hizbullah guerilla units.

The PLO were driven out of Egypt, Syria and Jordan – those countries bordering Israel – while Lebanon was forced to tolerate their presence and permit their anti-Israeli activities (provoking Israeli counter-operations against Lebanese targets).

The Lebanese government made feeble attempts to keep the PLO in line and then, for reasons never made clear, the Christians, under Maronite leadership, made some kind of an alliance with Israel in 1975 in order to keep the Palestinians in check. Instead, there were heinous massacres which some "Christians" committed against innocent civilians (with Israeli backing) that created such a furor in world public opinion that the Israelis were forced to withdraw their forces, leaving their allies behind under a Syrian "fraternal" hegemony.

The Lebanese Christians paid a high price for all this during the subsequent 15 years of civil war that basically destroyed the Lebanese social and economic infrastructure. The numbers of the dead, injured, maimed, displaced and disappeared came to almost half of the population there before this devastating period. Most Lebanese children were unable to attend school and many of them were forced to the streets to fight or loot. Lebanon, that "little piece of heaven" in the words of the great Lebanese troubadour, wadia' as Safi, was lost. The summer resort area for the Arab Middle East was nothing more than a sad memory.

Tragic was the Arab League's compliance with the mutual slaughter that took place during these long years. Arab intellectuals, in and outside Lebanon did little to resist this mayhem. All hopes that Arabs would adopt modern objectives and secular criteria for measuring their attitudes toward events were to no avail.

In 1981 a think-tank in Beirut, the National Arab Institute, organized an intellectual debate for top scholars from both sides of the war six years after it had started. Of the six speakers, four were Christians. A Muslim, Ridwan al Sayyed, editor of *The Arab*

Thought (al Fikr al A'rbi) spoke on the Muslim tradition of tolerance in history, concluding that Lebanon should return to the old *Dhimmis* system.

The general Muslim attitude was expressed by Mohammed Thafer al Qassimi who criticized Dr. Costantine Zurayk, a famous Christian thinker on Arab nationalism. In his opening remarks Zurayk had said this civil war was not a conflict between Islam and Christianity, but between the progressives and the reactionaries on both sides. Instead of evoking a positive response from this "progressive" forum, Qassimi rather blamed the Christians in Lebanon. To prove his point he intimated there was not a problem between Muslims and Christian in Egypt, Sudan, Iraq, Jordan, Morocco, Algeria or the Arab Peninsula. Rather, any problem in Lebanon was created by foreign provocateurs and adopted by Christians (Khouri 1981:117-123). All this was news to the Copts, Armenians, Assyrians and South Sudanese who thought they were being treated as second-class citizens.

This regrettable dialogue-of-the-deaf is indicative of the absence of real public discourse in the Arab world (Khalid 2000). Zurayk, a celebrated national thinker, had been calling for unity in the Arab nations since the 1950s. With the decline of the Arab national movement in 1970 after Nasser's assassination, he began calling for unity between all Arab peoples. By the end of his life, he was more modest in his dreams, but still lived with hope (Zurayk 1998).

The depths of frustration and the disappointment of the liberal Arab nationals is well expressed by Albert Hourani, famous historian at Oxford and authority on the Middle East in his classic, *Syria and Lebanon: A Political State,* published in 1946:

> There is in the Syrians and Lebanese a certain greatness, which has been too long asleep and is now awakening. For two generations the educated youth have sought opportunities in Egypt and in the New World. But both these spheres are now largely closed to them and the second of them could, at the best of times only, be entered at a great price: the loss of their native land and acceptance of the life of stranger and an exile. It is not strange therefore that the thoughts of young Syrians and Lebanese, especially of those among them who feel responsible for

the future of their country, should be turning eastward and southward; and that they hope to find in the other regions of Arab Asia opportunities at once for the exercise of their talents and for the fulfillment of their duty to their people (1946:117).

Hourani felt that both Syria and Lebanon held a unique position in the Arab world because of their large Christian population and their ancient connection to the Christian culture of the West which allowed them to be a bridge between Muslim Arabs and the West (op cit 79-80). Yet Hourani emphasized the need for Syrian and Lebanese Christians to be mindful of their roots in the East.

How sad that his appeal was ignored. Riyadh Najeeb al Rayyes, an enlightened Lebanese Muslim intellectual noted that the Lebanese Christians made the mistake of rejecting Arabism out of fear or a sense of superiority, allying themselves with Israel. This, for the first time since the Crusades, put the entire Christian existence in the area at risk (Al Rayyes 1988:18-19). However, Rayyes is not being quite fair nor objective.

Lebanese Christians only started seeking Israeli help after their Arab neighbors had foisted the PLO on Lebanon, thus exposing them, alone, to suffer Israel's reprisals for years. Also, the Lebanese–Israeli alliance was signed in 1982, five years after Sadat's dramatic visit to Israel when a peace agreement was signed between Israel and Egypt–the most important Arab State. Still, Al Rayyes admits this 1982 Lebanese-Israeli peace agreement was supported by the Lebanese-Muslim members of parliament (Al Rayyes ibid 21).

From his safe haven in London this Lebanese liberal felt free to suggest that future relations between Arabism and Islam should be based on these preconditions: the Arab national movement should crystalize within a secular democratic struggle and it should revolutionize the Muslim religious way of thinking in order to fit in with modern accepted thoughts on rationalism, science and freedom. These preconditions would rule out any mixture of the concepts of Islam and Arabism. He felt it would be impossible to manipulate this mixture (of religion and nationalism) in the service of ideologies and political maneuvers (Al Rayyes ibid 67).

Despite the failure of either side in Lebanon to achieve victory in this war, the country managed to calm down a bit without adopting any new ideology or political theory. The Lebanon of today varies little from that of the 1940s. The political system is built on a coalition of the oligarchies of the main religious societies and it daily faces the danger of renewed violence and social explosion on sectarian lines.

An increasing number of Christians tend to accept the idea that their salvation can come only from a modern state built on a secular egalitarian base. The Druze leadership concurs – or at least their charismatic leader Kamal Junblat declared his willingness to facilitate such a solution. Unfortunately the Sunni Muslims' mufti, Sheikh Hussein Quwatli, does not agree and proclaims that the "Muslim establishment position is firm. Muslims will be loyal only to a Muslim authority" (A'ashqouti 1991:47).

The Maronite community sacrificed much to fulfill its aspiration to secure the independent state of Lebanon as a political entity in modern times. These Maronites were forced during a long millennium of Arab-Muslim domination to learn the Arabic language and to mix with Arab-Christians and Muslims. They used Arabic in daily life but preserved their ancient language, the Syria-Aramaic dialect, for their liturgy.

Still they never universally acknowledged themselves as Arabs, and to this day Maronites, despite the fact that Lebanon was a founder-state member of the Arab League and the cultural and commercial center of the Arab Middle East, refuse this distinction. Of course they have deep-rooted, historical reasons to eschew the Arab title since their ancestors fought hard to maintain their freedom and in the process made alliances with the Byzantine emperors and the Crusaders against the Muslim caliphs and governors.

Given this bloody background it is easier to understand how Lebanese-Maronites, both laity and clerics, early in the 20th century met warily with Zionist leaders. The Lebanese patriarch Antoine Pierre Arida (head of the Maronite church from 1932 to 1952) and other pro-Zionists top officials, according to the Zionist Central Archives, were involved in talks with them for decades. At first the Jews were not sure it was in their best interests to sign an agreement with these anti-Muslim Maronites, but later the Zionists adopted the attitude that "beggars can't be choosers" and this shaky trust led to secret talks, unofficial understandings and coöperation between the two sides.

The first Zionist-Maronite treaty, drafted after World War I when Lebanon was under the French mandate, was to be signed in December 1936, but the French high commissioner for Lebanon, Domienn de Martel, rejected it categorically, saying it was not in Lebanon's best interest. The second attempt to formalize an official alliance between the Zionists and the Maronite oligarchy was signed by Patriarch Arida's authorized representative and nephew, Sheikh Toufic Aouad, and Bernard (later Dov) Joseph from the Jewish Agency. Aouad gave Joseph a letter signed by his uncle declaring he was "authorized to negotiate" and come to any agreement that was in the interest of both sides and to "collect any sums of money" (Zittrain 1994:92).

The Maronite-Zionist Treaty initialled by these two in May 1946 did little to alter the Zionist policy in Lebanon. Yaa'cov Shimoni of the Jewish Agency, who wrote the treaty, was quoted saying," The [political] department wisely concluded the best possible accord with Arida and then carried on as if the Treaty did not exist" (ibid 149). Yet Eisenberg, an American Jewish scholar, has concluded this was a lost opportunity, for these Zionists misjudged a chance to turn shared interests into mutual political advantages or perceiving that "of all their enemy's enemies, the Maronites offered the most willing candidates for friendship" (ibid 160).

The Israeli Archives do not, for the time being, offer us any evidence about whether or what sums were paid out, despite the fact that Zionist sources are usually quite generous in disclosing details about their paid friends, as has been found in Elyahu Sassoon's memoirs. This colorful character was in his early youth an active member in the Arab national movement in Syria serving the first Hashimite king in Damascus.

Later he moved to Palestine where he was recruited to work for the Zionist Movement and eventually became one of Israel's top emissaries to the Arabs. He tells of using money "to convince" Lebanese and Syrian editors and even some Arab delegates in pan-Arab meetings to publish pro-Zionist articles and to embrace "positive" attitudes or simply deny anti-Jewish accusations printed earlier. Sassoon claims to have planted no less than 260 articles over a few years in scores of Muslim, Christian, Lebanese and Syrian newspapers (Sasoon 1978:72-108).

The Maronites were not the only Arabs willing to ally themselves with the Zionist settlers in Palestine. Moshe Sharet, Israel's second prime minister (1954-1956) was during the 1930s searching for allies against the Arab Palestinian leadership and aspired to establish an "anti-Mufti" political party. A Lebanese Muslim prime minister volunteered for this mission, provided the Zionists would finance a newspaper for this joint project. Sharet was willing to bargain, but three months of dallying left the Lebanese Muslim prime minister no longer in a position to attract the Zionists as a potential ally.

Other Zionist sources claim to have influenced some leaders of the Palestinian Druze minority, who advised their co-religionists in Lebanon to refrain from joining Arab anti-Zionist fighters by sending them long pleas by reliable emissaries (ibid op cit 75-76). Another, Archbishop Augustine Mubarak, Maronite bishop of Beirut, was the only native Christian leader willing to declare his pro-Zionist policy openly. For decades he was convinced a Jewish state in Palestine would come to support and consolidate Lebanon as a Christian state, and he was brave enough to say so in public international forums such as the UNSCOP (United Nations Special Committee on Palestine) in August 1947.

Ex-president Emile Eddie and Archbishop Mubarak were so eager to win Zionist neighbors for Lebanon that Eddie let the famous Jewish journalist Francis Ofner convey to David Ben Gurion the message that the Maronites would support a Zionist demand to annex the southern zone of Lebanon to Palestine (Ofner 2001).

In 1946 Mubarak suggested to Chaim Weizmann of the Jewish Agency and Ernest Bevin, British Minister of Foreign Affairs, that as a first step towards establishing a Zionist-Maronite alliance the

British should annex the (mainly Shiite) southern region of Lebanon to Palestine and not to Syria (ZCAS 25/6319) so that a Maronite zone would border Israel. Not only did the Zionists reject these offers out of hand, Chaim Weizmann was quoted as laughing at the offer, saying his father had taught him to refuse a gift of anything that eats. The British, as well, did not pursue this alliance.

Archbishop Mubarak and his followers were the only Arabic-speaking natives of the Middle East who publicly said something in favor of the Zionist schemes, but they really were not that isolated. Many religious groups and individuals bargained with the Zionists in order to benefit from all the Jewish wealth flowing into the country, but Maronite leaders felt secure enough under the French mandate to pronounce their point of view openly, causing a lot of unhappiness and pique in widening Lebanese and Arab circles (Khalidi & Farroukh 1953:26-33; Schulze 342-4).

Archbishop Mubarak is long forgotten and his theories have become irrelevant in Israel today where the policies for solving the problems of the Jewish people center on returning Jews "home" to Zion and normalizing their relations with "others" – mainly the Muslims.

Israel's failure to win a peace agreement with King Abdullah I of Jordan and his assassination in July 1951 on the eve of his signing an agreement changed everything. Israel's political "axiom" – that the first Arab state to conclude peace with Israel is unknown but the second, Lebanon, is already waiting – faced a challenge, and the Israeli leaders felt the urge to correct this. David Ben Gurion seems to be the first who believed his government should actively help the Maronite Catholics of Lebanon establish a Christian state (Sharet 1978:377).

Moshe Dayan, a favorite Ben Gurion disciple, adopted his approach and suggested in 1955 that Israel should win (or hire) a Maronite army officer ("even a captain") to declare himself the redeemer of the Maronite nation, whereupon this would trigger an Israeli military advance to occupy the region and establish a Christian government allied with Israel. "The entire zone, south of the river Litany will be annexed to Israel – and every thing will be fine" (loc cit. 996). Ben Gurion suggested that a special committee of officials (from the ministries of defense and foreign affairs) follow up on this policy of "liberating" Lebanon–and it was established on May 28, 1955 (loc cit. 1024).

An Israeli-Lebanese agreement was finally signed during the last civil war (1975-1989) and was in place when the Israelis invaded Lebanon during the operation "Peace for the Galilee" in 1982. The declared target was "the PLO infrastructure in that country" as Menahem Begin and Ariel Sharon put it. Certainly they were keen to put an end to the PLO's military power, but they also invaded Lebanon to put in their ally, Bashir Al-Jemayyel, as president and, after all these years, to form an Israeli-Maronite alliance.

At the last minute this plan failed because the president-elect was assassinated. Even worse than his death, was the brutal massacre by savage criminals of innocent Palestinian civilians in refugee camps outside of Beirut as "a revenge" for the assassination of this admired leader. This heinous crime, perpetrated by some "Christians" who had allied themselves with the Israelis, destroyed the last hope for an Israeli-Maronite alliance.

A de facto alliance began in 1975 when Lebanese Christians from an isolated enclave in South Lebanon known as Marj A'yon came to the fence near Metula on the eastern sector of the international border between Israel and Lebanon asking for medical treatment for those wounded in violent skirmishes between armed groups of Palestinians and Lebanese Muslims on one side and right-wing Lebanese Christians on the other.

The Israelis, happy to find allies against the PLO, adopted a "Good Fence Policy" which supported the conservative Christians and helped drive the PLO fighters out of Lebanon in 1982. But there were repercussions which encouraged the massive exodus of Lebanese Christians to America and Europe over a 25-year period. Some of this was motivated by the Israeli presence–but the public alliance and its failure brought many to despair of hope for future relations between Christians and Muslims since so many native Christians had allied themselves with military Zionist aggression.

Those remaining Christians tried to close ranks and keep their distance from Muslims while living in "Christian" ghettos. Some of these joined right-wing anti-Arab groups. Savage and cruel skirmishes broke out in a bloody civil war that lasted 15 years (1976-1991). Finally things became somewhat less tense when Lebanon was afforded recognition in the Arab League as having special status—a partnership of Christians and Muslims in a political entity where Christians had special privileges, like being the major shareholders determining the fate of the land with a Maronite president and commander of the national army.

Other Lebanese Christians had fewer options. A tiny minority in the south near the Israeli border (where Israel and PLO guerrilla fighters were constantly warring across their villages) faced the conundrum of either joining the war on the side of the Palestinians (and deserting their villages) or making peace with the Israelis who occupied the region and staying in their villages. The Christians, and others as well, in an effort to maintain their villages, joined forces with the Israelis. This "alliance" survived for 25 years until 2000.

The Israelis felt no loyalty to this agreement yet decided to keep their grip on the Lebanese "security belt" as long as it suited their purposes. This "buffer zone" was deemed expendable in May 2000 and returned to Lebanon. This change meant many of Israel's "allies" had to flee their villages in Lebanon and become refugees in Israel. In the aftermath of Israel's hasty withdrawal, the local militia, 2,200 strong, crumbled and disintegrated.

The South Lebanese army, according to official sources, was composed of 500 Christians, 500 Sunni Muslims and Druze, with 1,200 soldiers from the Shiite sect—the same group which supplied the "enemy" Hizbullah militia. Without Israeli officers, these soldiers were free to choose sides and obviously most of them joined their Muslim counterparts at the first sign that Israel's forces were pulling back. The SLA collapsed. Some 7,000 Lebanese, SLA personnel, invalids, widows and orphans of those 700 Lebanese killed during the last 25 years of Israeli-Lebanese "alliance" (most of them Christians) found refuge in Israel—pending their return home or moving on to safer havens in Europe or America. Over 2,000 decided to risk going back home to Lebanon.

The vast majority of the Christian soldiers and a minority of the non-Christians in the South Lebanon Army became refugees in Israel simply because they did not trust the fighters of Hizbulla Lebanese militia to treat them as equals. Unfortunately the result of this long and ferocious civil war and Israel's alliance with some Christians was a consolidation of the Shiite Muslim militias – Amal first and Hizbullah later – into a major political force in that country and the Syrians' success in spreading their hegemony over Lebanon – a move welcomed by many moderate Christians grateful to Damascus for its intervention in putting an end to the chaos, savage atrocities and bloodshed.

Thus the Israeli attempt to turn Lebanon into a friendly neighbor had little hope of success because instead of being Christian, now over 90% of South Lebanon's population is mainly Shiite Muslim. This sect, famous for centuries for its docility, has become hostile and aggressive under the influence of a popular uprising in Iran, always the Shiite's center, against the corrupt regime of the Shah. This raised the clergy to power. Also, Christians were an insignificant minority in Sur (Tyre) and Sidon, both major towns, and composed a majority in fewer than ten villages with a population of some 30,000 in an area of more than a half-million Lebanese, most of whom were Shiites.

Another cause for Israel's failure to shape Lebanon to their liking was their unwillingness to pay their share of the partnership. The population of the *only* Maronite village peacefully occupied by Israeli forces in Palestine during the 1948 war was driven away into refugee status. Also the Lebanese Christians could not unite with Israel against the Palestinians, who were universally backed by all Arabs.

This unanimous moral support for Palestinians was only natural since Israel, the main cause of their tragedy and loss of their homeland, had never come up with any proposal that would address the minimal Palestinian rights and needs for a homeland. Some 350,000 Palestinian refugees still live in refugee camps in

Lebanon waiting to go home, but the Israeli government makes sure not to allow such a repatriation. The Lebanese feel no need to solve Israel's wrongs and refuse to grant these refugees permanent status.

In addition, compelling economic motives contribute to this failure. The Lebanese, both Muslim and Christian, for centuries were economically dependent on Arab clients who used their services as a bridge and commercial link to and from Europe – for banking, tourism, entertainment and cultural benefits. Israel had their own economic links and would not substitute for any customers the Lebanese lost in this arena. Worse, Israel was seen as a potentially dangerous rival economically.

The Gospels are replete with history that bears on Syria as a Christian Holy Land. When Jesus took his disciples to a lonely place for respite (Luke 9:18 & Mark 8:27), after praying he asked them: "Who do people say that the Son of Man is?" After the others had given various answers, Peter said, "You are the Messiah, the Son of the living God." To which Jesus replied, "Blessed are you, Simon son of Jonah! For flesh and blood has not revealed this to you.... You are Peter, [Kepha] and on this rock [kepha] I will build my church, and the gates of Hades will not prevail against it" (Mt 16:13-18).

The site in which this event took place is near the old Greek town of Paneas (today's Banias). In the aftermath of the Ottoman empire's disintegration at the end of World War I when new borders were drawn between Syria, Lebanon and Palestine, Banias became a border town inside Syria near the Palestinian border. Since the 1967 war, Israeli soldiers have occupied this deserted town and annexed it to Israel as a part of the Golan Heights.

Another chapter of Syria's role in Christian history involved the anti-Christian Shaul from Tarsus who was blinded by a brilliant light on his way to Damascus and then became the great Paul, apostle to the nations. Also Syria was home to ancient Antioch, called the great city of God in the book of Acts and the first See of St. Peter as head of the Christian church before its move to Rome. The importance of Antioch was evident in the notes of a historian who accompanied the first Crusade. He found there 1,200 churches, 360 monasteries and some 153 bishops serving under its patriarch centuries into the Muslim occupation (Tudobed op cit 259). Today this town is almost totally deserted and has been annexed to Turkey.

Under Muslim rule, Syria was famed as the homeland of St. John the Damascene (675-749), St. Simeon, the first of the stylites or pillar saints (390-459) and eight popes in Rome. The change in government turned the native Christians into a minority. Their unique fame in the last hundred years, after the savage pogrom they suffered in 1860, is their active role in the call and movement for Arab unity – regardless of any sectarian faiths.

The vast majority of Christians here are members of the Arab Orthodox Church of Antioch (since they became independent of the Greek hegemony). The Christian Orthodox in Jerusalem, Israel, Palestine and Jordan all aspire to independence from the Greek hierarchy. A growing number of Christians in Syria are Armenians and Assyrians who have found shelter here after fleeing atrocities suffered in neighboring Turkey and Iraq.

The first Syrian constitution stipulated that Syria, as an Arab country, should have a Muslim president. This constitution was amended in 1958 under the rule of President Shukri Al Quwwatli who proclaimed Islam as the state religion of Syria (Al Arnout 2000:21). A plebiscite adopted in 1973 declared Syria a "Popular, Democratic, Socialist, Sovereign Republic" whose "territory is not to be surrendered" (a pledge made to show the military regime's intent to liberate the occupied Golan Heights). It also affirmed Syria as a member in the Union of Arab Republics (which ceased to exist officially in 1977 after Sadat's famous visit to Israel) and part of the Arab homeland. Another stipulation of the constitution says Muslim law (*fiqh*) is the main source of judicial law and that Islam is the official religion, yet religious freedom is promised to all (Al Massareh 1973:389-390).

Syrian Christians, who make up about 10% of the population, are active in public life and tend to play a major role in radical groups (Syrian Nationals, Communists, Socialists and Arab Nationalists). Such activities indicate that the Syrian Christians and Orthodox feel a strong need for radical change, which drives them to participate in public life. Patriarch Hazim of Antioch, leader of the biggest and most important Christian church in Syria, has said: "Our church was lacking in educational institutes to teach its doctrine and so that drove our youth to be educated in foreign schools and thus to play a major role in other fields. This very problem encouraged the church to establish its own academic institute in Tripoli, Lebanon." A Muslim militia seized the Belmond University during the civil war, but Prime Minister Dr. Salim Al Hus later returned it to the church in 1991.

European Christian mission schools were active in Syria from the 18th century and until 1958. The United Arab Republic government (a short-lived union between Egypt and Syria from 1958 to 1961) closed these institutions under the pretext of nationalizing the education system. When this ended, a change of heart on Christian education dragged on another 13 years until finally in 1974 a decree was made allowing the return of assets to their former owners (Al Massareh January 1975:82).

One motivation moving Syria towards becoming a secular regime is the utter intolerance which the Baa'th Party under President Hafiz al Assad had toward fundamental militant Islamists ever since their June 1979 attempt to seize power in Syria. Assad, a member of the small Muslim Alawite faction, (who consider Ali equal, if not superior to Mohammed), has dominated Syria since 1970 even though most Syrians are Sunni, or conformist, Muslims inclined to oppose an Alawite government.

On the whole, Christians feel relatively safe in Syria, but far from being free and equal. Patriarch Ignatius IV Hazim worries about the future of Christians in Lebanon and Syria because of the escalating waves of emigrations, yet he still is confident there will always be a Christian presence in this Holy Land country, finding it "inconceivable that Christians will live in all lands except that in which their Lord and Savior chose to live." He estimates a total population of 2.2 million Christians of which a million are Orthodox. The Syrian government, following its secular principles, refuses to ask citizens about their religious affiliation.

A large community of Christian Syrians live in diaspora in South America. In Argentina Carlos Minim, son of a Syrian Muslim immigrant who converted, was elected president. The largest single Syrian society of some six million people lives in Brazil which the immigrants began calling "New Andalusia" remembering the Arab colony which flourished in southern Spain until 1492 (Radawi op cit 52). For awhile this community was served by myriad publications in Arabic, but these soon closed down as the new immigrants became acculturated. Still there are some ten publications in Arabic still circulating in Latin America.

The Syrian consul-general in São Paulo, Majid al Radawi, published a book urging the Syrian community abroad to maintain their Arab links for the sake of national and cultural values, but since many of these immigrants fled the Middle East for their lives, escaping official oppression and persecution, they are less than receptive to such slogans and rhetoric. Besides, the international news tends to remind them that oppression still persists in Syria.

It is safe to claim that the Syrian and Lebanese Christians suffered more than Egyptian Christians did. Of course it must be admitted they lived in more troubled lands with at first its proximity to Byzantine and then later the Crusades that brought suspicion on their community. Modern times did not bring much relief as the Europeans expanded their power base to the east. Although they were recognized as equal citizens – not just tolerated *Dhimmis* – this only ignited the popular anger and massacres of 1860 in both Syria and Lebanon and the recurring civil wars in Lebanon since its independence.

Fortunately, Syria's Christians did not form a separatist movement aspiring for isolation from the Muslim majority as happened in Lebanon. Instead they played a major role in the national movement and subsequent struggle for independence and shared the same fate with others. As the Syrian authoritative regime for most of the last five decades has fought the Muslim fundamentalists, this has made Syrian Christians feel secure from any immediate violence along sectarian lines.

On the other hand, the regime's political alliances with the Soviet bloc and Iran sentenced the Syrian economy to stagnation so the Christians were forced to share their Muslim compatriots' extreme poverty. This has driven many of them to seek employment in the Arab oil-producing countries. With the demise of the Soviet Union, many in Syria today are wondering how Bashar Al Assad, who succeeded his father as president when Hafiz Al Assad passed away in 1999, will lead the country. Some are heartened by the fact that he received a doctorate from an English university, and hope he will be more resilient, but still there is concern among the Syrian Christian community.

10

Iraq – Lost Paradise

"And should not I pity Nin'eveh that great city, in which there are more than 120,000 persons who do not know their right hand from their left, and also much cattle?" (Jonah 4:11).

Iraq is a modern state established by the British in the aftermath of occupying the ancient Mesopotamia of the Ottoman Empire. The name was first used in 1920 when the British united the three districts of Baghdad, Basra and Musol. The first local government was appointed in 1921, and the new state borders were internationally recognized in Brussels in 1925. Here a small long-suffering minority of oppressed Assyrian Christians who had allied themselves with the British during World War I lived in the southern regions of Turkey and the northern district of Musol/Iraq.

British and other European missionaries and merchants had interacted with the Assyrians since the 13th century – but this had resulted in dividing the church in the east (called Nestorian at times and Assyrians at others) into Syrian (Catholic and Orthodox) and Chaldeans (Catholics). They shared an Aramaic-Syrian liturgy and spoke the language Jesus Christ used during his earthly life with their original church. When British troops first occupied Iraq, the oppressed Assyrians welcomed them as co-religionists.

The British "evacuated" Iraq in 1931 before solving the Assyrians' problem. The League of Nations enjoined the Iraqi government in 1932 to settle those Assyrians who were unable to go back to their homeland in Turkey inside the northern district of Iraq. The Iraqi government, doubting the Kurd/Assyrian loyalty, decided rather to disperse them, curtailing the traditional authority of their religious leader to spiritual matters only. This was deemed unacceptable and a state of unrest dominated the relations between the Assyrian/Kurds and Iraqi government that climaxed in the 1933 massacres.

Thousands of men, women and children were killed, and many of those who survived abandoned Iraq to settle in the USA, Australia and Europe. The survivors were marginalized. The rare Assyrians who won fame were those radicals who played major roles in extreme revolutionary parties – Peter Basil and Yousef Salman (Al Fahd), members and leaders of the Iraqi Communist Party, and Tariq Aziz, deputy prime minister in the Baa'th regime.

The Baa'th regime made an attempt in 1970 win the support of the Assyrian community. A treacherous invitation was proffered to exiled church leaders to return home – with government pledges to confer rights to local governance and equality to the Assyrian community if they opposed the Kurdish rebellion. The Assyrians did not succumb to this dubious offer and the church Patriarch mar Shaa'on left Iraq in 1970 to return to the USA. The Iraqi regime, refusing to be denied, was implicated in the Assyrian prelate's assassination five years later (Shabera 2001:38).

The Iraqi population, currently estimated to be 21 million, contains a Christian presence of some 5% – about a million people. Most Iraqi Christians belong to the traditional churches – the Assyrians, Armenians and Aramaics – but many Assyrians adopted the Catholic doctrine and became Chaldean Catholics. Others have joined Evangelical Protestant churches. Since Saddam Hussein's invasion of Kuwait in 1990, Iraq has been under a rigorous economic blockade – supposedly to punish the Iraqi regime for invading Kuwait, producing chemical weapons and threatening the oil fields of Saudi Arabia and the Gulf State.

Originally, Saddam Hussein invaded Kuwait to claim it as Iraqi territory lost when the Western powers were carving up the Middle East. In actuality, it is was a grandiose gesture made by that pan-Arab leader with grand aspirations to rebuild an Arab empire stretching from the Persian Gulf to the Atlantic Ocean. The imminent threat to the oil field in the Gulf, so essential to the industrialized nations, prompted quick military response from the USA, France, and Britain – and also from Saudi Arabia, Syria, Egypt and Morocco.

Obviously this alliance could mislead naïve and honest people into believing that Saddam Hussein's lethal adventures against his compatriots, the Kurds during the 1970s, justified uniting all people of goodwill from the two universal faiths, Christianity and Islam, to oppose this evil. Unfortunately the results were less than felicitous. After defeating the Iraqis in Kuwait, the Security Council decided to punish the enslaved peoples of Iraq, but not their prison wardens. The UN teams made efforts to remove the country's weapons of mass destruction – an operation which has proved elusive for all.

The only clear result was the misery and suffering visited on the Iraqi citizens. Mike Nahal, the Middle East Council of Churches' representative in the relief organizations operating inside Iraq, published a report in 1994 describing the distress of the Iraqi population and its effect on the Christians. "There was an increase in the anti-Christian feelings and attacks were perpetrated against churches and injuries to Christian communities at the hand of extremist Muslims." He found special reasons for worry since "Iraqis, on the whole, tend to be secular and tolerant." This wave of hate crimes made the Iraqi government enact and publicize on a wide scale some new regulations, such as a three-year jail sentence for anyone "who maliciously desecrates a holy site or insults the religious beliefs of other citizens, ridiculing their worshiping rituals, or simply utters blasphemy" (MECC Report Jan-Feb 1995),

According to official figures, the number of Iraqi Christians had been increasing gradually, except during 1977 – 1987 when they declined rapidly due to the hardships created by the war with Iran.

In that decade, a strong wave of emigration resulted in the loss about 50% of the Christian minority. The 1965 census found that over 4% of the Iraqi population were Christians; of these, half lived in Baghdad with the others dispersed in small numbers in most districts of the republic. Iraq's most prominent Christian is Tariq Hanna Aziz, deputy prime minister and minister for foreign affairs. Other Iraqi Christians of note include the Jesuit monk Father Louis Sheikho and Anisettes al Carmili (from the Carmelite order) who have both contributed to the general Arab renaissance in the last century.

Jabra Ibrahim Jabra's pilgrimage is probably representative for Middle East Christians. This Palestinian writer, born in Bethlehem, as an Assyrian Christian has felt more at home in Iraq where he has lived most of his mature life, translating English classical literature, writing about the archaeological ruins connected with his people's religious heritage and national civilization, and dreaming of his childhood days in Bethlehem, Palestine.

His is not the exceptional story of a sensitive writer. Iraqi Assyrian emigrants whom I have met around the word tell similar tales. Their homeland is referred to as "paradise" and trying to explain why they left this paradise is painful. Of course, this is not unique to Iraqian emigrants. Still the Iraqis do carry with them the sense that they come from the land which witnessed the birth of the world's great culture, and somewhere in time Iraq, they believe, was "the site of the Biblical Garden of Eden."

This nostalgia is also apparent in the texts of ex-Iraqi Jewish writers who, in the aftermath of the 1948 Arab-Jewish War, settled in Israel after being driven from the homeland where their ancestors had lived for 2,500 years. Many insist on calling themselves Iraqis and although they write in Arabic or Hebrew, they mainly concentrate on Iraqi issues, unlike other Jews in Israel who came from North Africa, Egypt, Syria or Lebanon and seem totally assimilated into Israel's cultural life.

The Eastern churches' historical relations and local patriotism to Iraq made their leaders in 1925 appeal to the League of Nations in support of the Iraqi delegation's claim against Turkey. Iraq won that diplomatic battle so the ownership of the oil-rich district of Mousul was ultimately annexed to Iraq (*Al A'alam Al A'rabi* 4/9/1925).

This is not to claim the Iraqi Christians influenced the big powers in dividing this territory, but because of them, during the 1920s many Europeans had heard of the Turkish atrocities against the Armenians and the Assyrians. This added to the warm relations that existed between the Church of England (under the leadership of the archbishop of Canterbury) and the promising young Mar Shimon, the first British-educated head of the Assyrian church of the East. Observing this, one distinguished Iraqi statesperson, Fadel Jamali, wrote in his memoirs: "Without the British support Mousul could have been annexed to Turkey" (Al Jamali 1965:239).

There were also special ties forged between missionaries from the West, mainly the British and Americans, and the Assyrian-Nestorians, "the Protestants of the East" as the Church of England missionaries described them after their first meeting in the 1820s. A report about them written by the British chaplain then in Constantinople, Robert Walsh, published in the *Missionary Herald* in 1826, highlighted these "Protestants of the East." Most likely this account was based on information the traveler Claude James Rich made to the American churches when he asked them to send missionaries to share in winning these ancient Christians to their faith, "since these Protestants of the east were facing the imminent danger of being led astray by the ever-watchful, wily and active missionaries of Rome" (Waterfield 1973:102).

Claude James Rich, an employee of the British East India Company, was deeply touched by the Iraqi Christians' poverty and by the absence of icons or holy relics that Orthodox churches of the East traditionally had in their churches. He passed on this impression to his home church in England who were enthusiastic by this miracle of discovering a "prodigal son."

Alas, this encounter with the West was not all good news to the Assyrian church, for soon Catholic missionaries had divided this church by encouraging some to establish a Chaldean church to be united with the Roman Catholics. When the Protestants arrived later, they made an effort to win the entire Nestorian church to their fold but later changed their tune. One Presbyterian missionary decried the Assyrian church saying "the old church is a fossil. It is the grave of piety and Christian effort. It can never be reformed. Hence, for our Christians to live at all, they have been compelled to leave it" (Waterfield ibid:133).

Such criticism of the Nestorian church was only the first blow. In March 1843 Western missionaries, including the representative of the archbishop of Canterbury, G.P. Badger, assured the Assyrian leadership of British assistance against the oppressive Kurd authorities. This pledge was hollow, for when the Assyrians, armed with these false hopes, decided in 1846 to take up arms against the Kurdish government, some 10,000 of their original 50,000 troops were massacred (Waterfield ibid:107). No British support appeared. Granted, the Assyrian-Nestorian population was dwindling before they met these European missionaries, but the arrival of Westerners appeared to accelerate the process. Still more devastating days lay ahead after World War I with the British occupation of Iraq. The Assyrian-Nestorians, having endured much suffering in the mountains believed a bright future had arrived at last, but those hopes also were soon dashed.

The first Iraqi constitution, promulgated during the post-war British rule, bestowed on the Assyrian Christians recognition for their special cultural rights. Immediately after Iraq was granted its nominal independence in 1931, these Assyrians paid the full price for being naïve enough to depend on foreign powers. They suffered in the most severe way, especially for their association with the British and for serving in the British "Special Units" to enforce law and order in Iraq and help secure its northern borders. Anti-Assyrian massacres started in July 1933 when King Faysal of Iraq was on an official visit to King George V in England. The new government ministers, who had been humiliated a few months prior by their pro-British monarch, decided to win back their prestige by showing their strength and by fomenting indignation of the populace against the British and their allies, the Assyrians. Faysal wrote his government advising them to deal gently with the Assyrians, but they ignored this counsel (Khadori 1960).

Khadori, a Christian Iraqi who had emigrated to the USA, blamed General Bakr Siddqi, commander of Iraqi forces in the north of the country, for the massacres. Other Arab sources tend to minimize the significance of this massacre. It is not mentioned in many current books of Iraqi history. George Antonius, author of the classic *The Arab Awakening,* devotes only a few words to the "savagery with which the Assyrians were visited after their armed insurgence in the summer of 1933, and the massacre which took place is a shameful blot on the pages of Arab history" (1965:377).

It is hard to give credence to the claim that this tiny Assyrian minority rose in arms spontaneously against the Kurds who outnumbered them several times or against the Iraqi Arab Muslims who were ten times more numerous than they. The Iraqi population, according to Antonius, numbered at the end of the First World War more than three million, including 120,000 Christians (but only 35,000 Assyrians). What could persuade such a tiny minority to declare a state of war? The entire scenario is most unlikely, unless their leaders were complete lunatics or suicidal. And Antonius knew this. To convince his readers of these victims' guilt, he added: "The extravagant claims put forward by the Assyrian patriarch and a truculent group of chiefs made agreement impossible and thus the responsibility and the blame goes to the Assyrians' intransigence and to the ill-advised attitude of certain Assyrian leaders."

Antonius is willing to lay some "share of the responsibility on British shoulders, too, partly because of the open favoritism [of the British military which was tacitly] interpreted by the Assyrian leaders to mean a greater measure of support than was intended, and partly because of warnings of troubles which British officials in Iraq kept dispatching back home to their superiors in the Colonial Office during the years preceding the outbreak of hostilities against the Assyrian minority" (Antonius ibid:367).

So Antonius virtually contradicts himself by admitting it is unfair to blame the Assyrians for the massacre that befell them. Since the British colonial office knew for years about this dangerous situation, there are many culprits in this massacre. Antonius tries to exonerate his Hashimite friends, so he claims that during the massacre the Iraqi monarch was busy (in London) solving family problems in their hostilities with the Wahhabis, the Muslim fundamentalists who established the Saudi Kingdom in Hijaz and Najd (today known as the Kingdom of Saudi Arabia).

Even though one might gloss over this lacuna in George Antonius' description, it seems inexcusable in *The History Book of the Church of the East*, published 50 years later and written by two Lebanese Catholic clerics, Fathers Yateem and Deek, who refer to the massacres against the Assyrians during the 19th and 20th centuries at the hands of Kurdish tribes and Ottoman soldiers without mentioning the perpetrators: "Most Christians were executed during the years of the First World War, the faithful, bishops, and priests were killed" (Yateem & Deek 1991:348). Nameless perpetrators committed these atrocities, it seems.

Ignoring the Assyrian genocide soon became common. Nicola Zeyadeh, a famous Arab-Christian historian today, goes further and refrains completely from mentioning any massacres or anti-Christian oppression under the Arab rule. But then he does admit in the introduction that his book was "commissioned" by the Saudi royal prince Salman Ben A'bd al Aziz. The Prince read the first copy, rewarded its author, after which the author revised the text and supplied it to the publishers in Damascus (Zeyadeh 2000:9).

Antoine Weissel, a Dutch scholar, maintains the Assyrians had been encouraged (by European Christians, the Russians and the British) to fight back against their aggressive Kurd neighbors and that since 1843 they have suffered many casualties in these conflicts. He also claims these local wars climaxed in the relatively well-known Armenian Massacre during the First World War and an infamous and less publicized Assyrian massacre at the hands of Iraqi forces during the summer of 1933 (Weisels 1995:95-96, 219). This heavy death toll liquidated the last hopes of the Assyrians for a national entity, paving the road for the British-Iraqi alliance and the consolidation of the British share in Kurdistan's oil fields.

The actual criminal perpetrators were the Turkish sultans first and the Iraqi military elite later. We must never forget that the

"Young Turks" who toppled the sultan-caliph on their way to steer the Ottoman Empire on a new course, committed the worst atrocities. Their target was clear: force all their subjects to become Turks. They began this criminal genocidal policy against the Assyrians and later perfected it against the Armenians. Their aim was to clear the land of any foreign aliens, any potential organized resistance groups or any non-Muslim elements. For reasons never made clear, some historians hesitate in blaming the Turks for the Armenian genocide, searching instead for some mitigating circumstances, and even more (Christian-Arab) historians look the other way when they come near Turkish, Kurdish, and Iraqi attempts to annihilate the Assyrians.

The last Assyrian patriarch, Shimon the 23rd, was appointed to his post according to Nestorian-Assyrian tradition, which was to appoint the first cousin of the presiding prelate as heir to his uncle. Shimon 23rd was crowned in 1920 when he was only twelve years old and immediately thereafter became patriarch of the church. He went to study in England but on returning to Iraq after graduation, he "failed to meet both the clergy's and the people's expectation" and was exiled to Cyprus. After 1940 he took up residence in San Francisco, California, and in 1975 he was assassinated. The connection between this ambiguous affair and the massacre of the Assyrians is unclear, but those who point to this story (like George Antonius) blame the absence of any Assyrian leadership as the main cause of this sordid crime.

The Israeli-Marxist historian Aharon Cohen has detailed the Assyrians' tragedy. He estimates that in 1900 some half million Assyrians lived in North Iran and surrounding Turkish districts, especially in the southeast districts like Eardrum, Van and Mousul. During World War I the Turks and Kurds killed half of their population. In 1919, the British encouraged the survivors to live in Iraq, recruiting many of them into the occupying forces. In the aftermath of the Iraqi independence, the Iraqi Army attacked them and vast numbers of them were mutilated, tortured and killed. The few survivors tended to move to Syria, then under French rule. According to Cohen, by 1958, their number had been reduced to some 50,000 in Iraq (1958:39-40).

Another Israeli historian, Yosi Olmert, gives a differing account, but adds further details about the Assyrian suffering down through the ages in mountainous southeast Turkey and northwest Iran. Ever since the 14th century the Assyrians have suffered persecution. In the mid-19th century Kurdish neighbors encouraged by the Ottomans persecuted Assyrians, especially in the years 1830-1840. It is no wonder that Assyrian leaders in the early stages of the First World War made strange choices.

In May 1915 the Assyrian tribal chiefs met under the leadership of the church patriarch, Mar Shimon 22nd, and decided to support their Christian neighbors, the Russians. Soon the Russian Army collapsed and its generals decided to stand by the Bolshevik Communist Party, dropping the cross and raising the hammer and sickle. The Assyrians were thus abandoned and found themselves roaming the mountains, looking for a way to approach the British forces in Iran and Iraq.

At some point British intelligence officers arrived and promised them British support. The Assyrians left this meeting with the understanding the British would guarantee their independence, but the British insist this was never part of the deal. The one place where there remains no ambiguity or misunderstanding is that the Assyrians were faithful and trusted soldiers for the British in Iraq up until 1931 when the British handed most of the responsibility over to independent Iraq authorities.

In August 1933 the Iraqi Army proceeded to massacre the Assyrians while their English allies were still in their bases inside Iraq. Many of the Assyrian survivors ran for refuge to Syria (Olmert 985:15), not to the British Air Force base in Habbaneyeh in Iraq. Ever since then Assyrian authors have tended to be anti-British, with good reason. The British-Assyrian relationship brought great suffering to the Assyrians, and British soldiers have even been accused of helping the Iraqis (Shabera 1994:16). One Assyrian writer tells of 13 separate massacres that befell the Assyrians with the toll of the victims (during and after the World War I and before the Iraqi massacre of 1933) numbering some half million people (Shabera ibid:14).

Tawfik Suwaidi, an Iraqi Muslim political observer and leader during the monarchist period (1924-1958), went before a League of Nations' special committee convened to discuss the Assyrian problem and their miserable conditions to present the official Iraqi version of what happened (Sowaidi 1999:242-245). Without going into any details or accounts of what happened, he merely said, "The Assyrians were rude" and were "wiped out." How this happened, by whom and how many victims fell when the Iraqi Army savagely attacked these civilians does not enter into conversation nor seem important to this French-educated Iraqi. "They came to Iraq hoping to establish a national home in which they aspired to revive the glory of their ancestors," he says, not bothering to explain where they came from. "They [believed] the British would help them establish a national homeland in the north of Iraq which would turn this into a dangerous center with windows opening on all that would take place in Turkey, Iran, Iraq or Syria."

Great Britain's imperial intervention on their behalf resulted in setting a League of Nations special committee that forced Iraq to pay a million Iraqi dinars to help the few that survived settle in the north of Syria, but though historians may differ on the details, one thing is certain – the Assyrian-Nestorian Church of the East which had survived for more than a millennium on its own, once the Europeans and especially the British "discovered" its existence, became an endangered species. Interestingly, the British-appointed special inquiry board found the British innocent of the Assyrians' blood.

But claiming innocence according to a European criminal code, does not exonerate a nation from moral responsibility for failing to assure the lives of allies for as long as it maintains a military presence in Iraq or while it is training and arming the Iraqi national army.

To understand the motives and the general atmosphere leading up to this tragedy, one must recall that for a long time this country was part of the Ottoman Empire. Not until after World War I was it declared a separate entity under the British mandate. The first problem facing the new royal regime – under the British rule –

was the absence of a legitimate historical hierarchy – and the lack of the essential tools and symbols needed to run a state on a national level. Kurds, Assyrians and Turks inhabited the north. The center, in Baghdad and its environs, was inhabited mainly by Sunni-Muslim Arabs, while the south was for the most part Shiite, with the Iranian influence more dominant then than it is today.

Under the mandate, the British were supposed to unite this land. They decided the best solution for Iraq was to establish a royal dynasty – which would also help them find a remedy for dealing with the problem they were facing with their Arab allies from World War I – the Hashimites. This dynasty held the keys to Islam's holy towns in Hijaz (in Saudia today) as a kind of Turkish vassal, but the British in Egypt had managed to win them onto their side against the Ottomans. Immediately after the war the British were unable to fulfill the ambiguous pledges they had given the Hasimites: to establish an Arab kingdom in the Middle East.

At this point the Zionists introduced their pledge, known as the Balfour Declaration, for a Jewish homeland in Palestine. The French opposed attempts to create an Arab kingdom in Syria and the first Hashimite king crowned in Damascus in March 1920 was deported from his capital three months later. The British were not in a position to rescue their ally because they had signed a secret agreement with France (Sykes-Picco) dividing the Middle East Ottoman provinces between them and their French allies. The French were granted by the League of Nations the mandate over Syria and Lebanon. The Wahhabis fundamentalists conquered the Hashimites in Hijaz.

Thus, the British were faced with the problem of their Arab allies, the Hashimites. To solve this, they compensated the deposed king of Damascus, Faysal Ben Hussein, by offering him the throne of Baghdad. This king was unknown to most of his subjects, and the Iraqis who were appointed to the main political posts were unable to form a national leadership. Some of them were known as local chiefs, but none of them had national stature so there was little general support or enthusiasm about this move.

In the absence of influential political parties, the Iraqi Army became the main theater for ambitious souls who aspired to leadership. Rashid Ali al Gilani, prime minister during the massacre in 1933, was an ex-army officer who later led a pro-Nazi and anti-British military coup. Nuri Said, Iraq's most prominent politician, came from the ranks of the Ottoman Army officers. The king himself had won fame as a soldier fighting the Ottoman Turks with the legendary British intelligence officer, T.E. Lawrence (better known as Lawrence of Arabia).

This chaotic scene was the backdrop to the massacres. Absent even the elementary requirements for a modern state (i.e. national leadership with aspirations to succeed and a proper civil society with its institutions), Iraq was fragmented by overwhelming tribal traditions, blood feuds and divergent communities and religious sects (such as the Sunni and Shiite Muslims, the Arabs, Kurds and Persians besides the Christian and Jewish minorities). Added to this was the traditional significance of Baghdad, an historic Arab cultural and political center, and the emerging importance of oil production as a strategic asset in world politics. The tribal war imported to Iraq by the new Hashimite king (since his family was at war with the Wahhabis in neighboring Saudia) was virtually the last straw.

The British negotiation on the issue of Iraqi independence carefully secured England's interests, but protecting the Assyrians was not on the agenda. They were slaughtered while British troops were in Iraq securing their military air base in Habbanya, making sure it was in good condition in case the empire's interests were endangered. That need arose soon enough, for in 1941 pro-German elements toppled the government, endangering the oil supplies. At this point the British forces were deployed and their Jordanian Hashimite allies were called across the borders to help them enforce law and order on behalf of British interests.

Thus the lack of stability in modern Iraq plus the failure of the British to care about their ex-allies made possible the atrocities against the Assyrians in 1933 and the Jews during the military coup of 1941 – encouraging both communities to leave the country. The Federal National Union of Assyrians-Chaldeans in the USA had been established in 1933. Some 99% of the Iraqi Jews emigrated to the USA and Great Britain – but mainly to Israel when that was possible after the Jewish state was established.

Not all Assyrians left Iraq. Some persisted and survived in the mountains of the north, alongside the Kurdish tribes. In the late 1960s a group of the Scientific Exploration and Archaeological Research Foundation traveled to the area in an attempt to locate Noah's Ark. Instead they found Assyrian Christians living and fighting side-by-side with the Kurds against the Iraqi Army. Otto Meinardus tells of an Assyrian woman-fighter who was leading a force of 5,000 to 7,000 men in their battle against the Iraqis (*Eastern Churches Review* Spring 1970:53).

The *Catholic Near East* magazine wrote a summing-up of events accompanying the British presence in Iraq:

> The 20th century has been particularly difficult for the Christians in Iraq. The horrors of World War I forced scores to flee their homeland. Between 1915-1918 the Ottoman Turks massacred more than 50,000 Christians. Herded into refugee camps, thousands died in the cholera epidemic of 1918. The Assyrian Church of the East (Nestorians) suffered the heaviest losses. It is estimated that half of its congregation, including the Catholicos, numerous bishops, priest, men, women and children, were murdered or died of disease. [With the result that] today there are nearly 150,000 Iraqi Christians in the United States. Most of them settled along denominational lines: The Chaldean Catholics in California and Michigan, Nestorians in California and Illinois, and Syrian Orthodox and Syrian Catholics in New Jersey and New York (January 1991).

Lack of stability tends to be the motivating factor for people to emigrate. Besides coming to the U.S., Assyrians emigrated to England, Australia, Sweden, Holland and Germany, among others. The Assyrian writer Abram Shabira claims some 300,000 Assyrians are in the United States with 90,000 Nestorians in Chicago alone. In Detroit are a similar number of Catholic Chaldeans – a relatively new sect of Assyrians who accepted the Vatican's authority and doctrine. In California a special Assyrian TV channel operates 24 hours daily. The first Assyrian elected to the United States Congress, Ana Eisho, was from this state.

A similar situation exists in Sweden, currently homeland to 70,000 Assyrian refugees where Aslant Carimo, a lawyer, won a seat in parliament as a Social Democrat (*Al Quds,* 13 December 1998.) In Germany, however, the 60,000 Assyrians residing there are *Gastarbeiter* (guest workers) or simply *Turken Ohne Kpftuch* (unveiled Turks).

Left in Iraq at the end of the 20th century were some 100,000 Assyrians, many in the north inside the "Safe Zone" imposed by U.S. forces. Unfortunately, Assyrians feel safe neither here or north of here in Turkey. Their suffering and persecution seems to be as far from ending as Turkey is from being a civilized nation.

Al Hikma, a small Assyrian quarterly published in Jerusalem by church clergy, recently carried an article describing the persecution and suffering of monks in the isolated monasteries of Tur A'bdin, adding an appeal to Turkish authorities not to meddle in monastery affairs. Later issues described the grievous suffering of those in Kurdish territory as the Turks continue to deny them their national rights. The author Helga Anshutz describes visiting the Turkish-Iraqi border area and finding an Assyrian village with 100 people and 25 churches. In the Saint Cabreal and Zaa'faran historical monasteries she found monks trying to hide old and precious manuscripts from armed robbers roaming the area.

The Turkish armed forces, unable to control the region, appoint local Kurdish collaborators to "guard" the villages against the rebels, but these Kurdish traitors of their liberation movement are often undisciplined, using their arms to extort ransom money from poor Assyrian farmers whose children they would kidnap, demanding fantastic sums for their release (*Al Hikma* 4:1998).

The failure of the Turks to maintain law and order here stimulated more waves of emigration. Anschulz suggested that UNESCO declare the Assyrian monasteries as sites of universal human cultural value in hopes this might contribute to their preservation. *Al Hikma* (the Wisdom) continues to lobby for aid to the members of this ancient and proud church who have suffered tragically this past century, surviving as best they can. Church membership in north Iraq and southeast Turkey came to 40,000 in 1950, but in 45 years their numbers here have dwindled to some 8,000 members.

Al Hikma also tracks how these Assyrian families fare in their diaspora, noting how adamantly they work at keeping a footprint in Iraq by building new churches. Their presiding patriarch Ignatius Zakka I A'iwas is actively involved in healing wounds and soothing the suffering. They have established an Assyrian web site to help their far-flung family keep in touch and allow the church's members to exchange ideas. There are also some 100,000 Assyrians living in Syria who belong to various Assyrian Christian churches including the Nestorians, the Assyrian-Orthodox and the Chaldean-Catholics (BBC/Arabic 30 June 1998).

Those Assyrians who remain in Turkey are squeezed between two majorities and suffer both at the hands of the Turkish military and the Kurdish rebels who find them an easy prey. In a typical village, Idill, their population has dropped 90% in 15 years and the current bishop says his congregants are less than half their number in 1985. The Middle East Church Council organized a visit to the Assyrians living inside the Kurdish areas and found that Turkish authorities harass Assyrians in schools, prevent them from using their national language and make them feel that, despite the law, they are not regarded as equal citizens (MECC Report April 1991:7-9). Fortunately there are many places in Western Europe and America where Assyrians are, relatively speaking, warmly welcomed and promised a new homeland.

Today, at the beginning of the third millennium, Assyrians in Iraq make up a small and docile minority and are treated as such by the government. Since Iraq fought for eight years against the Orthodox Shiite regime in Iran, Saddam Hussein had a rare chance to pose as a progressive-secular leader by granting the Christian minority elementary rights as citizens. In 1972 the Iraqi Revolutionary Council decreed that Assyrians were to be given special cultural rights and in 1981 a law was passed allowing them to manage their church endowment and material assets (Liqaa #2.1997). The famous Assyrian writer living in exile, Apram Shabera, concluded Saddam was not anti-Christian but anti-Assyrian (Shabera 2001:46). As the war against Iran dragged on, and as Hussein increased oppressive measures to sustain his rule, many Iraqis – including Assyrians – sought refuge out of their homeland. The invasion of Kuwait and the Security Council sanctions imposed afterwards made the situation all the more grievous.

The American war "to free" Iraq in 2003, was another dramatic experience for the Iraqi people. The vast majority of all Iraqis were praying for Saddam Hussein's removal from office, but a clear majority of Arabs felt the American government was far from being an altruistic custodian of oppressed nations. The fact that President George W. Bush called his anti-Saddam intentions a crusade added to the Muslim animosity to this war. The opposition to the war by Vatican and major European leaders – and the scene of the massive demonstrations against the war in Paris, Berlin, Rome, London and New York – calmed the Muslims' rage and saved many Christians from attacks by extremist Muslim mobs.

The first day's fighting brought the "news" that Tariq Aziz, the only Christian in Iraq's ruling squad, ran away. Some felt this might trigger an anti-Christian wave of violence – but a few hours later Tariq Aziz countered this danger by appearing at a public news conference aired on TV. He declared that as an Iraqi born in Baghdad, he planned to live and die in his birth place. Still some within the U.S. propaganda machine kept chasing this only "Christian" – accusing him of being an American spy in Saddam Hussein's inner circle who was granted asylum in a palace in London.

This unfortunate policy of scapegoating the lone Christian makes observers suspect the motives here. A supposed Christian "friend" quoted in his book something taken from a right-wing Israeli daily. The claim was that Richard Butler, chief UN inspector searching for Iraq's weapons of mass-destruction, told an audience in Israel that Tariq Aziz "confided" to him that Iraq's biological weapons were being readied to deal with the "Zionist entity" (Burge 29:2003), even though at the time Iraq was adamantly denying publicly their having any weapons of destruction.

Fortunately, most ignored such blatant lies and no pogroms were begun in Iraq or a neighboring Arab state against Christians during the war. However, the American military's decision to disband the entire Iraq Army put 300,000 professional soldiers in the ranks of the unemployed and compounded the U.S. administration's failure to enforce law and order promptly after capturing Baghdad. Many peaceful civilians – including most Christians – saw these poor decisions and concluded, in spite of their fear of looters, marauders and thugs, that the best thing they could do was to keep distant from the "Allied Forces."

The future of Iraq under the renewed British-American military occupation seems risky, at best, and the prospects for Iraqi Christians remain ambiguous. The press reports they are petitioning the military regime to recognize all Iraqi Christians in the new constitution as the Chalidssyrian community, with their national language Aramaic respected. Iraqi Christians are asking for an autonomous zone for their million-strong community in Ninveh, north of Baghdad. No one knows what response they will receive, but half of the 200,000 Christians in the southern town of Basra have already fled their homes, looking for refuge in the north, away from the deadly Shiite gangs who target them as enemies.

As far back as 1958 the military regimes ruling Iraq were worse than the royal period established in 1921 to govern the newly independent state. Even harsher were the periods of unrest during Iraq's military attempts to demonstrate their strength by toppling their government, oppressing the opposition or invading their neighbors, Iran and Kuwait. Thus the holy land heritage and the Christian shrines in this country have been losing more and more of their natural guardians. Perhaps they are destined to become "museums." The next chapters give a rather detailed account of this on-going struggle in the heart of those holy lands – in Jerusalem, Israel, Palestine and Jordan.

11

The Lord's Compatriots Today

The stories passed down from my parents and their friends, dating back to the beginning of the 20th century, revolve around the cruelty of Turkish despots and oppressors. This produced a prejudice in me that made me ignore the advice I received from my revered tutor at Oxford, Albert H. Hourani (something I rarely did), who told me I was being too unkind to Sultan Abd al Hamid by labelling him an anti-Christian despot. Mr. Hourani, who brought a broader view of history to the scene, had concluded that, compared to his predecessors, Abd al Hamid was almost a reformer. I felt that he based his conclusions only on yellowed papers from official archives while I based mine on reliable first-hand sources – the victims of this despot's regime.

Our disagreement convinced me that often history books and personal experiences don't match. I had no doubts about Mr. Hourani's capability and integrity and felt privileged to have him as a tutor and thesis supervisor in Oxford. I knew he was much better versed than I on how to read history and judge events, including the shortcomings of historical characters, and to what level we can trust official documents in archives, but he also knew personal history could be simultaneously useful and misleading. Through oral history we can learn the subjective assessments of the people involved, but they also can miss the larger picture and blur the overview.

My parents and their neighbors had to compare the Ottoman rule of their youth to that of the British, who came after them with a far more liberal policy of law and order. Palestine under the British was, despite the looming Zionist threat, more affluent than in any other period in its recent history, but under the Ottomans, Palestine at the turn of the 20th century was at a nadir in most areas – the people were economically destitute, the population was dwindling and terror-struck by oppressive and exploitative rulers.

The Ottoman sultans and their notorious administration exploited their subjects, leaving poor farmers with no margins to tide them over bad years caused by inclement weather or devastating calamities like a locust invasion that stripped the fields and vineyards. These impoverished peasants then suffered from the "yellow air" epidemic which followed – their term for cholera. History books recite the cold figures telling us that before 1908 and the toppling of the sultan, the Palestinian population was cut in half by plagues of locusts and cholera. But it was my father's stories that put flesh on those stark statistics. The Ottoman government not only ignored the plight of their subjects, but also pressed them into military service to fight their wars in faraway countries like Greece, Bulgaria and Yemen against rebellious tribes or freedom fighters who were trying to rid themselves of the same oppressors.

My father old us that in our small village during these years they needed a new cemetery because in a community of a few hundred people they were daily burying three to five people. The combination of the Ottoman rule, the plague of locusts, the cholera epidemic, heavy taxes and a corrupt administration managed to devastate our miserable population in the Holy Land. The British under the command of General Allenby were seen as a godsend to rescue them from the Ottomans' tyranny.

The first British high commissioner to Palestine, Herbert Samuel, described the land in the 1920s: "The population had been depleted; the people of the towns were in severe distress; much uncultivated land was left untilled; the stock of cattle and horses had fallen to a low ebb; the woodland, always scanty, had almost disappeared; orange growers had been ruined by lack of irrigation; commerce had long been at a standstill" (Sereny & Ashery 1936:68).

According to history books, the Turk-Ottoman rule lasted 400 years in Palestine, but actually the Turks, Seljuk, Kurds and other non-Arab Muslims have dominated the Middle East since the ninth century. During most of that time Christians (and Jews) were discriminated against on religious grounds. *Dhimmis* paid the *Jizya* and were expected to be humble and respectful to the Muslim lords who protected them from foreign danger. This practice was briefly halted early in the 19th century when Egyptian soldiers, with French officers, occupied Palestine, Lebanon and Syria, and threatened Turkey by introducing egalitarian concepts. Unfortunately, European allies, mainly the British, rescued the Ottoman sultan and forced Ibrahim Pasha and his French allies to withdraw back to Egypt, taking his modern ideas with him.

Seventy years later, in 1908, the Ottoman government could no longer dismiss the fallout from the French Revolution and so adopted a modern constitution, similar to the French one, electing a parliament for the first time in the region's history. The reform was short-lived because the new parliament met only for two sessions (Assaf op cit 10) before a "tentative" state of emergency brought back martial law – which lasted 31 years. The sultan, faced with "Young Turk" colonels challenging his authority, had capitulated because the empire was deteriorating and national movements in the Balkan and Arab colonies needed to be suppressed. The state also needed money to pay its debts and finance a "reform" for its failing military forces. The sultan's short-sighted advisors made no attempts to discover the cause of their problems: a tyrannical regime that neglected the basic civic and health needs of the society.

The health of the Palestinian population during the last two centuries has been a long litany of suffering from a variety of diseases: malaria, typhoid, dysentery, measles, trachoma and rheumatism. To grant them their due, the Ottomans established two small, primitive hospitals in Jerusalem and Nablus during the last years of their reign, but for the vast majority of the population, government medical services were virtually non-existent. The first Anglican mission included physicians who treated Jews in Jerusalem. Rich Jews from England hastened to dispatch their own medical units to preclude Christians from treating their co-religionists. The Edinburgh Medical Mission opened the first hospital in Galilee to serve the rural community and subsequently a variety of Christian missions from different countries built hospitals or clinics throughout the region offering free or heavily subsidized treatment to all.

Not to be outshone, religious Jews made an attempt to compete, but no one could touch the legendary Scottish physician, David Watt Torrance (1862–1923) who bravely visited villages and Bedouin encampments infected by epidemics. He is still remembered with great affection by many in Galilee, including Jews, who were treated by him during these perilous years. The Tiberias municipality named a town square after him and its "official" history recounts his heroic life (Avisar 1973:122, 234-337).

British rule brought the first public health service to the region in 1918 with several epidemic stations, hospitals and mobile clinics carried on the back of camels. By 1920, the mandate's department of health provided newborn care plus services for children and adults who were not attended by the mission medical services in 22 hospitals and 23 outpatient clinics. The British established ten hospitals in Palestine, mainly for Muslim patients. A Muslim, Dr. Kamel Dajani from Jaffa, built the only private 50-bed hospital in Palestine. With improved medical services, life expectancy rose steadily until it was over 50 by the end of British rule.

Infant mortality rates also dropped sharply during this period. The Muslim population showed the worst indices between 1927 and 1932 with the first year 174 deaths per 1,000 live births, followed by 133 deaths for Christians and 71 for Jews per 1,000 births. By 1939 to 1946 these numbers had improved for Muslims: 123 deaths, Christians: 90 deaths and Jews: 50 deaths. After 50 years of Jewish rule, the infant mortality rate has dropped further and the life expectancy has ascended to new highs—but the order is preserved: Jews can expect to live 65 years, Christians almost 59 years and the Muslims some 50 years. Of course the majority of the current Jewish populations has emigrated from more advanced Western countries where early health care is normative, but other factors contribute: Muslims persist, more than Christians, in having large families and often live in rural areas where medical services are harder to come by.

When the Ottomans ruled the area, education was regarded as a frivolous luxury and educators were given little respect. Their first law relating to education, enacted in 1846, permitted a few religious schools to teach Arabic grammar, literature, dictation and geography—opening these schools to lay teachers. In 1869 another law adopted the French school system, dividing them into elementary and secondary schools, but imposing the Turkish language as the only instrument for teaching. Arabic was only tolerated as a subject. A French researcher found that by 1896 there were 242 government schools in the region plus a hundred "foreign" schools—including French, Italian, Armenians, Greek, Russian, British, German and American. The government was educating 10,135 pupils, mostly male Muslims, and concentrating on religious subjects, whereas the Christians taught 6,130 pupils with 40% of those being girls on a whole gamut of topics (Al A'ora 1935:156-167).

Observers of the Ottoman Empire concluded they awakened late and did little. Not until 1913 was education compulsory and then the ensuing war made this a moot objective. Consequently most Palestinian Arabs were illiterates when the country was occupied by British troops. Most of those who were literate had graduated from a Christian mission school so the Christian population was much more literate because Western missions emphasized education. The Ottomans cared little for education and threatened missionaries if they accepted Muslim pupils into their schools.

Educational reform came with the British rule of Palestine. The number of native pupils attending schools doubled five times between 1920 and 1947 whereas the Arab population doubled once from about 650,000 to 1,300,000. Besides reading, the British introduced new scientific subjects and modern ideas, plus foreign languages that made it possible for graduates to pursue advanced degrees in faraway lands. My ancestors were *Dhimmis,* exempted from military service but required to pay the head tax (*Jizya*). When the *Dhimmis* status was removed in the middle of the 19th century, a system was introduced so those who chose not to serve in the army could opt out by paying the *badal* for a substitute who served the Turkish soldiers by digging trenches or feeding their horses. But even those who paid the *badal* and stayed home were occasionally conscripted into local service – like cutting down the village's natural forests for the military's use.

At times, Ottoman officers would order villagers to commit heinous deeds like cutting down their sacred old olive trees and carrying the wood on their donkeys to nearby railway stations, so their economy's lifeblood was sacrificed to substitute for coal in the Turkish trains that supplied the anti-British war efforts to occupy Palestine. These olive trees had survived from Roman days, providing sustenance to our poor villages, so injury to them was considered as bad as killing a child – my father used to say.

I was named A'tallah (which means God's gift) because my parents lost their first son two years prior to my birth. I was treated with the utmost love parents could bestow on a child – but all that could suddenly evaporate if my father felt I failed to control our oxen that were tilling the land around our olive trees, and they caused damage to a branch. Then he would heap insults on my young head to impress on me the proper care of this great heritage.

The olive tree is also considered sacred, both to Muslims and Christians, because it was an olive branch the dove brought back to Noah's Ark to herald God's making peace with humankind and the termination of the flood. Traditionally it is also believed that when the Roman soldiers were on their way to arrest Jesus, a blessed olive tree opened its trunk and invited the Creator of the entire universe to hide inside. The Lord therefore, it is claimed, blessed the olive oil and the olive tree, which is the reason our olive trees have survived for centuries despite fire and pestilence.

The heroes from my childhood were the brave men who disobeyed the draft, refused to enlist as soldiers and fled to live in deep caves in the forests or else managed to emigrate and rid themselves from the Ottoman's yoke. Unfortunately, no one suspected at the time that the European powers were just waiting for the Ottomans to disintegrate so they could divide up the spoils.

In 1908 some Ottoman colonels seized power in a coup d'état claiming their goal was to reform the failing empire by restoring unity and establishing an efficient central government based on secular principles of equality for all. They also promised to end the *millet* system which granted non-Muslim minorities like the *Dhimmis* inner autonomy under their church leaders. This system proved to be both a blessing and a curse, for while it protected church leaders and the faithful from the coercive and corrupt state apparatus, it prevented any social mobility for individual members of those minorities in public life. The Greek-Catholics who split from the Greek-Orthodox *millet* in 1725 waited over a century to be officially recognized as a separate *millet* – a recognition which was essential in giving their clergy official status in the church. For the state, this *millet* system kept the minority groups in an inferior status.

Arab leaders, both Muslim and Christian, suddenly discovered a mutual purpose: a unanimity in resenting the Young Turks' reforms and an antagonism at their attempt to force their Arabic-speaking subjects to accept the Turkish culture and language as official. The Arabs, proud of their language that predated the dawn of Islam and the institution of Arabic as the language for all Islamic rituals, opposed this policy, fearing it was a precursor to the Turks declaring a secular state and turning Muslim Arabs into another second-class *millet*.

The news of a reformed constitution providing egalitarian

treatment for everyone did not trickle down to Galilee. None of my father's neighbors ever heard of a change in Ottoman policy, nor did the Europeans living in Jerusalem learn of the "new constitution" until August 1908. R.A.S. Macalister, a British scholar living in Jerusalem wrote, "The news arrived that *al Horrihya* (liberty) was proclaimed and immediately the town was full of shops selling rifles, guns and weapons. The chaos dominated all aspects of life, including law and order enforcement for years, until the break of the First World War" (1921). Another eyewitness in Jerusalem, Bertha Spafford-Vester, pointed out that although this proclamation made everyone a Palestinian (so that all Muslims, Christians and Jews became Turkish subjects), "only Muslims were drafted into the army, while a nominal sum exempted Jewish and Christian Turkish subjects from military service.... This was the first shock experienced in Palestine as to what 'equality' meant" (1950:222).

Few commented on the legal changes. One exception was the Palestinian intellectual, Khalil Skakini, active in the Greek Orthodox church and prominent in the struggle of the local Arab faithful against their domination by the Greek clergy. He and his colleagues believed the new constitution might allow for an elected body to oversee the church administration, but his experience proved that in the Ottoman state, money buys unlimited influence in the highest regions, and nothing changed except for the names of the rulers (Sakakini op cit 33-34).

The Armenians were the ones who felt drastic changes. The traditional oppression they had suffered became more brutal as the Turkish generals, defeated in WWI, decided to inflict genocide on them. The historian Richard G. Hovennisian described their tragic case to the World Affairs Council of Pittsburgh in 1982: "The Armenians, more than any other group, celebrated the fall of the Sultan, believing that the Young Turks would fulfill their pledge to confer equality to all. They were soon to be disappointed in the most extreme way. The Turks exiled, pillaged, raped and killed Armenians." American diplomat Adam Gibbon Herbert referred to the massacre as "the blackest page in modern history" and the historian Arnold Toynbee described it as the murder of a nation.

One must acknowledge that a massacre of this magnitude and brutality did not take place under the Muslim caliphs. Islam cannot be blamed for these Turkish crimes just as Christian Germans are innocent of the Nazi Holocaust. Interestingly, German officers at the time of the Armenian genocide were training the Ottoman armies in the use of modern arms.

The German commander of the Turkish and German troops (who fought against the British forces that would invade and capture Palestine) reported on the atrocities to his superiors in Germany, but these reports were not made public (Kressenstein 2002: 122-123). This soldier's war diaries reveal that at some point he believed the Turkish excuses for the massacres, but later he came to acknowledge that the "Young Turks" had a design to drive into the desert all non-Muslim elements in Jerusalem, including all Christian and Jewish residents. When asked by his government about this, he recommended to his political and military commanders that the German government should threaten to withdraw all their officers who fought on the Ottoman side lest they implement such a plan (op cit 222-4). One must note that the Muslim and Christian Arabs in Syria offered food and shelter to the Armenians who survived starving during their deportation. Armenian communities still live in many major centers of the Middle East – Aleppo (Syria), Beirut (Lebanon) and Jerusalem.

Turks still take no responsibility for the murder of over a million Armenians and until recently have resolutely refused to compensate the victims. This 20th century failure in the world community was a precursor to the Nazi crimes during WWII and other subsequent acts of genocide. Kerin Yappe, a League of Nations' representative in Aleppo, helped repatriate over 10,000 Christian Armenian and Assyrian girls kidnapped during the Turkish atrocities. To this day you can meet Armenians whose mothers were kidnapped and forced to marry Muslim Turks before being rescued. In her book Bertha Spafford-Vester tells the moving story of an Armenian woman, forced to marry a Bedouin as a child, who used to beg for help from any American and British visitor to the glorious ruins of Petra (op cit 223).

The Turks returned to rule Lebanon in 1914, imposing martial law, besieging the Lebanese mountains and cutting the population off from the outside world. When a plague of locusts hit this area, hunger was so devastating, it reputedly turned some Lebanese into cannibals. Mothers, crazed at watching their children starve, committed triage, killing and cooking some, hoping to stave off starvation for the others. The ferocious locusts left no grass in the fields or green branches on the trees. My father, in his early teens, ate boiled locusts and whatever grass could be found in the fields. These grim scenes dominated the Holy Land during the last days of the Ottoman Empire and set in motion the welcoming of the European and Christian rulers.

No wonder the British occupation was so welcome. James Parks, summing up the influence of the West in 19th century Palestine, comments on the many schools, hospitals, orphanages and similar institutions which, although open to all, usually benefited the small Christian minority because the Muslims were either afraid of or indifferent towards everything except for the medical services of Christian clinics and hospitals (1970). Muslim parents were reluctant to deliver their children to mission schools and any who were tolerant of such opportunities faced religious and governmental repression from their religious leaders.

Though the founders of these schools had hoped to welcome and win all children to their faith and culture, the Ottoman rulers imposed limits on Muslim enrollment and so a Jerusalem school opened in 1884 only on condition that Muslim boys would not be accepted (Tibawi 1961: 155-165). Still, many Muslim elite pushed to get their children into these schools even under Ottoman rule. When the Ottoman Empire collapsed, upper- and middle-class Muslims tried to give some European education—especially to their girls—in Christian boarding schools. American University of Beirut graduates were soon counted among the highest echelons of Arab society, both Christian and Muslim.

Just what effect this education had in this region has never been addressed seriously. Some Muslim intellectuals, like Hisham Sharabi at Georgetown University, or Mustapha Khalidi, Omar Farrouqi and Zain Ed Din Nur Zain are quite hostile, feeling that these institutes either were in the service of foreign forces or offered a cold shoulder to Islam. Still, they are quite proud and grateful for their own educational opportunities and their superior position in society. Despite hundreds of new Muslim and Arab academic institutions built in the past 50 years in all Arab communities and states, the American University in Beirut and its younger sister in Cairo still are considered the most prestigious academic institutes in the Arab Middle East. The University of Bir Zait in Palestine, founded by Anglicans with English as its official language, is also regarded highly. Muslims and Christians alike consider the American, Italian or French primary and secondary schools in Nazareth superior educational institutes and willingly pay tuition to have their children study there, even though education is free to all in Israel.

For these reasons most Palestinians — Muslims, Jews and Christians — welcomed the British mandate. Since the British forces were allied with the sheriff of Mecca, the Hashimite, this soothed Muslims who considered the Ottoman sultans as Islamic caliphs. The Hashimites, they claimed, were more appropriate to the post since they came from Mecca and said to be direct descendants of Hashim, the Prophet's uncle. Native Christians felt the British would respect the holy places. Balfour's Declaration and the pledge to Chaim Weizmann to assist Zionist-Jews establish "a national homeland" did not appear imminent nor realistic. After all, the entire Jewish population in Palestine in 1922 amounted to 83,000 persons, 10% of the total citizenry in the country. Besides, this Jewish community was constantly engaged in internecine quarrels. The extremely religious anti-Zionist opposed the Sephardim who totally rejected the socialist ideologies of the new Ashkenazi "pioneers". Also there were millions of Arabs in neighboring countries.

A decade later when the British mandate's high commissioner ordered a comprehensive census (1931), the results were indicative of Palestine's drift. The Jewish minority had doubled its ranks to 175,000, now 17% of the population, while the Christians had increased by only 26% and the Muslims by almost 30%. This shaky demographic balance caused extra tensions. Thus began the first battle in the long, bloody struggle over Palestine. Still the British and the Palestinians were living their illusions. The British helped Muslims organize as religious autonomous *millet*, just as the Muslim states had treated non-Muslims. The Muslim high congress was appointed with Haj Amin Al Husseini, the mufti of Jerusalem, chosen by the British high commissioner in Palestine to preside over the Muslims, who were the great majority of the Palestinians.

Prior to the English occupation, such a post had not existed in Palestine since Islam was not just another religion in the country, but the official ruling group. Traditionally, it had dominated the state and had been authorized to enact the laws for the entire population. Most Christians, being naïve and innocent, regarded the British mandate authority as the government of "their own." But from the start, the more sophisticated regarded them a clear and present danger. The *Al Carmel* newspaper in Haifa and the *Falastin* in Jaffa published by Palestinian Christians were fiercely and consistently anti-Zionist even before the British occupation. Their editors kept calling on Palestinians to wake up to the danger.

This attitude was shared by most Arabs, and their ferocious opposition to Zionist plans generated sharp responses from the Jewish press. The Hebrew daily *Ha Herut* wrote, "Najeeb Nassar [the editor of the Haifa newspaper] is so wild that he is not entitled to be called an editor. Whatever is published in his newspaper represents no one except the Christian youth who hate Jews out of religious and racist motives" (Nov. 4, 1910). Rabbi Haim Nahum sued this same editor for insulting the Jewish faith but an Ottoman judge found him innocent of the charges (Assaf op cit 46).

The Christian Arabs had always been outspoken against Zionist plans because they knew Jewish immigration to Palestine would damage Muslim and Christian interests—who had enough problems dealing with each other. Of course, no one could predict the coming Nazi persecution of Jews, and no one knows what would have happened after World War I if this Holocaust had not made the Zionists' call a viable solution.

One can say that the pressures of economic depression between the two world wars and the genocide in Nazi-occupied Europe produced, some 30 years after the British occupation of Palestine, a Jewish state in most of Palestine – and a real catastrophe for most Palestinian Arabs. A few voices had given early warning of the "Zionist danger." The Muslim mayor of Jerusalem Yousef al Khalidi (1844-1906) exchanged correspondence with Theodore Hertzel, who subsequently tried to calm Palestinian fears about Zionist's intentions. This Jerusalem mayor ingenuously tried to convince the Zionists' prophet that his plans to dominate Palestine were in vain "despite the sympathy of the Ottomans and Muslims, because of the Orthodox and Catholic (Christians) hatred towards Zionism" (A'adel Mannaa' 1986:22).

The pro-Zionist British liberal, James Parkes, attempting to understand why the Christian Arabs sided with Muslims, concluded the "Arabic speaking Christians were obliged in many cases to purchase their security during the violent troubles of the 1930s, by being passionately more pro-Arab than the Muslims" (op cit 267).

What most failed to recognize was that the Christian Arabs, al though not treated by the Muslims as equals, had never been offered any reasonable alternative. They had no choice but to stand for their country and for the Muslims with whom they shared a common language, heritage and hope. Even after many of the educated Christian Arabs emigrated to the West, they were faithful to their identity as Arabs and sincerely patriotic to their homeland.

The Zionists accused the British of favoring Christian Arabs and the general consensus expressed in the Jewish political literature during the British mandate in Palestine was that British officials, especially in the foreign office, were pro-Arab and not fulfilling the pledge of the Balfour Declaration to help the Jewish settlers dominate the country and turn it into a "Jewish homeland." One claimed the British were sympathetic to the Arabs because they were more docile and obedient servants and were especially biased towards Arab Christians because they were co-religionists. Such claims ignore the Palestinian deportation to refugee camps in 1948 at a time when British forces were deployed in strength in Palestine – belying any possible "pro-Arab" English bias.

For myriad reasons, the British promised the Zionists a "national homeland" carved out of Palestine. To placate the Muslim community, they appointed a grand mufti, giving him total authority for running the Muslim-dominated society plus vast areas of cultivable rural lands, shops and buildings in urban areas, plus administration of religious services, courts, rituals, schools and thousands of employees in all religious functions. The pledge to the Zionists, added to the uniting of Muslims under the leadership of one authority, made certain there would be clashes between the various groups within the population of Palestine.

The British opted to maintain the status quo from the Ottoman days for the Christians, acknowledging the same eight churches the sultan had recognized, giving the clergy administrative and legal autonomy for performing marriages, burials, deciding divorce cases and settling inheritance issues in their special courts. They also guaranteed the traditional order inside holy shrines – like the Nativity Church in Bethlehem and the Holy Sepulcher in Jerusalem, carefully dividing the rights and timetables for prayers in these shrines between the Greek Orthodox, Roman Catholics, Armenians and Copts.

Fortunately for Nazareth, the several different Christian churches do not claim the same sites. The Roman Catholic Franciscans own the historical site of the Virgin Mary's home where she received the Annunciation from the archangel Gabriel; the Greek Catholics possess the site traditionally recognized as the location of the Jewish synagogue where Jesus began his public ministry by reading the passage from Isaiah that prophesied of his being anointed to preach good news to the poor, the captives, the blind and the oppressed (Lk 4:18-19). The Greek-Orthodox, the largest Christian community in town, have the church on Mary's Well – the water source from which the holy family supplied its water needs and where the angel reputedly encountered the virgin at this well.

A'aref Al A'aref, the Palestinian historian, says the British control of Palestine after World War I encouraged Muslim-Christian coöperation in public life, and the Zionist threat only added urgency to this national solidarity (op cit, 488) which even withstood the catastrophe of 1948 – as Rosemary Sayegh pointed out in her research on Palestinian refugees in Lebanon (1980:16).

The Narrow Gate Churches

By enforcing law and order, the British brought to Palestine a fresh atmosphere of national feeling among the Arabs, calming the emigration waves so that many Christian Arabs in exile were willing to come home. However, when they asked the mandatory authorities to recognize their rights as Palestinian citizens, they found the British mostly uncoöperative unless they could produce documents proving they were "Ottoman subjects." Thus my uncle, who fled the Ottoman military services, was refused nationality in the country in which he had been born.

On the other side, emigration from rural to urban areas was accelerated during the British mandate, for they were in urgent need of a working force for various projects—deepening Haifa's harbor, establishing a local police force, staffing railway services, military bases and a public works department to erect new roads or maintain existing highways. Many villagers left their farms to live in towns, lured by the money or the lights, only to discover that urban living was not all it was touted to be. Yet, individual freedom, running water, medical services, electricity, plus a modern educational system encouraged many Christian Arabs to leave their traditional strongholds in the mountains and live in towns—the illiterate to be part of the labor force, the more educated to become urban proletarians and clerks in government offices.

Some small Christian communities in Palestinian villages were soon deserted: Sajara Christians moved to live in the nearby town of Tiberias; the Um al Fahem community relocated to Nazareth, while the Cabul, Sha'ab and Damon communities went to Haifa. Other villages lost their young people to the urban centers. My village of Al Jish became a virtual ghost town during the 1940s with almost all the young plus many of the employable men moving to Haifa for school or work. Only during the holidays would our village become lively and joyful again.

Muslims were less affected by this trend because their conservative attitude toward women precluded the men leaving women unsupervised in the villages. Also many Muslim villagers were illiterate, a condition that made it difficult to find work outside of agriculture or hard labor, so little attracted them to the city slums. Many Christians worked in town but kept their family in villages since they were unable to rent proper apartments for their families in a town.

When General Allenby had occupied Palestine in 1917 the entire Christian community numbered 70,000. On entering the Jaffa Gate to the walled city of Jerusalem he declared: "Today the Crusades have ended." After ruling for 30 years, the British departed from Haifa's Bay leaving behind approximately double this number—150,000 Christians—a "made in England" blessing. British rule also had introduced and consolidated in modern Palestine the concept of equality for all citizens without an inherent bias based on religious affiliation. The British made a central government responsible for imposing law and order along with educational and basic welfare services such as mother- and baby-care clinics.

During this period Christian emigration almost came to a halt (abetted by new U.S. regulations that restricted immigration during the 1929 economic crises). The Christian community's growth in Jerusalem included members of the British forces and their dependents plus survivors of the Armenian massacres seeking refuge in Jerusalem's Christian institutions, especially for those who had not found havens in neighboring Syria or Christian Lebanon. In the second half of the 1940s, the number of Christians residing in Jerusalem reached 27,000. The Zionist wave of immigration tripled eight times between 1922 and 1948 while the Muslims and Christians only doubled their community's size during the 30 years of British rule.

The Palestine official census of 1931 had showed a list of 47 villages carrying the name *Dair* (Arabic for monastery), yet today Christians do not reside there, except in a few cases where they make up a small minority, but the name is indicative of a past Christian presence. One village contained a mixed Muslim and Christian population—Dair Hanna in central Galilee—another contained a Catholic monastery and boarding school—Dair Rafat, near Jerusalem. A list of locales published in the 1980s still includes 50 sites with "Dair" included in them. Those not inhabited by Muslim Arabs are now ruins or taken over by Israeli-Jews (who changed their names). Five connoted Christian monasteries near Jerusalem,

Bethlehem and Nazareth, but only one lone village still has Christians and Muslims still living side-by-side as they did in 1931.

The list of ex-monasteries in the Jerusalem area include Dair Amman, Dair Salaam, Dair Ash Saikh, Dair Amro, Dair al-Hawa and Dair Yassen. In the Gaza region there were Dair al Balah and Dair Snaid. In the environs of Ramleh you find Dair Qaddis, Dair Ayyoub, Dair Abu Salama, Dair Tarief and Dair Muhsin. Jenin contained Dair Abu Da'eef and Dair Gazaleh and Safad had Dair al Ghsoun, Dair Al Qassi and Dair Hanna. In Nablus there were Dair Abu al Sus, Dair Estya, Dair al Aqraa', Dair Ballout and Dair Sharaf. Near Ramallah were Dair al Qarea', Dair Yarba', Dair Masha'l, Dair Debwan, Dair al Sudan, Dair A'mmar, Dair Ghassaneh and Dair Nezam. In Hebron were Dair Razeh, Dair Samet, Dair al A'sal Tahta, Dair Al a'sal Fuqa, Dair al Dubban and Dair Nahhas.

This same list mentions three sites by the name *Khirbet ad Dair* (the ruins of the monastery) in the neighborhood of Hebron, Bethlehem and Jerusalem. As could be expected, many local names are indicative of the mutual religious heritage of Jews, Christians and Muslims. Saint Elias (Elijah), the biblical prophet-warrior, is esteemed and venerated in Christian churches and at special sites *(maqam*, in Arabic) where he is honored by Muslims as well as Jews. Palestinian Christians are also biased in favor of Saint George *(Jiryes,* in Arabic, *Girges* in Egypt), the holy knight and martyr born and buried in Palestine. Both George and Elias are popular names for Christian babies today in Palestine.

These historical names are indicative of a Christian presence in these Palestinian villages down through the centuries. In some, Christians numbered in the hundreds, as in Sakhnin, in others there were fewer. In all there were over 80 Christian communities in Palestine plus some 20 isolated monasteries — again of varying sizes. Small ones, such as mar Elias on the Jerusalem — Bethlehem road or Al Khader south of Bethlehem, had only a handful of monks while others, such as Beit Jamal and Dair Rafat, had over a hundred monks and postulants in residence. Yet throughout Palestine, Christians lived alongside Muslim, Jewish or Druze neighbors — accepting them as genuine natives of the homeland of their Savior.

Of course, Christian communities tended to congregate around regions considered to be holy sites where the Lord and his family lived. Native Christians had lived in these particular sites before, during and after the Crusades and had survived in these sites even after the 1948 war. They constituted a majority in the towns around Jerusalem, Bethlehem and Beit Jala in the south and Ramallah in the north. Nazareth in Galilee was also surrounded by Christian communities — Raineh, Kafr Cana and Tura'an (east of town) and Yaffa, Mjaidel and Maa'lool on the west. In fact, a Christian presence was found in every town in Palestine, albeit of differing sizes. There were more Christians in the growing, prosperous communities and fewer in the ancient, socially conservative and economically traditional communities of Nablus, Hebron and Gaza.

It was on the west bank of the Jordan River in what is now called Palestine/Israel that Jesus lived most of his earthly life. Occasionally he had crossed that river eastward to Bethany (now called Beth barah) where he was baptized by John the Baptist (Jn 1:28) and to the Gadarenes (now called Um-keis) on the east bank of the Jordan River (Mk 5:1). This country, known today as the Hashimite Kingdom of Jordan, had always been home to some native Christians — probably direct descendants of the Hebrew Christians, or the Church of Circumcision. Tradition tells us that the latter group fled from Jerusalem during the Roman siege in 70 A.D. and settled in a town called Pella in the eastern Jordan valley (currently called Ta baqat Fahel). Others may have descended from those who heard the good news from St. Paul immediately after his eyes were opened in Damascus. The Apostle to the Nations tells us he spent three years with the Arabs. (It is probable that Jordan is part of the region once called Arabia, since the term meant "Nomads" and most Jordanians lived as nomads until the mid-20th century.)

Other Jordanian Christians are believed to be descended from the Crusaders. The first British Commander of Jordan's Arab Legion (1925–1929) worked assiduously to collect information about Jordan's tribes and *Hamula* (extended families). His research led him to Muslim families with Greek-Christian names (such as Ettaexia) and he met a Muslim family called Motran (Arabic for bishop) which was "famous for having blue eyes." Lt. Col. Fredrick J. Peak also found four families who knew that their grandfathers were Christian but had converted to Islam at some stage (1998).

Peak compiled data showing that some 45 extended Christian families still survive in 30 towns and villages in the region of Transjordan—as it was known until the Hashimite kingdom was established after World War I. The Hashimites managed to unify the country with generous help from their British allies (and Lawrence of Arabia). Before this, what is now known as Jordan seldom knew an orderly rule of law, and was subject to the whims of Bedouin nomad sheikhs.

The current Christian community in Jordan comprises some 5% of the population of five million, most of whom live in the capital and are, relatively speaking, prosperous. The government tends to favor these industrious, peacekeeping citizens, some of whom have served as cabinet ministers and in top governmental posts or have played significant roles in the country's economics, culture and health services. Christians have held public office in the region ever since the 1908 constitution set up the first *Majlis A'omomi* (Syrian house of commons) in the Ottoman Empire and elected two Christians out four representatives—Yousef Al Sukkar for Salt and Owdeh Qsos as Kerak's representative (Muhafaza 2001:46).

Most Christians in Jordan are Orthodox—some 100,000 adherents—but church leaders have been in a constant struggle with the Greek clerics who resist the Jerusalem patriarchate's control over the parishioners. This conflict is probably the cause of their rather poor educational institutes and the few number of active priests. The official church yearbook claims 26 parishes (six in Amman) but little support comes from the Orthodox patriarchate for the 13 schools they run in Jordan and little heed is paid to data about these schools, or even the number of staff and students in them.

The vacuum created by the contentious Orthodox has been filled by the Roman Catholics or "Latins" who seem to flourish, operating ten parishes in Amman and 32 in outlying cities and villages of Jordan. Roman Catholic parishioners in Jordan, Palestine and Israel total 72,000, with over half of these in Jordan. The Latins keep a presence in the area running a wide variety of schools.

The third largest Christian church in Jordan is the Greek Catholic Melkites who established most of their parishes in the first half of the 20th century when Jordan was part of the Galilee bishopric. Currently they have 29 parishes (six in Amman and 23 outside the capital) and more than 30,000 members. Beyond these there are other smaller churches, including old native churches such as the Maronites, Armenians, Syrians, Chaldeans and Episcopals, and then the more vibrant and evangelical churches such as the Baptists, etc.

Although these all play a growing role in society, they are still very much marginalized and kept from putting down deep roots in the local community. A serious problem they face is the anxiousness of their members to emigrate at the first opportunity. Since many of these church people learn English and often pray or sing in that language because of the missionary presence, their focus seems to be outside their own communities.

Jordanian Christians are generally genuine natives who tend to live in outlying towns. Here, too, they are more educated thanks to church-supported educational institutes that have served them for over a century – before any state education even existed. This education has promoted an industrious community, along similar lines to their co-religionists across the Jordan valley in Palestine/Israel.

Traditionally Jordanian Christians have encountered fewer European pilgrims since, aside from those headed to Petra, seldom do such groups come their way. This has exposed them less to European and American influences – which seems to encourage emigration. This changed during the 1948 war which drove many Christians from Jaffa, Ramleh, Jerusalem and other Christian communities in central Palestine, to look for refuge in Jordan, especially Amman. When these refugees realized they were not soon returning home, they began looking abroad for opportunities and led a new wave of emigrants to Australia, Canada and the USA. This, of course, impoverished the Christian communities left behind.

12

New and Old Churches

*"Avoid stupid controversies, genealogies, dissensions
and quarrels over the law, for they are unprofitable
and futile"* (Titus 3:9).

The Holy Land native Christians' most grievous problem is
the lack of unity in their ranks and the rivalry between their churches. Many causes are cited for this division, but I find no significant spiritual gain or justification for the prolonged absence of
friendly relations and practical coöperation between them. History
is the first reason for the division, but the animosity stems mainly
from "issues" such as what calendar to follow in determining the
dates for celebrating Christmas or Easter.

More tragic is the competition among the hierarchy of the
various churches to ascertain who is entitled to be mentioned first
when politicians such as the mayor of Jerusalem come to visit or
who is to conduct Christmas mass at the Church of the Nativity
in Bethlehem. So these churches compete among themselves as if
they were in a popularity contest, urging congregants to leave old
churches for new, demonstrating few signs of being Christ's body
for those observing during the celebrations of the Annunciation,
Christmas and the Glorious Resurrection (known to the West as

Easter). Catholics and Protestants celebrate on the same dates, but the Copts, Armenians and Greek Orthodox follow their own calendar.

Recently a grass-roots movement in a few Galilean villages demanded all Christians there celebrate Christmas on the 25th of December and the Glorious Resurrection according to the Orthodox calendar. This plea fell on deaf ears, so most Christians in Christ's hometown celebrate his birthday, death and resurrection on a variety of dates because the churches are incapable of agreeing on such marginal issues, despite complaints from their parishioners.

Fortunately, one feels slight breezes of ecumenism that have started blowing in the last decades. More "mixed" marriages between members of Catholic and Orthodox Christians are registered. Some "political" acts demonstrating Christian coöperation and common interest are taking place, along with new types of Christian activities which encourage young Christians to believe their future in the homeland of their Savior will be secure. The Greek-Orthodox church, the major one in Palestine for the past 2,000 years, is currently at a turning point and one hopes it is moving in the right direction.

Any attempt to trace Christianity's history in the Holy Land begins with the acknowledgement that until the 20th century the Greek Orthodox church of Palestine was the mother church of the area's Christians. Established by the first apostles and church founders for the faithful natives, this church's language has been Greek from the beginning since this was the cultural language of the land (and the language of three of the four canonical Gospels). This church represented the official mainstream Christianity as it was interpreted by Constantinople, and it was with this church that most opted to stay during the major schism that occurred at the beginning of the second millennium. When Constantinople fell to the Ottomans in 1453, the Palestine church found itself cut off for many centuries from the rest of Christendom and from official relations with others in the Christian world.

At the turn of the 19th century, 90% of the Holy Land's Christians were Greek Orthodox, but by the beginning of the

20th century they made up only 65% of the Christian community (Colbi 1964:68). Now, entering the third millennium, the Orthodox share of the Christian community has dropped again to some 44% (Thordson 1996:95). Estimates put the Greek-Orthodox faithful in Palestine/Israel at 57,700 – while all Catholics (Greek, Latin and other unionists – Maronites, Syrians, Armenians, Copts and Chaldean Catholics) total some 65,000. The Protestants, Anglicans, Baptists, Lutherans and others (including Hebrew Christians) add another 7,000. These figures show there is a consistent tendency among the Orthodox to withdraw or emigrate, as has been noted.

Living in a war zone is not pleasant given the public exchange of abuse and accusations by the Arab natives and the Greek clergy for over a century. The struggle between the Greek clergy and the natives in the church can probably be traced back as early as 1534 when Greek monks in Jerusalem established the Fraternity of the Holy Sepulcher, a "closed" society which helped a Greek named Jermanos ascend to the See of Jerusalem (1534-1579). During his 45-year tenure, Jermanos and his "brothers" made sure any vacant post in the church would be filled only by Greeks (Hawaweeni 1893:7). Thus native Orthodox adherents have for years heaped accusations on the Greek clerics for many misdeeds – including hypocrisy on the part of the monks who claimed to be celibate but still managed to produce offspring who were sent to church schools to prepare them to follow in the footsteps of their fathers.

There have been many allegations made during the last century by both Orthodox clerics and parishioners, whose main focus seems to be controlling their various schools and administering their assets and estates. The principles of Christ are forgotten as various sides demonstrated a willingness to use any legal or semilegal means to achieve their goals. Lamentably, hurling base insults and accusations against one another has become standard – and historians say these are not new phenomena. Apparently the first act of Patriarch Basilious (1645-1660) after being crowned head of the church of Jerusalem was to inform the Ottoman authorities that his rival, Patriarch Barthlemous, was a Russian spy. That charge caused this cleric to suffer the most savage Ottoman penalty – dying impaled on a long peg.

It is unclear whether this account is valid. A more reliable anti-Greek accusation that has circulated for decades purports that Greeks bribed the Ottomans and British governors, plus the Jordanian and Israeli officials, to delay the enactment of regulations that would give the laity some influence and control in the running of their church. Although the Ottomans promised this reform and the British enacted a law during 1934, it was not implemented because of the "inappropriate" hostilities that had occurred before and during World War II. The Jordanians passed a similar law in January 1957 but revoked it with the first change in the cabinet five months later.

The Israelis never promised the local Christian population any concessions and were keen to secure good relations with Greece, as well as keep local Orthodox weak, so they were uninterested in helping these Arab pioneers – who produced the first anti-Zionists in the region – in their quest for self-government. Thus the Greeks managed to keep their iron grip and ownership over anything of material value in the church – and unfortunately many national treasures from the Arab-Christian's history have fallen into the hands of those who wished to trade in historical artifacts. Thus the late King Hussein was able to bequeath an historic Yemenite-made, gold-ornamented sword which had belonged to the Greek Orthodox Patriarch Benedictus II to Moshe Dayan, Israel's minister of defense. He also had presented the late King Hussein, as a young monarch, with his first Cadillac.

Such generosity proved useful. When the leftist, pro-Nasser government of Suliman Nabulsi enacted a Jordanian law demanding that Greek clerics share their revenues and church administration with the local laity, as well as promoting Arab clergy to the posts of bishop both in Amman and Jerusalem, this government soon lost favor in the eyes of King Hussein. A few months later the new government of Samir Rifaa'i erased the law (Kaldani 1993:130-131).

It was thus the Greeks kept control and left the native groups grumbling. A "Popular Congress to Support The Arab Orthodox Case" held in Nazareth in 1998 decided the congress should take "severe steps" in case the patriarchate refused to share with the local parishioners the administration of the church's policy and not promote Arab clerics to full membership in the Holy Sepulcher Fraternity and other policy-making posts. Such steps would include boycotting the patriarch and his representatives. Three years later nothing had changed but the only step taken by church members was to appeal to an Israeli court asking that the law enacted by the British Mandate – 60 years before – be enforced.

When the Orthodox patriarch passed away in February 2001 the Greeks did not loosen their grip and there was much machination when the Orthodox faithful tried to get involved in the election of his successor. It finally came to light that the Israelis refused to recognize the newly elected patriarch Eironimous I because of an attempt to have a Greek-supported patriarch put in place. The latter had agreed to sell church real estate on the West (Israeli) side of Jerusalem to the Palestinian Authority. These claims and counterclaims came to an end when the Israeli police found that some Israeli "merchants" had fabricated the documents. The new patriarch had to wait two years before finally being recognized by the Israeli government in January 2004 (under Greek and American pressure). The anti-Greek camp appealed to the court with new accusations. All the while the native Orthodox faithful find themselves frustrated in their attempts to have their representatives serve as church leaders.

So the Arab Orthodox population continues to drift away. The Greeks seem uninterested in promoting or educating the local clergy and many of the native clerics are an aging population. There is little to attract younger men to the priesthood. Historically the Arab Orthodox priests have suffered virtually as paupers. In 1810 the Swiss traveler John Lewis Burkhardt visited the Holy Land and passing through Ezra' in the Houran (south-west of Syria today), he hired an Arab Orthodox priest as guide. In his account he noted the poor priest carried around on the back of his donkey everything needed to conduct mass in the villages they passed through for he was the only priest in half a dozen villages (Burkhardt op cit 63-65).

Today all 14 metropolises, five archbishops, three bishops, 48 archimandrites, 22 monks, seven secluded priests and five deacons in the Order of the Holy Sepulcher Fraternity are Greeks (Kaldani op cit 131). The one native Arab bishop is Sylvester Al Far; he occupies the post of deputy to a Greek bishop in Amman. The highest Arab in the patriarch's court in Jerusalem is Archimandrite Dr. A'tallah Hanna who acts as the patriarchate's spokesperson to any Arab audience.

The Greeks seem unperturbed by any accusations, unless they have to go to court to answer charges of corruption and selling church property. They attack the motives of any who question their leadership. In an interview with *Ha Arertz*, Israel's elite newspaper, the patriarch accused elected leaders of his parish of wanting to dominate church lands so they could sell them in order to finance the "cost of purchasing the alcohol they consume" (*Ha Aretz* 25/9/1992).

After World War II, Russian Orthodox Christians returned to the Middle East offering military, economic and cultural aid. Hundreds of doctors and engineers who live in the Holy Land today received their education in Russia (or one of the Soviet Union's satellite states). The Greek clerics were wary of the Russian Orthodox presence because they were concerned that local Christians would turn against the Greeks (Papadopoulos op cit 846-847).

The first Russian missionaries had arrived in Palestine in 1843 and Russian clergy were quite active in Syria and Palestine until 1914. Today, almost a century after the Russians left Palestine, the Orthodox faithful still feel loyalty to them remembering their attempts to help the local church and their support of the Syrian Orthodox Arabs who were trying to rid themselves of the Greek domination and the assaults of Catholic and Protestant missionaries who were hoping to convert the Orthodox communities to their own flocks.

Traditionally, the Greek clergy have kept themselves aloof from their faithful. Even though their members have consistently been leading activists in the ecumenical movement, the clerics insist they are the only rightful Christians. In the summer of 2000 the patriarchate even published a pamphlet for distribution in the church stating that Orthodox and other Christians cannot come together and unite on any administrative basis for "such a unity would in fact be dropping the core for the sake of the crust" (*Usra Wahida*: Summer 2000). The Orthodox hierarchy thus remains adamant there be no leniency on ostracizing other Christians, no sharing with them in a mass or mutual celebrations of Christmas and Easter unless the leaders of other Catholic or Protestant churches accept the Orthodox dogma since this church, "with the utmost modesty," believes it is the sole church "which is *the* one, holy, catholic, apostolic church that the (Nicene) creed refers to."

Though the Greek patriarchate neglects Arab faithful, leaving their small and ancient church buildings in disrepair and ignoring their needs for religious education in most villages, they do bestir themselves to make such pretentious pronouncements. Even Nazareth, the town with the largest Christian (and Orthodox) congregation in the Holy Land, has no school of any significance since the closure of the Russian seminary in 1914. Interestingly, during the time the Russian Orthodox were active in the Arab Orthodox community, the Greeks opened a few schools in Galilee plus a seminary at the Cross Convent in West Jerusalem.

World War I brought great disaster both to the Russian and the Greek clergy in the Jerusalem Patriarchate. Between 1911 and 1951 official church records make no mention of any construction or upkeep in the Jerusalem patriarchate except for repairing the damage from the 1927 earthquake in the Holy Sepulcher's roof which was carried out by the "Greek government" between the years 1931-1933. Finally in Jerusalem the patriarch established "an exemplary" school for the benefit of the children of the church, which he "personally paid the costs in 1983" (Taqweem Sanawi op cit 56). Three years later he did the same in Amman, Jordan.

It is unclear how this holy man who had been in church institutes since 1938 when he was 15 years old, managed with this humble life to spend millions of dollars building schools, churches and palaces, claiming all the financing came from his personal purse as an act of charity to his parishioners (Taqweem ibid 73). It would appear that such gestures meant to win the approbation of the faithful were funded because of the interesting code and regulations of the Holy Sepulcher Fraternity. The real source of this vast wealth is explained by the Greek author Necephore Moshopoulos in his book *La Terre Sainte, La Question de Palestine et le Patriacat de Jerusalem, ses Driots ses Privileges,* Athens 1957, pp. 64-68) (Kaldani op cit 22-23). Apparently the Holy Sepulcher Fraternity members consider themselves sole owners of Orthodox church properties and thus the only beneficiaries from them, the income of the faithful's offerings, alms, vows and endowments to the Holy Land churches from pilgrims, et al.

Beyond this, to assure income during times of conflict and privation and to avoid making the pilgrim travel to Palestine in times of great risk, the Jerusalem patriarchate made sure the faithful could offer their vows to the Nativity and Holy Sepulcher Churches and make contributions to the various patriarchate delegations in Constantinople, Athens, Nicosia, Moscow, and California (Taqweem op cit 79-80). At earlier stages these delegations included offices in Russian cities and in Romania. The patriarch, according to this code, is the absolute chair of the church and the fraternity, and the fraternity is the sole heir of its members. "The fraternity may offer, within its ability and resources, and out of its own free will, the needed financial support to assist in preparing existing churches or in building new ones."

One of the main problems that divides the Orthodox church's clergy and faithful stems from an Arab term and its translation to Western languages. *"Roum"* is a term Arabs (including the Koran) use to name the Greek-Byzantines who ruled Palestine during the early days of Islam. Today the term denotes the Orthodox church. The Greeks won the linguistic battle, so in all known languages the Orthodox church in the Holy Land is called the Greek-Orthodox church. Even in Arabic, most publications call that church Roum-Orthodox despite the fact that over 99% of their church members in the Holy Land call themselves Arabs, speak Arabic as a mother tongue and fail to understand their church leaders rituals in the Greek language. The Greek clergy insist the church is Greek and the church's assets belong to Greek nationals – thus they refuse to appoint Arabs to membership in the Holy Sepulcher Fraternity since this might force them to share with Arab natives the church's material assets. Many faithful Orthodox Christians voted against the Greek clergy's hegemony with their feet by joining other churches.

A constructive step by the Orthodox Arab community against this Greek dominance occurred in November 2000 when an Arab bishop was ordained for the Amman diocese and a new Arab Jerusalemite church was born. This move was supported by the Antioch's patriarch with the warm blessing of the American branch of the church. The Greek patriarch of Jerusalem opposed Bishop Demitri Khouri, a native of Taybeh (near Ramallah in Palestine), so the Jordanian government stepped in and ordered the closure of the church on the grounds that the church owner violated the law. Jordanian law recognizes only the Greek-Orthodox, and considers the Jerusalem-Orthodox church a new native Orthodox church which is not licensed.

The dwindling of the Orthodox church in Palestine during the last century can be blamed on the Greek clergy. Compare this decline with the resurgence of the Greek (and Roman) Catholic churches who maintain the old traditions and rituals of the historic Orthodox church but submit to the authority of the Holy See in the Vatican, accepting the pope's authority while ordaining Arabs to all ranks and posts and using Arabic in religious rituals.

This church officially began in Palestine in 1701 when the Vatican delegated Sidon's Orthodox bishop Anathimos Saffi to serve Orthodox parishioners willing "to reunite with Rome." This appointment came after three decades of negotiations with members of the Orthodox church in Syria who showed interest in joining the Catholic church. Anathimos Saffi was the first to approach Rome and five years later a group of Orthodox monks left their convent in Belmond, asking for papal support and becoming the first order of monks in the new church. Bishop Sylvester Dahhan from Beirut wrote in 1701 to Rome telling the Vatican of his longing for a united church and declaring his acceptance of the Catholic faith. Not until 1724 was the Greek Catholic church recognized by the Holy See as an independent entity.

The beginnings of this church are actually rooted in historic rivalry in the ranks of the Middle Eastern Orthodox clergy. Two contending candidates for the Antioch patriarchate claimed to have been legitimately elected patriarch. One, Seraphim Tanas, supported the idea of reuniting the church under papal authority, so Rome recognized him as the first patriarch of Antioch for the Greek Catholic church. This declaration was far from making the secession a *fait accompli*. The Levant was part of the Ottoman Empire and its *millet* system placed all Christians in the empire under the jurisdiction of the Greek Orthodox patriarch. The Greek Catholics had to wait almost a century for the Sultan *Firman* (edict), which recognized them as separate *millet* (1834).

Some 260 years after that first move to secession in Israel, Greek Catholics are more numerous and have far more educational institutes than the Greek Orthodox. Those giving allegiance to Rome are supported by a strong Franciscan presence, as well as other European Catholic educational institutions which welcome all Greek Orthodox living in Israel into their fold. Over half of the Greek Orthodox in Israel have left their church, joining other groups. Dr. Johnny Mansour, biographer of Archbishop Gregarious Hajjar, noted that this industrious Greek-Catholic prelate added nine new parishes to the 22 which already existed in his diocese before his arrival in Galilee (1901–1940) plus nine more parishes in Trans-Jordan. Mansour attributes much of later Roman-Catholic success to their establishment of hospitals and schools (1985:43-44).

Only in Syria has the Orthodox church held its ground against Catholicism. There the Roman Catholics had traditionally been a small minority and today, even combined with their Greek Catholic allies, they have only a quarter of the Orthodox church's membership in the country. The difference between the Orthodox in Syria and those in Palestine is the language of the high clergy, for the language of the church rituals in Syria is Arabic, while the official language in Jerusalem is Greek. An Arab choir cannot glorify the Resurrection of the Lord in their mother tongue. Here again, church history and its struggles for cultural survival are deeply affected by national cultural sentiments. The failure of the clergy to use the mother tongue of their flock is seen as demeaning to the congregants. The priests are not culturally sensitive to the congregation.

After the end of the Crusades, the Franciscans were the first European Christians to win official recognition from both the Muslim rulers and the Vatican as the Guardians of the Holy Land (*Custus del Terra Sancta*). Their presence around the holy places was soon validated by building churches, schools and shrines. They also helped revive the Christian communities in Palestine by providing community and a safe haven for native Christians from the mountainous strongholds – Galilee, Lebanon, Syria, Jordan as well as refugees from Iraq and Turkey.

The Franciscans settled in Jerusalem and Bethlehem where they have maintained a presence continuously since the 13th century. They were insecure about traveling in a country where the government's sole concern appeared to be collecting taxes and not protecting wayfarers. Therefore, the Franciscans infrequently visited Nazareth, the town of Annunciation and the home town of the Holy Family. Finally, in the 16th century they settled in a rented house in Nazareth, but their main presence remained in Jerusalem where they built schools, clinics and churches.

In 1620 when the Franciscan monks tried to build a church in Nazareth, hostile neighbors would come at night and destroy whatever construction had been done that day. Finally these monks turned for succor to the Maronite patriarch in Bkerky (north of Beirut) who prevailed on a dozen poor and pious Maronite families in that district to accompany the monks on their return and live in Nazareth where the monks had promised them permanent jobs. The Franciscans thus managed to build the first Annunciation church since the Crusaders' defeat and the destruction of Nazareth. When the church building was finally inaugurated ten years later, a local parish had been established made up of European monks, ex-Maronites who had come to town to defend the project, plus a few others who answered the bell's toll.

This pattern of coöperation between the native Christians and mission operations has been repeated in most other Western attempts to settle in the Holy Land. Catholic educational institutions in Israel, Palestine and Jordan have prepared some 55,000 students of all classes and educational levels to face life's challenges. Preschool nurseries through university and Biblical research institutes have taught students – not always Catholics. Many were Muslims or children of other Christian churches who believed these institutions offered the best education. Some 2,000 Catholic men and women have dedicated their lives to service in the Holy Land running 300 institutions of learning, medical services, or various works of charity for the needy, disabled, aged and orphans. The Franciscans have been joined by other orders such as the *Freres des Ecoles Chretiennes* and the Carmelites (who originally came during the Crusades in 1157 and then returned to the Holy Land in 1631).

Although the monks arrived in Palestine first, it has been the nuns who have done the yeoman's job. In their quiet witness of a Christian presence they have generally impressed the Muslim society for their humble and dedicated service. Noteworthy are the *Soeurs du Rosaraire,* a native order of nuns that has been serving in the community since 1880, the order of *Saint Josef de l'Apparition.* The Franciscans opened their first schools for the existing native Christian community in the 15th century in Bethlehem, Jerusalem, Nazareth, Ramleh (in Palestine), Damascus, and Aleppo (Syria). At first the pupils were taught Latin, Italian and other subjects related to the Roman Catholic creed to prepare them to become guides and translators for pilgrims or to benefit from establishing commercial links with the European visitors.

By 1633 the Franciscans had decided to open more advanced schools in Bethlehem, Ramleh, Damascus and Aleppo. Concurrently French monks established the first inn to serve pilgrims in Bethlehem and they also introduced handicraft training to native Christians – something which many Bethlehem women excelled at

The Narrow Gate Churches

and profited from for centuries. A permanent training center was opened in Jerusalem's Saint Savior compound in 1879 to train 50 students at a time. Today the Catholic church runs 14 hospitals in the area under the Jerusalem Patriarchate (Catholic Church Report 1997:182-184).

The Catholics concentrated on helping their new parishioners, especially those living in Bethlehem and Jerusalem as well as some of their Muslim neighbors. Pope Pius VI even published a special bull (*Inter Caetera*) urging the world's Catholics to support the Franciscan fathers in their campaign of raising money to support their activity in the Holy Land. Unfortunately today the Franciscans resist coöperating with scholars, even Catholics, and will not share their historical documents. Dr. Hanna Kaldani, a Catholic priest, was unable to peruse 150-year-old documents in their possession (Aerts 1933:51-52).

A few within this order have published documents which disclose that the *Custodian de Terra Sancta* were literally supporting the faithful in Jerusalem with daily bread and housing at substantial cost in order to protect the presence of Roman Catholics there. In 1933, Conrad Aerts urged Catholics around the world to contribute to the mission needs in the Holy Land. Many of the needy were Armenian and Assyrian survivors of the Turkish and Iraqi Massacres. Aerts assured his European readers they were not asked to give their money in vain – the Holy Land church would pay back those generous donations by 20,000 holy masses said per annum in the holy shrines of Palestine (Kaldani op cit 196).

This tradition of bartering prayers for cash was not a Catholic invention; it has been a Jewish practice for centuries. Some Jews still earn their livelihood in the traditional holy towns of Jerusalem, Hebron, Tiberias and Safad by dedicating their lives to learning and praying while co-religionists raise money to support their humble needs. During hard times this sad endeavor has turned a few local Jews in Palestine against newcomers.

For many Jews and Christians, the Holy Land turned out to be a land of poverty and misery. Similar incidents are mentioned in Paul's letter to the Romans (15:25-33) but in recent generations the native Christian society have not had to care for their own needy but instead have profited from the fierce competition between the Catholic, Protestant and Orthodox churches.

Too often the well-to-do have gotten in line for the Red Cross International Relief intended for the needy and the affluent have eaten the free bread prepared by the Catholic bakery for the poor in Jerusalem. Fortunately this "help" was not embraced by most of the Christians living in outlying villages. They worked hard to build their homes, feed their children and educate them as independent Christians—avoiding the image of keeping their faith for the sake of free bread from the foreign missionaries. My family, and most Christian villagers in Galilee, never received or asked for material help from the foreigners. This type of dole has been tapering off and the church community is concentrating on meeting the real challenge of providing academic education, proper housing and the training of modern young Christians to stem the tide of emigration—which is where the real danger for Christians in the Holy Land lies. If the emigration trends of the last few decades continue, this community (which has survived 2,000 years of persecution and hardship) will be left to the clergy, monks and nuns who guard the sad stones of the holy shrines.

Bethlehem University, established as the first Catholic university in Palestine dedicated to educating the local populace, is second only to Bir Zait University, founded to prepare young people for the American University of Beirut and for points abroad. The goal of the Bethlehem University was to train students to initiate or participate in local enterprises. Like Bir Zait, Bethlehem University is open to non-Christian students and even has Muslims on its staff, although Catholic clergy continue to hold the key posts. This university has contributed greatly to the local Christian community, providing housing projects for new couples, new hostels for the reception of pilgrims and many jobs for the local Christians.

Another "new" Christian presence in Palestine is the Anglican church, first established by British missionaries who came to Jerusalem to convert Jews to Christianity. After little success in that attempt, they decided to concentrate on converting Greek Ortho-

dox Arabs to the Anglican confession. More of these were attracted after 1958 when the British relinquished leadership of the
church and native converts were allowed to fill higher church
posts and the first Arab Anglican, Najeeb Quba'in, was ordained
bishop of Jordan and Syria under the Jerusalem Archbishopric.

Archdeacon Rafik Farah has written in Arabic a detailed early
history of the Episcopal church since the bishopric was established
in Jerusalem in 1841 (1995). Most who joined the church came from
Orthodox ranks, bringing little joy to the missionaries, for they
knew many of these new members joined in order "to facilitate
matrimony or other material benefits" as described by their English Bishop George Francis Blyth (1832-1914) in his report to the
faithful in 1890 (Farah 1995:128-139). A century later, between 1948-
1974 there were a thousand Arab members in the Anglican confession in Israel. Those emigrating, according to Archdeacon Farah,
balanced the new babies born into the ten churches in seven parishes (two of which later closed). But at the end of the 20th century the church had dwindled because of the war and emigration,
yet it still remained rich in physical assets inherited from missions
that had ceased their activities in the Holy Land.

The legacy of these mission efforts cannot be underestimated.
Many Arab leaders today in all fields are graduates of Protestant
educational institutes begun by Western missions. Writers, educators and activists acknowledge an immense debt to their mission
education and formation. In 1991 when Anglican-Episcopal Arabs
celebrated their church's 150th jubilee in Jerusalem they owned 32
institutions for education, rehabilitation, health services, housing
and pilgrims' inns. The troubles of the past decades have kept the
church membership at stasis, but it still maintains a powerful presence because of these establishments.

Another group of Europeans who in past centuries demonstrated interest in the Holy Land were Christian "Zionists" like
the German Templars who believed Christians should settle in the
homeland of the Savior and wait for his second coming. Others
believed they should build up the land of the Savior or give local

Christians a personal example. A similar motive brought Greeks to Palestine during the 18th century. They were tolerated by the local government of the Arab Sheikh Daher Al Omar but not really welcome. Soon they mixed with the local Greek Orthodox native Christians and the most famous son of this group was the late Yanni Qustandi Yanni, Mayor of Kafr Yaseef and chair of the first Arab national group to organize inside Israel, "The Arab Popular Front."

Back in the 1850s some American Protestants expecting the second coming of Christ in the second millennium arrived at Jaffa gates and built their small settlement of Mount Hope. The climate did not agree with them, so most of them left the country after a few years or perished, leaving their message and properties to the German Templars. These Germans (officially called *Deutsche Tempelgesellschaft*) were followers of Christopher Hoffman who had aspired to create the ultimate "people of God" (*Das volk Gottes*) where a family-church-nation would lead the way by personal example, preparing for the next coming of Christ.

Originating in Württemberg, they lived some 80 years in Palestine in special urban quarters of Jerusalem, Jaffa, Nazareth and Haifa, and established their own farming villages, almost like precursors of the kibbutz movement. After the 1948 war most of them were forced to leave Palestine/Israel due to bad feelings towards all Germans because of the Holocaust. A remnant of the settlers who adamantly refused to admit failure and leave were persecuted and humiliated by Israeli military units until they, too, departed (Ben Artsi 1997:12-13). In 1955 representatives of the Templars sold their properties to the Israeli government in 1955, but their memory lingers on as "German Colonies" are still found in Jerusalem and Haifa, and hotels they built in Nazareth, Haifa and Jerusalem still function, albeit under new management, but the architecture still tells the old story about the German settlers.

Although few remember the Templars religious hopes and yearnings for the second coming of Christ, many in the Arab community still admire their industry and good works. Unfortunately these German Christian communities became infested by

Nazi racist ideology and some German settlers forgot the message of Christian love which had propelled their parents to leave Germany in the first place. Thus it is easier to understand some of the hostility and strong sentiments the Jews formed against German presence, but it was a sad portent of how the Israelis were going to treat all other groups who lived in the Holy Land.

Other Germans besides the Templars in the 19th century included Catholic monks and nuns of various orders, like their French, Italian, Spanish, Austrian and British counterparts, who prayed, contemplated, opened schools, hospitals, churches, guesthouses and shelters for the needy in the Holy Land. Like other Europeans, they were keen to support the local church. Mainly they tried to extend a helping hand to local Roman Catholic institutes in Palestine, Lebanon, Syria, Egypt and Cyprus while bringing in substantial funds to keep these various works operating.

An American settlement of Christians was established in Jerusalem by Horatio and Anna Spafford, pious Christians from Chicago who embraced the British-Israel theory which purported that the Anglo-Saxon people are descendants of the lost tribes of Israel (Vester-Spafford 1950:24). This couple had suffered in the great Chicago fire in 1871 and then had lost four children tragically, so they decided to emigrate to the Holy Land with a group of friends and followers where they taught, nursed and offered help to the needy in Jerusalem. Later they were joined by a Swedish contingent and although they managed to survive under Ottoman rule, their descendants were dispersed during the British rule in Palestine. A century later their legacy remains in two institutions serving Jerusalem – the American Colony Hotel – still frequented by international journalists since it is more or less a neutral site in the divided city – and the Anna Spafford Children's Hospital which still functions inside the walled town. In time, these institutions were handed over to native Christians.

A few American evangelical missionaries keep trying to win "new converts" from the ranks of local Christians, but mostly they have turned their attention elsewhere. Although their "foreign mission work" appears quite marginal as far as expanding the

Christian community by adding new converts to the faith, they have contributed to the education and needs of the Catholics (Latin, Greek and Chaldean) and Protestants (Anglicans, Baptists and Lutherans, mainly) who originally were from the Greek Orthodox, Copt, Maronite, Assyrian and other native churches.

The Anglican church was the first to withdraw their Western leaders – and transfer the local church management to a new generation of native members. Catholic resolutions since 1965 to promote local Christians for higher ranks in the clergy, started by Pope Paul VI during his historic pilgrimage in 1965 to the Holy Land, resulted in the nomination of Dr. Hanna Kaldani as Nazareth's first Roman Catholic bishop since the Crusades. Subsequently John Paul II took another major step by choosing Michael Sabbah as the Jerusalem patriarch, emphasizing the opinion that natives are trusted, at last, to run the Christian church in the land of their Savior.

The question is whether the native Christians remaining in the Middle East today are healthy and consolidated enough to survive and whether they can stand alone during these perilous days and face the blowing storms.

13

Israel – and the Native Christians

I was born to a family of Greek-Catholics in a small village where Maronites made up the majority of Christians. Together these two churches were still a minority in my village, Al Jish. As we grew up, we believed that as Palestinian Arabs we were members of a great nation with a magnificent history and a promising future. This dream was shattered before my 15th birthday when Zionist Jews conquered Palestine and we became part of the Arab minority in Israel. The government officially insisted on calling and treating us as "minorities" – Muslims, Christians and Druze. This is the essence of our story.

The British mandate in Palestine came to its end on May 15, 1948. On that day, according to a UN resolution made on November 27, 1947, two independent states were supposed to be born, one for the Arab natives and one for the Jews. The Arabs, except for an insignificant minority, were united on one thing – the rejection of a division of Palestine and the refusal to allow the establishment of an independent Zionist state in their midst. The Jewish

Agency executives and other representatives of the *Yishuv* leaders met in Tel Aviv to listen to David Ben Gurion's solemn declaration of Israel as an independent Jewish and democratic sovereign state. This declaration opened a new chapter not only of Jewish history, but also for the native Christians of the Holy Land.

The British authorities in Palestine had failed to keep the peace in the six months between November 1947 and May 1948 so a bloody civil war broke out between the Jewish organized militias and some Arab irregulars (who expected strong backing from the Arab League states' regular armies). These hostilities transformed the demography of Palestine as Jewish forces occupied Jaffa, Haifa, Tiberias, Safad, Beisan, Acre and many other main urban centers. The vast majority of their populations became refugees and Arabs lost the first round in their struggle against Israel.

From their point of view, Palestinians were just trying to resist an unjust international dictate. The suffering of Jewish began before the Christian era when they were enslaved in Egypt and then later exiled to Babylon and Persia. Before the end of the first century A.D. they had been deported by Titus to Rome in an exile unprecedented in human history, both in its length and consequences. The exiles never lost their devotion to their homeland, the cradle of their faith and the focus of Judeo-Christian culture. Wherever Jews wandered during the next two millennia, while enduring great suffering, pogroms and harassment from many countries – including Spain, Britain, France, Russia and Germany – always they longed to return again to Israel.

The devoted "friends" of Israel today – many of whom once were numbered among their persecutors – have helped the Zionist movement repatriate Jews to Zion, overlooking the "small" problem of changes that had taken place in Zion during their absence. These Jews might have longed to return to a Canaan of their dreams, but that land had not waited for them. In fact, there were Jewish farmers and shepherds who had never emigrated, who for generations lived side-by-side with members of more ancient nations, who had always inhabited this land. These people had considered this their homeland far longer than James Balfour's ancestors regarded Britain as their island home or than most European peoples had been settled in their various countries.

That Jews have a right to enjoy life in every human aspect is something Palestinians did not contest, but they felt justified in refusing to pay for centuries of anti-Jewish crimes committed by others. Even when the United Nations decided on the partition of Palestine between the Jewish minority and the Palestinian Arab majority, Palestinians felt justified in resisting a decision they had no part in making. Their Arab neighbors promised to help them, but the result was a tragedy for the Palestinians and a shameful failure for the Arabs.

When the war between Israelis and Arabs came to an end a year after the first exchange of gunfire, the smoke of the hostilities was scattered by the western winds and the short spring season of 1949 brought forth the colorful wild flowers blooming on the Palestinian fields as usual. Nature took no notice of the Arabs' defeat and misery or the Jews' joy. Now Israel was no longer a historic myth or religious symbol, but a Jewish state and a new political entity, home to 34,400 Christians, mostly Arab Palestinians, who managed to maintain their homeland inside the new state.

This was also the first time since the birth of Christianity that Jews had been put to the test as a ruling power, to be judged for how they treated minorities living under their rule. It was also the first experience of Jewish-Christian relations in a country under Jewish rule. The Jews went from being classic scapegoats or traditional victims to being an overwhelming majority. Now they governed in the Holy Land for all the world to see and focus on the universal conflict between Judaism and Christianity – and the potential hope for a new formula of coëxistence of the two faiths.

Even though this was a struggle between competing religious populations, most leaders of the Jewish-Zionist party were atheists and anti-clerical socialists from European backgrounds. The only religious Zionists, the *Ha Mizrahi* movement, were a small minority group. Many of the young "pioneers" who disembarked at the Palestinian ports came loaded with prejudices – against European colonialism and against all Christians. They had a tragic heritage of being ghetto Jews who had endured the anti-Semitic feeling of many Goyim. Many Jewish leaders pragmatically tried to maintain cordial political relations with non-Jews, but whenever they were criticized, the Zionists discovered they had been given a major way to secure sympathy: the holocaust of World War II. The colossal crimes of the Nazi regime against the Jews and other "inferior" races were cited to absolve the Israeli-Zionists for any inappropriate actions taken against Christian Arabs.

Most of the 156,000 Christians who lived in Palestine before the outbreak of hostilities in 1948 were no longer in Israel by the end of that war – not even a quarter of the Christian population remained, but those who had stayed were living mainly in Galilee. Like their Muslim compatriots, many fled to refugee camps or managed to emigrate to the West. The fortunate few continued to live in their homes in Palestinian areas not yet occupied by the Israeli forces – like East Jerusalem, Bethlehem, Ramallah and Gaza City. Many of these Palestinians lost their property and then became refugees as well after the Six Day War in 1967.

Looking at the first comprehensive Israeli census conducted in 1961 (one taken in 1949 was highly inaccurate since it overlooked many displaced civilians, overcome by the agony of war, were uncoöperative or hiding in caves or forests). When you compare this census to those of 1931, 1972 and 1995 you get a fuller indication of the changes on the demographic level between the first and second halves of the 20th century. Analyzing all these census data shows that many ancient communities have been demolished, their inhabitants forcibly driven out either by war or fear. Many were blocked by force from returning home once the hostilities had ceased. Other areass were deserted by a population that felt insecure or went elsewhere in search of a better standard of living.

Another demographic phenomenon of this period is that there was a new Christian presence in various towns that previously lacked any before. Most of these "new" communities are formed by immigrants to Israel, but some include local Arab Christians who have moved to mainly Jewish localities in pursuit of better housing, jobs or improved conditions – especially in Nazareth Illit,

Beer Sheba and Naharria. In few cases, such as in Tiberias, the new Christians tend to be Christian-Zionists who came to support Israel's economy and welcome Jews home to quicken the Second Coming of the Lord. Some deported Christians settled in neighboring towns or villages inside Israel – like the refugees from demolished Beisan, Tiberias, Mjaidel and Maa'lol, who mainly settled in Nazareth and Yafa al Naserah. Others from Kafr Bira'im went to Al Jish, Al Maker or Haifa. Many forced out of Iqrit settled in al Rameh and a small number of the former residents of Al Bassa and Mansoura went to Mia'ilya or Mazraa'a.

Efforts to compare the results of the Palestine Census of 1931, the Israeli Central Bureau of Statistics census for East Jerusalem of 1967 and its "Demographic Characteristics of the Population in the Administered Areas" in the same year, plus numbers published in 1994 by the Palestine Academic Society for the Study of International Affairs, and church figures from the *La Terra Santa* for 1995 show that the figures are not comparable, and suggest that these communities are in continuous movement from villages to towns or out of the country.

No one can ascertain just how many refugees have been forced from their homes. As noted, under the British Mandate Christian communities in Palestine increased steadily and continuously. Their number was probably elevated also by the hostilities in Europe during World War II that made Christians seek safer homes. But the results of one year of killing and misery between 1947 and 1948 were disastrous to the Christian community. Half of the 156,000 Christians estimated to have been in the Holy Land in 1947 were living outside their homeland by 1949. Some 34,400 or 22%, of the original Christian population in Palestine became Israeli citizens and an optimistic estimate claims 50,000 survived in the Arab zones of the West Bank and Gaza.

The major flourishing and industrious Christian communities of Jerusalem, Haifa and Jaffa were erased or reduced to ruins. Small pastoral parishes disappeared altogether. The Christian presence was entirely abolished or drastically reduced in urban towns like Safad, Tiberias, Beisan and Beer Sheba. The loss was equally bad in rural communities. Ain Karim (St. John the Baptist's home-town) lost its Christian population. Al Bassa, the only Palestinian village in Galilee which housed a Christian high school, was de-molished. Birweh, Damoun and Suhmata in western Galilee were left in ruins. Abel al Qameh (near the Lebanese border), Mjaidel, Maa'lool and Sirean (on Nazareth's outskirts) met similar fates. Samach, on the Sea of Galilee's southern coast, was demolished.

Iqrit's and Kafr Bira'am's Christian populations were tricked into moving out of their homes. The irony of this tragedy has been noted by the locals, for the village of Kafr Bira'im was the *only* Maronite village inside Israel and the Maronite church was the only Middle Eastern community inclined to accept the Zionist Plan. These villagers and farmers welcomed the Jewish forces into their homes. In spite of their gracious attitude, a representative of the Israeli military forces appeared a month later and tricked them, asking them to move away "for two weeks" to some safe haven out of harms' way from the war zone. After that, they were prom-ised, they would be free to return.

When they were not allowed to go back to their homes, they appealed to Israel's High Court of Justice in 1951. To head them off, the Israeli forces demolished all the buildings in those villages, except for their two churches, but still the court ruled in their favor. The Israeli government, ignoring Israeli high court rulings still adamantly refuses to let these Christian villagers return home. When pressed by Maronite and Catholic church leaders on behalf of these parishioners, the Israeli government claims to be still in a process of discussing the issue. Even Israel's military alliance with the Lebanese Maronites against the Palestine Liberation Orga-nization, between 1976 and the year 2000, could not convince Israel's establishment to allow Kafr Bira'am's uprooted people (and their neighbors, Greek Catholics from Iqrit) to return and build the empty ruins of their villages.

During this period many rural villages disappeared. The list is disheartening: Ain Karem, with its monastery, plus Bassa, Birweh, Damoun, Kafr Bira'im, Iqrit, Mansoura, Mjaidel, Maa'lol, Suhmata, Siren, Shaa'b, Samach, Shajara, Abel al Qmeh all lay in ruins, its thousands of Christian inhabitants scattered to the wind. The suffering was not limited to Palestinian Christian communities. Their Muslim compatriots suffered the same fate. The only village of Armenians, Sheik Braik (Ceasaria), was evacuated. The German Christian settlers, the Templars, soon had to abandon their presence in the villages where they had settled (Bethlehem in Galilee, Waldheim near Bethlehem, Sarona by Tel Aviv, Wilhelma near Aloni Aba, Walhala outside Jaffa and Neuhardthof by Tira) and sail back home to Germany.

The Armenian settlement was a rare instance where Armenian refugees had attempted to start a farming community in Palestine. Most of them lived in urban areas, especially in Jerusalem (as did most German settlers who built their communities at the outskirts of Haifa, Jaffa, Jerusalem and Nazareth) but their villages occupied a prominent position on the landscape until World War II when the residents were deported from Israel in April 1948.

Native Arab Christians lived, more so than their Jewish and Muslim neighbors, in the urban centers and there they suffered their most painful losses. The Palestine official figures tell the gloomy story of these large communities in the central cities: Haifa, the country's main port, was home in 1945 to 138,000: 75,000 Jews, 36,000 Muslims and 26,570 Christians. The Muslim community was entirely wiped out and the Christians were reduced to less than 2,000. Jaffa, historic commercial center and traditional port of Christian (and Jewish) pilgrims on their way to Jerusalem, was home to 15,000 native Christians at the end of the British Mandate. Fewer than a thousand were still there after 1948. Acre, the last Crusader stronghold and a walled city that held out against Napoleon Bonaparte early in the 19th century, was home to 12,360 Palestinians before 1948. The Jewish minority in the town consisted of 140 people with a Muslim majority of 9,890 persons and the Christians numbering 2,330. After the war only a few hundred Christians still lived in the town.

Benny Morris in *the Birth of the Palestinian Refugee Problem, 1947-1949*, quotes official Israelis in an effort to prove there was no discriminating policy for or against the Christians. Yet he includes other documents which describe how eager the Israeli establishment was to rid themselves of the Christian (and Muslim) presence in their new state. One paper quoted advice given by David Ben Gurion to his aides saying they should try hard to convince Christians (from Tarshiha, for example) to leave, without creating an international crisis (1991:147-148). Throughout his book, Morris seems intent on proving there was special treatment for the local Christians, but he was honest enough to record a sordid episode from Safad.

The Arabs in this Arab-Jewish town with a small Christian minority refused to desert their town at the end of the 1948 war, and were willing to stay and face the risk of living under Jewish rule. However, this tiny group of 140 Arabs, including 100 Muslims "who were, in average, 80 years old" (Morris quotes the Jewish military governor of the town), were all deported two or three weeks after they surrendered. The Muslims were sent to Lebanon and the Christians were entrusted to the monasteries of the Charity of the Sacred Heart and Nazareth Sisters (ibid:301-302).

The vast majority of the native population of Lydda and Ramleh were forced to walk under harsh conditions to Ramallah – a few hundred were allowed to remain inside a barbed-wire camp in their hometown. The figures show the major towns of Jaffa, Acre and Haifa were hit severely, but still these towns are in better shape than Jerusalem.

After the 1948 war West Jerusalem became Israel's capital. Before this, Jerusalem had been home to 20,000 prosperous Christians living in its new residential neighborhoods with another 8,000 in the Old City. The war wiped out the entire community in West Jerusalem, and only a few hundred remained in church institutes as guards or maintenance workers in charity institutes (Rose:1993).

East Jerusalem, the Arab sector of the Holy City, became part of Jordan between 1948 and 1967. The fate of the Christian community here was somewhat different for they, unlike the Muslims who mainly came from rural backgrounds, were an urban populace. After 1948 they became Jordanians and Jerusalem now found itself treated as just another city in the Hashimite kingdom, not the capital of a state. Therefore, many lost their jobs as civil servants or in its related branches. Jordan, a poor country, had as its top priority the development of its capital Amman. Jerusalem was regarded only as a place for tourists and pilgrims. Many from Jerusalem, both Muslims and Christians, moved to Amman to be near the headquarters of the various government departments, radio and TV stations, national newspapers and other media outlets; others emigrated to Gulf states or to America. As a result, Jerusalem's Christian population did not increase during the 20 years of Jordanian rule.

Jerusalem's west and east sectors were united under Israeli rule after the 1967 War. This "reunification" turned out to be another devastating blow to its Christian population. Many left at this point in pursuit of a more peaceful homeland or as a result of the Israeli policy of "iron fist" retaliations against any Palestinian resistance against the occupation. Jerusalem's Christian community was cut in half, despite the merging of several neighboring villages, such as A'in Karim, Silwan, Beit Hanina and al-Tour.

After the Christians were wiped out in 1949 from the historic towns of Beer Sheba, Beisan, Safad and Tiberias, a few other Christians, most not locally born, came to settle in these towns. In the poverty-stricken Beisan and the extreme *haridi* (ultra-religious) atmosphere of Safad, the few Christians there live in the underground. In Beer Sheba and Tiberias, a blooming community is growing, most of its Christians drawn from the ranks of those arriving in Israel as spouses in mixed marriages and their families. Others came as temporary guest laborers from Romania or the Philippines. Now numbering some 50,000 Christians, many will return to their homelands, but thousands will become permanent residents and citizens. The 21st century finds Israel at a crossroads on the issue of forming a new Christian community.

The hostilities from 1947 to 1949 caused the destruction of over 425 Arab villages, most of which had been in existence for two millennia. Christian communities were banished from some 80 towns and villages. These were shortsighted moves, for emigration is a real menace to the survival of any society. It caused a combination of brain drain and human hemorrhaging that disturbed the society deeply with the remnant being an aging community. British soldiers and their families, civil service personnel and accompanying civilians, who had served the cultural and commercial companies, all left the country. Many Greek and Armenians had felt the war was not theirs. These industrious, hard working and, along with the German Christian settlers, productive workers had contributed much to the country's essential physical needs, technology, vocational training and infrastructure necessary for the tourism industry. Like the Jews in Germany they did not regard themselves as disposable items.

The entire Arab population, including those lucky ones who succeeded in maintaining their right to live in their own homes inside Israel, lost property, social status, family members and friends. From being normal people living on their own land, they became a tolerated and suspect minority. A conservative estimate suggests 80,000 Palestinian Christians paid the price of that war by losing their homes and property and becoming refugees unable to return home, just like their Muslim neighbors. Some put the estimate higher (Zoughbi 1998). One academic researcher claims 23,000 Christians and 22,000 Muslims were driven off in "an ethnic cleansing operation" from the Israeli sector of Jerusalem during the 1948 war. Other sources claim more. Christian relief groups said 100,000 Christians were in refugee camps (King 1981:58).

It is a mistake to conclude, however, that those who became Israeli citizens were the fortunate survivors of war–while those who found themselves outside the borders were the miserable refugees. Many of Israel's new citizens suffered from the whims of Israeli policy that operated outside their own legal system. From the earliest days of the Zionist Movement, the Israeli goal was to continue taking over Arab lands. After declaring their sovereign state, the Zionists were unstoppable. Most of the Arab lands were confiscated under a series of "laws and regulations" (Mansour 1997).

Christian and Muslim farmers, having lost their sources of income, had little choice other than to work as day laborers on the now-Jewish farms or to build homes for new Jewish immigrants. Civil servants lost their jobs as they were forced out of their former villages and homes. Palestinians discovered themselves to be Jordanians when Jordan and Iraqi forces annexed part of Palestine to "save" it from Israeli occupation, renaming it the West Bank. Palestinian natives in Jerusalem, Bethlehem, Ramallah, Hebron, Nablus, Jenin and neighboring villages lost estates, workshops, jobs–to become unemployed Jordanians.

Christian relief groups meeting in Beirut in May 1951 under the aegis of the World Council of Churches decided to concentrate their efforts not only on Christians but to extend a helping hand to all refugees, regardless of their faith (King op cit:58). (This policy prevented keeping separate statistics on Christian refugees.) Those Christians who managed to remain in Bethlehem or Arab (East) Jerusalem still lost their homes and property in the Jewish section of Jerusalem. An Israeli official paper, distributed by the prime minister's office, claimed the Christian population of Jerusalem in 1949 was 25,000 whereas by 1967 because of the Jordanian occupation their number had been reduced to 11,000.

These figures are clearly distorted. In 1947 the city of Jerusalem actually was home to some 30,000 Christians. As a result of the hostilities, the Israeli West Jerusalem sector was entirely cleansed of its Christian (and Muslim) communities. After the British departure from Palestine, most refugees moved east to the Arab sector, but many were unable to find any shelter there and had to go further afield to find any source of economic survival.

Only 15,000 Christians lived inside the Arab East Jerusalem sector in 1949, including those refugees who found "temporary" shelter in monasteries and hospices. The vast majority of these kept looking for a place outside their home country. The local community could not offer them any reasonable livelihood. Many from the native population of Jerusalem, Ramallah and Bethlehem resumed their tragic, century-long tradition of packing their bags and looking for new homes away from the war and hatred in Palestine. Many settled in Latin America, especially in Chile. Some Israeli officials claimed the Jordanian government should bear all the blame for the Christians' emigration between 1948 and 1967

(Schmelz 1992:10, Eliav 1992:22), but this is unfair. Many Muslim Palestinians also were waiting for American visas, but others left Jerusalem and headed to the Gulf states.

Christians who emigrated from Ramallah, Jafna, Bir Zait and Taybeh tended to settle in the United States because Ramallah had a well-known Friends' school (Quaker) and their graduates had been indoctrinated to see the USA as a "promised land." What made so many Palestinian Christians leave their own (and their Savior's) homeland? According to my personal experience and knowledge, the blame for this crime falls on ignorant Palestinian Arabs and on the leaders of the Arab states leaders and of Israel.

During WWII, when I was a youngster in a remote village in north Galilee, I remember vividly the UN deliberation at Lake Success on the Palestinian Issue and the consequent resolution to divide our country into an Arab and Jewish state. At that point, our people were outraged that foreigners in London, Moscow and New York decided to solve the Jewish problem at our expense. Why should they divide our small 25,000 square kilometer home? Why not make the Germans pay for the Nazi crimes? A few days after the UN decided on the Partition Plan, a visitor came from the nearby town of Safad to my village. He was introduced as a representative of the regional national committee. He tried to the villagers no danger would threaten us from the Jewish gangs, since "we" (the Arabs) had seven regular armies.

This kind of mantra was repeated often in those days since there were seven Arab League member states: Egypt, Iraq, Syria, Jordan, Lebanon, Saudi Arabia and Yemen. No one dared ask what "real Arab military potential" meant, because anyone who asked questions risked facing a military tribunal as suspected member of a defeatist "fifth column."

Of course, later it was disclosed that Egypt did not even possess a military map of Palestine, and the poor Egyptian soldiers dispatched to the war front in Palestine were fed dry bread and salty cheese bought in Gaza's open markets. Happy Yemen (Felix Arabia) was so poor their delegation could not attend the opening ceremony of the Arab League. Saudi Arabia's army was non-existent (as were the crude oil fields). Jordanian's army was under British command. The Lebanese army was too small even to hold a military parade on their independence day. The Syrian army was incapable of controlling its three-year-old state borders, making it impossible to prevent the smuggling of drugs across its long frontiers with Turkey, Iraq, Jordan and Lebanon. The likelihood of a war to help Palestine was never believable.

In short, the Palestinians were promised help from bankrupt or corrupt childish political systems. In some cases, as has become clear today, Arab kings were complicit with the Jews, as was King Abdullah, founder of the Hashimite kingdom of Jordan. It began to resemble a Gilbert & Sullivan production when the Arabs appointed this king as commander-in-chief for their armies, while everyone knew the real commander of *his* army, known as the Arab Legion, was an English soldier (John Bagott Glub Pasha) as were most of the top officers in this army.

Why did 1.5 million Palestinian Arabs need foreign help against 750,000 Jews? This answer is quite simple. The Palestinians had no experienced military leadership to mobilize them, no basic military training for their troops and no experience – which they could have acquired if they had served with the Allied Forces in WWII (as 27,000 Palestinian Jews did) or had crossed the borders to one of the Arab states that were quite keen to train them (like Syria).

The grand mufti, Haj Amin Al Husseini, dominated the Palestinian leadership by proxy, using terror squads sent from his exile in Egypt. There was no real preparation on the ground except for a few thousand rifles and light weapons "rescued" from the German-British battlefields during the World War II battles in al Alamain by Libyan desert Bedouins. Arab individuals who believed they should protect their families and homes until the arrival of the "Arab armies" bought these weapons privately.

I was an eyewitness to the Yarmuk and Alawite Brigades of *Jaysh Al-Inqaz* (the Salvation Army) – military forces mobilized by the Arab League during the 1948 war – as they arrived at the front lines near our village. Most were impoverished farmers whose first military training took place right there. We watched them go through exercise drills not unlike the physical training classes we teenagers had at school. Totally naïve about the dangers they would be facing they asked us – local teenagers – what Jews looked like and whether they were really cowards (as they had been told).

This was the army being prepared to face the Israeli military units – equipped and hardened fighters from their war experiences. These were able to fight efficiently and establish the boundaries on the ground that had been designed by their political leadership. With a few exceptions, such as in Haifa where the Arabs surrendered in the early stages of the war, the local Jewish leadership made an attempt to persuade their Arab neighbors not to leave town, but in most other cases the defeated Arabs were urged, pushed or simply driven away by force and terrorism, as in the cases of Safad, Tiberias, Lydda, Beisan and hundreds of villages, including Christian villages (such as al Bassa and Suhmata in western Galilee and Maa'loul and Mjaidel, near Nazareth). There were also cases in which atrocities were committed in villages to drive people away, as in A'ailabun.

In a few places the Christian population risked staying home, but Israelis then tried to trick them into leaving for a short period – which later became permanent – as in Iqrit and Kafr Bira'am. As news of atrocities and deception spread around Galilee during the autumn of 1948, Arabs were desperately waiting for promised arrival of "Arab armies." More and more hazarded staying put, despite the news of the Dair Yassen massacre and the fear of atrocities against the innocent civilian population, especially against the chastity and honor of women (Al Azm 1967:20).

Many military operations were waged against the Arab population. The Dair Yassen incident is considered a double tragedy for Palestinians and is recalled as proof of their leadership's failure. This was a small village on a hilltop on the road between Jerusalem and Tel Aviv, now renamed – Qiryat Shaul. According to Jewish Hagana militia commanders, Dair Yassen was a peaceful village in "good relations" with its Jewish neighbors during the war. The Jewish population of Jerusalem, however, was feeling threatened by some Arab villagers and volunteers under the command of Abd al Qader Husseini (a rare member of the urban upper class who was willing to take personal risk and share in war operations) and the forces under his command were endangering the Jewish supply route between Jerusalem and Tel Aviv and the coastal strongholds.

Dair Yassen turned out to be an easy target for Irgun Tzvai Leumi and Luhami Herut Yesrael, two right-wing militia groups who early in April 1948 took the town. Civilians, including women and children, were killed, and the survivors were humiliated by a four-mile forced march down the road to East Jerusalem – in an attempt to win popularity and improve the morale of civilian Jews feeling under siege. Then 93 of the Arab villagers were brutally murdered in cold blood in order to terrorize the others and panic them into moving faster into the Arab sector of town. Today the remaining natives of Dair Yassen claim they fought back – and killed some Jews – when they were attacked, but this claim is hard to believe because all other reports say the attack surprised the villagers. Any such statements 50 years-after-the-fact seem like an attempt to save the community's self-esteem – after long years of being pointed out as a cultural icon of misery and suffering.

Dr. Hazem Nusaibah, son of a respected Muslim family from Jerusalem and a scholar who served the Jordanian government in high posts, confessed in an interview on a BBC documentary program ("The Fifty Years War: 1988") that he, on orders from Jerusalem's Arab leadership, wrote the first press release describing the massacre in Dair Yassen. He used the most horrible terms he could muster, describing the raping of women and the slaughtering of hundreds (including babies in the presence of their mothers) in order to incite the Arab nations to come to Palestine's rescue or else bring about some international intervention. Unfortunately, the effect of this horrible news was counter-productive, for it caused devastating panic inside the ranks of the local Arabs. More and more Arabs began to flee from their homes so as not to face the "Dair Yassen fate."

Some months later a feeble show by the Arab armies came during their first military confrontation with rather small Jewish outposts. This was added to cheering news from Nazareth where no massacres took place during its occupation (July 17, 1948) and the local population was permitted to stay. But at this period, news came of ill-treatment suffered in Lebanese refugee camps and the removal of many refugee groups from Lebanese areas bordering with Palestine to far away camps in Syria. The Palestinians understood they had few alternatives to consider: life in refugee camps in exile stripped of their human dignity and property or risking death under Israeli rule.

Yet more and more people opted to stay.

This development did not please Israeli's leaders. They surely must have rejoiced when so many of the Palestinians had moved at the first sounds of war. However when civilians, especially farmers, seemed determined to stay, the Israelis were eager to see them keep moving in order to make space for the Jews pouring into the country from European concentration camps. Yigael Alon, commander of the Palmach forces, was one of those who did their best to revive Dair Yassen's hysteria by adopting military scare tactics to panic civilians into becoming refugees (Morris op cit:511-512, Alon 1990:42).

An infamous officer from this era, Samuel Lahis, was deputy commander of a battalion during the Hiram Operation. His unit occupied villages near ours in the upper Galilee Mountains. Lahis ordered all villagers in Hula to gather inside the village mosque and proceeded to blow it up. His commander, Colonel Dov Yremia, absent at the time, heard the details of this crime from one of his soldiers, Abraham Hass. (Hass was the idealistic leader of some Bulgarian Jewish volunteers who had arrived in Palestine to help their Jewish kinfolk against "feudal Arab leaders" establish a "progressive" state. Later Hass became a Communist Party activist in my village.)

Colonel Yremia brought charges against his deputy–but the court-martial sent Lahis to jail for only a few months and he finished his career in the 1970s as director general of the Jewish Agency. Before Lahis was promoted Dov Yremia, a peace activist since the 1982 war in Lebanon, reminded the Israeli public of La-his' treatment of his prisoners of war in 1948 in an attempt to block his chance for this high national post—to no avail.

Atrocities occurred in our village as well—but on a smaller scale. Most of the native Christians and many of the Muslims farmers were unwilling to flee, believing the thick walls and strong buildings of Saints Peter & Paul Greek-Catholic Melkite Church would provide protection from Jewish guns and that a church is an unlikely place for the murder of civilians. True. But even though the Israeli soldiers did not kill anyone sequestered inside the church, they killed a neighboring couple in their own home. The husband had been wounded a few days earlier by a stray bullet so his wife was nursing him. Soldiers passing near the house heard sounds and decided to quiet them by a hand grenade, killing both Rida and Foma Bekhit. Other villagers, including Youseph Mohammed Qassem, my friend and classmate, were killed in an air force attack. Years later Aibi Nathan, a celebrated Israeli philanthropist and peace activist, apologized to me, for he had been one of the pilots on that raid.

The incident forever seared on our collective memory occurred on the second day of occupation when some young people, including my late sister Nazira, who had been hiding in the forest returned home. They were stopped by a military checkpoint and searched. The only "dangerous" material found in their pockets was some Palestinian bank notes and this "illegal" stuff was confiscated. The search was conducted with no hostile words being exchanged. Nazira heard Yousef Hashoul, a villager who had been living and working in Haifa for the previous decade, ask one of the soldiers if he was the brother of a soccer player he knew and admired. This seemed to break the natural tension between the soldiers and the civilians created by the presence of uniforms and guns. Hashoul asked the soldiers why the Palestinian currency was being confiscated. They replied that Israel had printed its own currency and all they meant to do was exchange the old for new bank notes. "But you did not write down our names nor give us a receipt" Hashoul responded.

Hearing this reasonable remark, the soldiers asked those whose money had been confiscated to accompany them "to the office" so they could receive receipts. The destitute members of that civilian group, including my sister, walked safely to the village. Before arriving at the church, they heard automatic gunfire down in the valley's fig groves. Later, the bodies of the four victims were discovered. Rafful Hashoul, his son-in-law Youseph Salim Hashoul, Faris Andrawes Haddad and his younger brother Elias Andrawes Haddad had been killed and mutilated. The brother of the soccer player and his friends had killed the soccer fan and his father-in-law and two of the sons of our blacksmith in order to steal some paltry amount of money. They even amputated the finger of a newly wed young man to get his gold wedding ring.

Later this incident was raised in Israel's parliament by one of the first Arab Christians elected to the Knesset, Amin Jarjoura (*Divrie Ha Knesset* 11/1949). David Ben Gurion responded by declaring his faith in the "purity of the arms" of Israel's armed forces and promised to investigate. Neither he nor any of his successors have ever acknowledged this tragedy again.

Dr. Tom Segev, a liberal Israeli writer, uncovered in the official Israeli archives clear evidence the Israeli army misbehaved in many other cases. Mostly these documents are still "classified," but the list of names given the files indicate the sites of the violations – Kafr Bira'am, Iqrit, Mia'ilia, Fasouta, Beit Jamal, Terra Sancta Convent, Rameh, Dair Hanna, Acre, Haifa, Jaffa, Holy Christian places, Tamra, Shafamr, Ramleh, Lydda and the 89th battalion (1984:85). Segev concludes by quoting another Israeli, Dr. Yousef Lam, a Knesset member of the Mapai Ruling Party, who said, "All of us misbehaved during the war, both against properties and against humans. We certainly did not behave as Jews should behave and we ought to be ashamed of ourselves."

It seems important to point out that the list of files referred to by Segev almost entirely relate to Christian places and institutions. A few are mixed towns but there is only one Muslim village in that list – Tamra. Later it was revealed that David Ben Gurion confessed in his private diary he was worried about rumors of the army's misconduct and had ordered the use of force in preventing impropriety on the eve of the occupation of Nazareth (1982:591).

Major Emmanuel (Mano) Friedman from Rosh Pina who served as liaison officer for civilians affairs and later as military governor in our village told me he was with the army during the first days of occupation and had made a report which detailed everything he had heard from civilian eyewitnesses. In response to this plus some notes of written apology he gave the families of the dead, he received an order to meet the minister of defense at the army headquarters in Tel Aviv where Ben Gurion personally threatened to court-martial him for defaming the army. Friedman refused to withdraw his accusation and soon after the meeting was released from military service. Nothing was ever done to compensate the bereaved families or punish the criminals.

Some two weeks after the occupation of our village, Friedman visited us. The news spread in the village that Mano Friedman was at the *mukhtar*'s *madafareh* (guest room of the village chief) and I have vivid memories of joining the crowd who gathered to hear him pass on the military orders that we were to leave our homes for a short period, for no more than a fortnight, since some military operations were expected and we might face real danger.

Some villagers asked where the army wanted us to go. Friedman suggested we might move north to Lebanon. Others asked about the neighboring village of Kafr Bira'am and we were told they also were ordered to go in the same direction. When it was discovered that our neighbors in Rameh were not asked to move, the question was put if we could join them for a fortnight. Friedman was a gracious man and was willing to negotiate, even though as a soldier he could have simply ordered and threatened. He agreed to ask his commanders, but advised us to prepare our suitcases in case the answer was that we had no choice but to move north out of our country.

My history and Arabic teacher, the late Shammas Atanass A'qel, joined Mano Friedman on his jeep trip to Safad, the nearest telephone in those days. Two hours later these two blond, fat men, Friedman and A'qel, returned in the open military jeep,

Friedman driving at full speed and A'qel standing, waving his tropical hat as they careened down the dusty street leading to Our Lady, the small Maronite church. People blocked the road asking what happened. Atanass, pausing like someone carrying dramatic news, refused to answer, tears coursing down his cheeks. He urged people to gather in the church where he announced from the pulpit that the army officers had changed their minds. "We shall stay forever in our homes. Our neighbors from Kafr Bira'am will come join us in Al-Jish for a two-week stay in the hopes the Lebanese border will calm down and they will be able to go back to their homes and property."

I doubt if any resident of my village ever prayed in a more devoted way the routine hymn of the Maronite ritual: "*Ya Um Allah ya Hanunu, ya kanz al rahmat wal maa'ouna*" ("Merciful, passionate mother of God, you are the treasure of mercy and help"). Was it divine intervention or was this the work of Bikhor Shitret, the first Jewish native of Palestine to serve as minister in Israel's cabinet who intervened on our behalf? Digging in Israel's archives proved to me that Shitret did in some cases come forward to defend Arabs (Benziman & Mansour 1992:63-66, Morris op cit :153-154).

What happened behind the scenes is illuminating. Shammas A'qel was a Maronite deacon who, because of personal matters, failed to get the parish approval necessary in the Maronite church for a married man to be ordained a parish priest. Instead he became a history and Arabic language teacher. His interest in history was deeply real and genuine which brought him into close relations with the late Yitshaq Ben Zvi, a respected man of letters in Israel's Labor movement, who was elected to be the second president of the state. Shammas A'qel and Major Mano Friedman managed to contact Ben Zvi and Bikhor Shitret, minister of minorities in Israel's first cabinet, who were surprised to hear of the military orders. These personal friends of my teacher were able to reverse the orders and secure our safety.

Our neighbors, friends and relatives from Kafr Bira'am came and occupied any empty houses that were in our village – mostly those homes which belonged to ex-villagers who had fled and become refugees. Still, there were not enough rooms for all of them, so, though most found shelter, others were obliged to cross the borders to nearby villages in Lebanon. "The two weeks, at most" were extended and those who crossed the borders became eternal refugees, while those who joined us are still displaced and waiting, a half century later, for a permit to return to rebuild their village.

Our Kafr Bira'am neighbors, I should add, deserve credit for being more active than any other displaced Palestinians in their struggle for rights and who have won a lot of sympathy for their cause. They brought their petition to the Israeli courts and got the high court to rule in their favor. Both of Israel's local newspapers and the international press have put the spotlight on their plight. The villagers have led demonstrations on Jerusalem's streets and at least ten published books have dealt on this issue, including a well-documented book by the Maronite priest Fr. Yousef Sussan and one that became an English best-seller, *Blood Brothers* which was written by the village's most famous son, Dr. Elias Chacour.

An almost identical case to that of Kafr Bira'am happened at Iqrit, a Greek Catholic Melkite village 20 miles to the west. Both villages were occupied in the Hiram Operation and both were unarmed and not trained to resist. Yaa'cob Lieshanski, commander of the Israeli military force that conquered Iqrit, has described what happened during his operations in the Western Galilee. "The villagers who fought against us had to leave their villages, but it was different in Iqrit, where no one fought against us. So when the residents needed rides to get to the liberated areas, I took it as a duty to act in their interest, because the village was near the border and the war was going on." Lieshanki was later appointed military governor. He tells of talks he held with the village's *mukhtar* regarding the possibility of moving to a temporary settlement. The *mukhtar* was willing to accept such a temporary arrangement until things "become clear."

Lieshanski's stand was clear. He supported the right of these displaced persons to return to their homes and church, but suggested their original land, currently used by Jewish settlers, should be exchanged for other empty lands. The high court accepted their plea against the government, ruling in their favor, as they did with Kafr Bira'im. So far, Israel's successive governments have failed for 50 years to obey the court's injunctions. The villagers' success is on paper only.

Another tragic story with a better ending occurred in the Christian village of A'ilaboun. Occupied in the same military operation as Iqrit and Kafr Bira'am by the IDF (Israel Defense Forces), it put up no resistance and most villagers sought refuge in the church. The local priest walked out with a white flag to meet the Jewish soldiers, pleading for the life and safety of his parish. In response, the occupying force commander ordered twelve young village men to stand in a line and told his men to shoot them.

When I investigated why this crime was committed, I was told by some Israeli officers who had participated in the operation and from Amos Mokadi that the massacre was not authorized by the command, but because the soldiers had met a strong resistance where some of their comrades were killed, they took revenge. Another officer elaborated and said the massacre was the result of "an eye for an eye" tradition because a few days before, some locals ambushed an Israeli vehicle not far from this village, killing two passengers, mutilating their bodies, even "playing soccer" with the head of one of them. An old villager whom I asked about the incident, said he had heard this excuse earlier, but claimed the criminal who mutilated the head of the Jewish passenger at Maskana junction (currently called Golani) on the outskirts of A'ailabun was not a resident of their village, but a soldier in the semi-military units of the *Jaysh Al-Enqaz*, the Arab League forces who were supposed to rescue Palestine.

Elias Saliba Sroor, an ex-headmaster of the village school and author of a book on the history of this village, offers another plausible explanation: A'ailabun was assigned to the Jewish state by the UN partition resolution of 1947, unlike most of the villages in the Western Galilee whose populations were allowed by the Israeli forces to remain unharmed. The soldiers in A'ailabun were supposed to force the population to join the refugees across the border. The shooting was premeditated in order to persuade them to abandon the town. Thus twelve innocent young men were shot in cold blood and their families and neighbors were ordered at gunpoint to leave. The villagers fled instantly, abandoning the corpses of the innocent victims to await the arrival of the parish priest and some other brave men who had been hiding in the fields. Together they buried Jiryes Shibly Al Hayek, Badia' Jiryes Al Hayek, Fadl Al A'ialabouni, Milad Fayyad, Fuad Nofal Zraiq, Zaki Nakhleh, Raja Miekhael, Hanna Ibrahim Al Khouri, Naa'im Zraiq, Mikael Mitri al Shami, Abdullah Sima'an al Shoufani, A'azer al Hourani and Muhammad Khaled.

The brave Greek-Catholic Melkite parish priest, Fr. Marcus Hanna Moa'llem, refused to leave the village and later showed up in Nazareth where he informed the Roman Catholic authorities about the sad fate of his parishioners. Monsignor Vargani, the Roman Catholic patriarchal vicar, and the Red Cross delegation raised the issue with Israeli officials through diplomatic channels which resulted in a change of heart by the Israeli officials. A'ailabun was born again and the villagers were allowed to cross the borders back from refugee camps and return to their homes, fields and normal life. It seems as though their lives had been saved in recompense for the death of these twelve innocent young men.

Tiberias, Safad and Biessan were occupied in the early stages of the 1948 war. The entire Arab population of these towns were forced to look for refuge elsewhere. The Muslims and Christians of Safad went to Lebanon and later continued on to Syria. According to Sefer Hapalmach's description of the battle, the Israeli forces shelled the town heavily with a noisy, homemade gun they called a *Davidka* to create panic and speed the exodus.

The Arab, Jordanian and Syrian semi-military units of volunteers retreated on orders from Jordan's King Abdullah, the commander-in-chief of the Arab League's fighting forces. King Abdullah discovered his avowed enemy, Haj Amin Al Husseini, was about to declare Safad as the capital of Arabic Palestine when the British Mandate ended on May 15, 1948. Safad, a small, historic town in the far north seemed to be an isolated post, far from Abdullah's military forces that were concentrated around Jerusalem.

King Abdullah had no intentions of aiding the goals of Al Husseini, who was setting himself up to become the king of Jerusalem, so he ordered those under his command to leave the defense of the north to the irregular volunteers left behind, even though, for the most part, they were unarmed and untrained, and at the first sign of battle were bound to run for safety. The noisy *Davidka* gun convinced those who hesitated.

In Tiberias the scenario was slightly different. Negotiations took place between the parties about a local cease-fire, but the British officials insisted on urging those Arabs who wanted to leave town to do so it before the British law and order forces had to leave. They entreated the Christians to move to Nazareth, while Muslims were encouraged to move east to Syria. The Arabs were apparently easily persuaded to accept this advice.

The same thing happened in Biessan when trained and armed Jews conquered this market town. Most of the Muslim population fled the country, heading east to Jordan while the small Christian community decided to remain. The commanders of the occupying forces offered them two alternatives: move east to Jordan or north to Nazareth, which was still in Arab hands. Most Christians in Beisan had relatives around Nazareth, so chose to go to that town. This I was told by Jamal Saa'd, a banker in Nazareth, and Canon Naim Ateek, founder of Sabeel Center of the Liberation Theology.

Officially al Bassa was just another village in western Galilee, but in fact it was larger – with a population of almost 2,000 in 1931 which by 1948 had grown to 5,000 – more than half of whom were Christians. Located in a charming site near both the Lebanese frontier and the sea coast, it attracted many new residents. The Greek Catholic archbishop of Galilee, Gregarious Haggar, chose this village for his diocesan high school. In many other ways, this township was flourishing. Smugglers also contributed to the wealth of its residents by circumventing the barriers erected by British authorities to prevent movement between Palestine and Lebanon during the Arab rebellion (1936-1939) and the early years of World War II when the pro-German French authorities ruled Lebanon.

The British hoped their barriers would stop the transport of arms or volunteers across the border, but in actuality they enriched the border villagers who were allowed to go through the gate daily in order to till their land that lay beyond the wall of barbed wire. Thus they daily had an opportunity to make extra income by smuggling goods across the border. In 1948, during the first stages of the war, representatives of al Bassa visited their Jewish neighbors in Kibbutz Hanita to forge an informal nonaggression pact between them, but soon this was breached – each side accusing the other of bad faith. Who attacked and who counterattacked is the question no one has been able to determine.

A few al Bassa villagers still live in their homes outside the old village. One of its few ex-residents still alive – Elias Al-Ghannam Wakim – told me he had been a member of the village's delegation sent to Kibbutz Hanita to negotiate an agreement of good relations between the two villages. Yanay, the Jewish *mukhtar* was friendly, but insisted the representatives of Al Bassa take upon themselves the prevention of anti-Jewish activities. The villagers promised to do so to the best of their abilities, but felt the Jews were negotiating in bad faith because they were asking something al Bassa farmers could not deliver. "How can we guarantee some Arab – or non-Arab – armed gangs will not shoot their guns in a country that is without a police force or any other law-enforcing agency?"

Wakim added that in his opinion, for the past half-century the Jews' main goal has been to lay their hands on more and more Arab land – especially since theirs tended to be the most fertile in the region, unlike that of neighbors in Mia'ilyah and Fassuta whose land was arid and hilly. "We were forced to leave because the Jews coveted our lands. The villages that were allowed to stay did not have good, fertile land." In talking about his ex-village, Wakim continues, "We were not a village. The villagers owned ten olive oil presses and a similar number of coffee houses. Thousands from nearby villages daily used our services and facilities."

Why did the Jews allow the Canaan family to stay in their grove in al Bassa? The answer is quite simple. It was the result of the Canaans' long cordial relations with some Jewish neighbors.

They were lucky enough to remain in their home, although they were never allowed improve their old family home to accommodate the needs of their younger generation.

Elias Wakim's son, a prominent Palestinian activist and successful lawyer, is the chair of the uprooted villagers' association in Israel and hopes for better days when an Israeli liberal government will recognize the rights of the displaced villagers to return to their homes. He is aware of the impossible predicament in Israel today, but still holds on to his dream, hoping someday it becomes a reality. So far, the association has held a conference and carried out research which discovered that Palestinian-displaced persons from 55 villages managed to stay in Israel after 1948 by receiving legal recognition that allows them to become Israeli citizens (without a permit to return to their previous properties and homes). The number of those evicted accounts for a quarter of the total Arab minority inside Israel. Wakim claims the number of Palestinian-Arab locations destroyed in the 1948 war was 418 sites.

The Israeli government's policy of handling the Palestinian-Arab minority that managed to stay in their own homeland after 1948 observed an old Jewish dictum: "Respect them, (but also) suspect them." The treatment of Christians followed this same precept – but even a bit more so. Since Christians were more educated and more connected with European circles, the Jews crafted a more lenient diplomatic approach to the farmers when they were not welcomed.

Joseph Weiss, chair of the Jewish National Fund and a Zionist official, with full approval of the Israeli minister of foreign affairs, Moshe Sharet, launched a plan in the early 1950s called "Yohanan Operation" of which the sole aim was to rid Israel of my family's presence, along with all natives of the village I was born in. This fanatic Zionist attempted to deceive and convince us to emigrate as a complete community from north Galilee to Argentina – by trying to talk us into bartering our lands for a similar area in the state of Mendoza owned by a Jewish "landlord" from that region. He was willing, he claimed, to compensate us for the churches, school building and other public assets we had in our village.

My father, I am proud to say, was the spearhead of those who rejected the idea on the grounds that we were privileged to be born in the land of our Savior and we will be blessed to be buried in its soil, as well. Later on, in the 1970s when the Central Zionist Archives in Jerusalem were opened and Weiss' autobiography was published, the truth was out – this had been a scheme concocted to encourage Christians to leave Israel (Benziman & Mansour op cit:58-59).

Israel's typical treatment of all native Palestinians, begun during the 1948 war, was that they were welcome as peaceful neighbors, provided they lived outside its borders. In principle they treated Muslims and Christians alike, but in reality the Israelis had few inhibitions about using brutal force with Muslims, while with Christians their treatment tended to be more humane since the Israeli government did not want to provoke unnecessary reactions in the European and American press and diplomatic circles. Of course these "double standards" must be remembered in the context that for the first 30 years of Israel's existence, their statehood was officially rejected on the all sides by their Muslim neighbors in the Middle East.

The Arab governments refused publicly to consider solutions that did not abolish the Jewish state, offering an insecure autonomy to those Jews who had lived in Palestine before 1917 (and the Balfour Declaration). This policy was articulated clearly to all sides and the Arabs were convinced that its 1948 military defeat was provisional. The educated and young tended to believe the corrupt and treacherous Arab regimes had effected the Arab failure. Such convictions fed national illusions that have persisted ever since.

Of course, the Jews who had won their independence for the first time after many prayers and struggles were not about to return to a life under a benevolent or not-so-benevolent despot. In a last-minute attempt by the Jewish leadership to prevent the outbreak of the 1948 war, or at least to convince their old ally, King Abdullah of Jordan, not to participate in it, Ben Gurion sent Golda Meir to meet with the king at his summer palace in Shuneh. The king suggested the Zionists accept him as their king with the promise he would grant them equality and autonomy. Golda Meir responded that on such lines there was nothing to negotiate (Ran 1996:215-216). On the other hand, most Christians of the world welcomed this new state, since they generally felt sympathy for the Jews after the heinous crimes of the Nazis – and in the face of the Arab's total rejection of Israel. Unfortunately, the world powers and Israel failed to adopt a reasonable, fair and firm policy to solve the problems created as a direct result of Israel's triumph.

The first Palestinian attempt to negotiate with Israel came in 1949 after the Palestinians discovered how wrong they were in trusting their Arab "kin." A delegation of Palestinian refugees met Israeli officials in Lausanne, Switzerland, but that encounter only showed Palestinians how Israel was no longer willing to recognize Palestinians as partners. Even their representatives, Aziz Shehadeh, Zaki Barakat and Nimer Al Hawwari, were not recognized by the Israelis as a delegation for the Palestinian refugees. They merely informed this group of Palestinians that Israel was willing to negotiate with a sovereign state, not with "people." Since the Palestinians were, in Israel's view, just some jurists representing private clients, they would only look at claims Palestinian refugees made for compensation for the property abandoned in Palestine (Al Hawwari 1999:377-384). The talks were aborted before they ever started.

The Palestinians were not the only ones attempting to deal with the Israelis during the early years of their rule in the Holy Land. Zionist diplomats negotiated with Egyptian leaders before the 1948 war and were willing to coöperate in a project dividing Palestine into two separate states – one Arab and one Jewish (Sasoon 1978:364-365, Cohen 1970:518-519). Jordan's King Abdullah was also willing to share Palestinian territories with Israel. For over 30 years many discussions, long encounters and detailed negotiations took place secretly between the two sides across the Jordan River. The first agreement between the Hashimite dynasty was concluded between Prince Fayssal and Haim Wietsman in 1919 and another quite feasible agreement was made in July 1951 on the eve of the king's assassination while walking inside the Al Aqsa mosques in Jerusalem (Rabinovich 1991:42-43).

Syria, too, was willing to talk to Israel and establish an alliance with the Zionists. This rather odd tale was told in detail in a small volume by Itamar Rabinovich, Tel Aviv University dean and ex-ambassador in Washington and head of its delegation negotiating with the Syrians during the 1996 peace talks in D.C. He said Hosni Zaa'im, commander-in-chief of the Syrian army, who led the first coup d'état after the Arab defeat in 1948, asked for a meeting with David Ben Gurion to discuss peace and an alliance between Syria and Israel (Ben Gurion rejected the offer). During the four short months in 1949 when this Syrian general ruled his country, he signed an armistice agreement with Israel, offered them a military alliance and met with Israeli delegates (but not the prime minister) (op cit:62-65). The Egyptians, Syrians and Jordanians "forgot" or concealed their contacts with the Israelis in the late '40s and early '50s. Beginning in 1952 and continuing for decades, they attempted to deny any past relations or plan any future contacts with Israel. Even a pleasant greeting from an Israeli at the UN headquarters in New York was considered an act of treason.

But the Palestinians were unable to forget. Most of them were now refugees in Arab lands, which precluded their taking part in the normal life of a citizen – nor were they permitted to act as an independent national group dealing with their new predicament. Still, the Palestinians' disappointing meeting with Israelis in Switzerland was not entirely futile from their point of view. At least they knew they had lost their country and also the right to win back their rights or influence their future. For some time exiled Palestinians were trapped in deep despair because of their new catastrophe, but soon they were looking around for a savior.

Some Palestinian refugees embraced secular and radical ideologies – such as Communism, pan-Arabism or Syrian nationalism. A few years after the *Nakba* (the Catastrophe), Palestinians discovered their most promising hero: Egypt's Gamal Abd Al Nasser (Arabic – Beauty [of Allah], slave of that who brings triumph) who promised he would create a united Arab state which would lead them to their rightful position as a super power. This was not sheer rhetoric. Some events that followed supported this claim. Nasser nationalized the Suez Canal, rejected the British and French threats and fought back and survived their military campaign (with the Israelis) in 1956 to recover the Suez Canal and topple the regime in Egypt. His alliance with the Soviet Union turned him into an international hero, not only for the Arabs, but for many Third World countries as well.

This charismatic populist attracted the attention and influenced many young Arabs who were yearning for a change. The Palestinians in their homeland and the refugees in Arab "host" countries were, more than other Arabs, entirely enthralled by the pan-Arab ideology of a united state. Actually, this ideology had been promulgated during a long century by Arab-Christian thinkers. First Najeeb A'azouri in 1905 articulated this vision. Later Michael A'flaq, the Syrian, wrote the Baa'th Party program during the '40s. The most respected thinker was Questatine Zurayk, guru of thousands of future potential leaders of Arab states. His career as a history teacher and author lasted for more than a half century, from the '40s until 1999. He played a major role as the Arabs' national authority, not just for those who attended his classes at the American University of Beirut but also for the thousands who read his book on this topic first published in 1948.

Other intellectuals, especially Orthodox-Christian Lebanese, heeded Anton Sa'adeh's secular calls for a revival of the old Syrian culture. Some, impressed by the USSR's military triumphs of World War II and the Marxist theory of using force to end injustice, poverty or exploitation, gave homage to Moscow for decades. The dramatic failure in 1956 of the imperialists Britain and France (with Israel) in regaining the Suez Canal was a boon for the Pan-Arab movement. Also Nasser moved, at least with lip service, about this time to the left on social issues which encouraged many Marxist-Arabs to join the ranks of his populist supporters.

Nasser's espousal of socialism was a gift to his enemies, for in recruiting the Western Allies against him, Israel became the bastion of anti-Communist resistance in the Middle East whereas Egypt was perceived as a dangerous hub of anti-Western interests. These radical swings in the Arabs' political stance did little to help an

Israeli-Arab accord. While Arabs regarded Nasser as a savior, most Jews believed him to be their main enemy and the Israeli establishment found little opposition from their public for any new policy of oppression or intimidation of its Arab minority. Mostly they adopted a policy of "divide and rule" with their Arab minority.

In 1949 there were 34,400 Christians living in Israel; 20 years later there were 58,000 – a 70% increase (Colbi 1969). At the same time, the population of their Muslim neighbors increased from 111,500 to 223,000 – an increase of over 110%. The Jewish population grew even more – from 1,013,900 to 2,344,900 persons – more than a 130% increase, mostly the result of immigration. The Israeli Central Bureau of Statistics (CBS) estimate of the Christians inside Israel jumped from 58,500 in 1966 to 71,000 in 1967 because some 11,000 Christians were added to the number, coming from the newly occupied East-Arab Jerusalem. By 1983 the figures showed there were 94,000 Christians in Israel and by 1995 the apogee was reached with a record high of 162,500.

Within a year their number was down to 123,400. Investigation revealed the decrease was caused by an Israel ministry's newly adopted policy. Until the 1995 census all European and American "mixed" couples, including any non-Jewish spouses, were registered as "Christian;" also many Russians and Ukrainians who had immigrated to Israel from the USSR were counted as "Christians" until they were able to prove they were Jewish according to the conservative religious rule, *Halakha*.

Many of these new Israeli citizens were diehard atheists or else refused to profess belief in a faith they didn't accept, so the Israeli statisticians adopted a "new" group: *Not classified by religion* which accounted for some 84,000 people by the end of 1996. Unfortunately, these were not free citizens who opted not to belong to any religious group. In most cases they were scared non-Jews who had managed to arrive in the land of Israel but were afraid to lose their civil rights or be deported should they declare themselves Christians or Muslims.

According to Israeli law, a Jew is someone born to a Jewish mother, so the case of the Carmelite monk Father Daniel Roufiesen illustrates the problems facing such people. Born to a Jewish family in Poland, F. Roufiesen accepted Christ as Savior during the dark days of World War II and later became active in rescuing other Jews from Nazi persecution. After the war he emigrated to Israel and settled in his order's monastery on Mount Carmel, serving as parish priest for a small, non-Arab Roman Catholic congregation in Haifa. When he appealed to the ministry of interior for an Israeli passport, according to the basic law of return which confers an automatic citizenship on any Jew at their port of arrival in Israel, the ministry ruled that a Roman Catholic or member of any non-Jewish religion couldn't claim the right of an Israeli citizenship according to the Law of Return. The Israeli high court of justice confirmed the ministry of interior policy and ruled against F. Roufiesen, claiming he lost his right to be recognized as a Jew when he departed from the Jewish faith.

The harsh way "non-Jews" were treated by officials became a hot issue in Israel's 1999 election. The ultra-religious party *Shas* that dominated the ministry of the interior and the Russian immigrants' political party *Yesrael Bea'alya* competed against each other. *Shas* activists made life intolerable for non-Jewish partners in an immigrant family, humiliating them and often refusing to recognize them as converts since the rabbi who had signed their documents was not strict or conservative enough. *Yesrael Bea'alya,* in trying to appeal to the ex-Soviets, demanded a more liberal approach.

Some Christian churches try to help those who want to live as Christians, but few immigrants come to any church. More of them "show up" after their death to be buried in Christian cemeteries, because orthodox Jews—who monopolize the religious services—refuse to bury non-Jews inside a Jewish cemetery, allowing their burials only "outside the fence," a policy too insulting for most families.

Some 50,000 Christians lived in the Arab Palestinian territories (under Jordanian and Egyptian administration) in 1949, mainly around Jerusalem, Bethlehem and Ramallah. The Jordanian government, as a rule, was not hostile to Christians, but they were too weak to help them feel at home in a changing society. Dr. Adnan Musallam from Bethlehem University claims Christians were let down by the Jordanians after they annexed the Palestinian areas west of Jordan River, calling it the West Bank. By 1949 Jordan had enacted a citizenship policy which did not recognize the rights of emigrants living abroad – as had the British denied all Palestinians who had emigrated from their homeland before 1920 the right to obtain Palestinian citizenship and passports (Musallam 1991:44-45).

The Jordanian census in 1961 showed the Christian community in the West Bank had dwindled to 46,000. Their numbers kept dropping so when the first Israeli census was taken in 1967, this area had 3,000 fewer Christians. It is fair to say Jordan's regime was not hostile to Christians. Especially at highest levels, the establishment was always friendly and tolerant. Although incidents occurred in the community that demonstrated heated animosity between Muslims and Christians, what made people emigrate was basically that Jordan was a poor country. The younger generation left to find better jobs in foreign lands. Many Muslims were able to work and live in relative ease in the oil-rich neighbors across the desert, but Christians tended to emigrate across the ocean.

This trend continued in Jordan throughout the second half of the 20th century on both banks of the Jordan River, even though the population of the West Bank of Jordan decreased faster than that on the east. Between 1952 and 1961 the population of the West Bank increased only 8.5% while across the river it increased 28.4%. The census figures show that whereas Christians a century ago represented 10% of the population in the Holy Land, today they make up only 2%. They have suffered from hunger, famine, wars, deportation and destruction but have also seen improved health, education and quality-of-life conditions. The European political and religious intervention in their lives has helped a lot. Part of this was colonial rule, but the rest came from religious missions and cultural influences aimed at helping native Christians improve their lives or find such away from the Holy Land.

The number of Christians in Jerusalem today is reduced to 35% of their size in 1948. European missions contributed to this attrition by introducing foreign languages and values that aided and gave them incentive to emigrate. Many of the Jerusalem Christian community were overly dependent on their respective Roman Catholic, Greek-Orthodox or Anglican churches. As these entities were weakened under Israeli rule, it became easier for dependent Christians to go elsewhere to find stability and security for their families. As their numbers diminished, their Muslim and Jewish neighbors in Jerusalem kept increasing phenomenally, making the Christian presence all the more negligible. Despair from all the conflict and hatred in the region also was an important factor.

The Narrow Gate Churches

14

Profile of a Community
Peaceful, Productive and Aging

Before discussing the way native Christians confronted the challenge of life under Israeli rule, we ought to know more about these Christians. The Christian Palestinian-Arab community is a minority inside Israel, which in turn is a Jewish minority in the midst of a vast Arab-Muslim ocean. This religious minority inside an ethnic-national minority surrounded by a large number of national states share nothing with each other but a common conflict. A cultural and social profile for such a community need be compared only with native-born Muslims, for it would be unfair to compare Arabs, either Muslim or Christian, with Jews who for the most part were not "born in Israel" but rather in the Diaspora.

Most new residents in the Middle East, parents and children alike, never wanted to live there, despite Israel's national anthem, *Ha Tiqva* (The Hope) which exhorts all Jews to aspire to live there. These aliens feel little connection to the natives—and they refuse to learn Arabic. Even those who come from Arabic-speaking countries such as Iraq, Morocco, Yemen, Egypt or other Arab states, don't send their children to schools that include Arabic as a subject in its program. Many members of North African Jewry claim they came from France. The majority of the immigrants from Muslim countries distance themselves from their Arab background and are hostile to anything that lumps them together with Arabs.

This self-imposed alienation takes extremes. There is the "modern" Hebrew accent young Jews adopt to set themselves off from their Arab neighbors—which emerges from the weakness most Europeans have for pronouncing guttural letters. Instead of trying to learn, they have adapted grammatical rules so now, for them, the mistake is accepted as the norm. They also distort original Hebrew by introducing foreign sounds and letters to substitute for those similar to Arabic or Aramaic ones, turning "modern" Hebrew into a hybridization of Germanic and Anglo-Saxon sounds.

Thus modern Hebrew spoken in Israel is far less Semitic than Hebrew of the past and most Hebrew speakers today find Arabic as alienating as Chinese (while for Arabic speakers Hebrew is easy to learn). Since the vast majority of those children born to parents that immigrated to Israel from Arab lands face no problem in pronouncing Hebrew letters, this self-imposed alienation is not a "popular" mistake. The Israeli education ministry contributes to this practice by not teaching Arabic in most Jewish schools, so the number of Jewish graduates from Arabic classes does not meet the needs of military intelligence. Most Israeli classes for Arabic studies in local universities are carried out in Hebrew because both students and teachers are not fluent in Arabic as a spoken language.

Another hurdle between Jews and Christians is caused by the Jewish communities' vastly disparate backgrounds. Although most Jews claim membership in the Jewish community, there is little agreement what this means culturally. Is the Yemenite Jew with unique physical features and rather peculiar pronunciation of the Hebrew language more Jewish than the East European who looks more like a Catholic Pole? In the daily habits, moral values and political and social trends there are huge gaps separating the religious from the atheists, liberals from rigid conservatives and puritans from those who openly advocate a permissive life and total license, so one tends to find more "traditionalists" and religious Jews in the ranks of the North African Jews than in European Jews. Yet the most liberals and the most rigid religious extremists are ethnically speaking white Europeans. Oriental Jews seldom are among fanatic settlers in the Palestinian occupied territories. Yigael A'mir, a Yemenite Jew and infamous assassin of Prime Minister Yitzhak Rabin (November 5, 1995), is certainly an exception to this.

Comparing Jews and Arabs is complicated. Arabs, both Muslim and Christian, are native descendants of the same ancient peoples, with a similar history for centuries and a common life experience. Both Muslim and Christian Arabs are urban dwellers and rural farmers, but Christians, because of their insecurities have been more urban than the Muslims. A minority of the Muslim population inside Israel/ Palestine are still nomad Bedouins – with the complicated cultural gap separating them from more sedentary communities. The 1931 census shows the literacy rate for Christian boys (age 5-14) as 54.3% and for the same Muslim age group it was 23.5%. This census showed that of the 47,981 Bedouins living in the Negev desert at the time, only 53 persons, including a single woman, claimed that they could read and write.

Christian Arabs have not practiced a nomadic lifestyle for the last thousand years, but they have a lot in common with Muslims who live in their towns and villages. Historians generally refuse the notion that the origin of most Christians living today in Palestine goes back to the Crusades. James Parkes claims many Crusaders merged themselves into the local population, wherever Christian or Muslim (Parkes op cit:9). The Muslim historian Imad al Din, eyewitness of the Crusader defeat by Saladin in 1187 and the fall of Jerusalem, writes the Muslims divided the defeated Crusaders to four groups: (1) those granted amnesty by the magnanimity of the conquerors; (2)those set free by of Saladin because they were Armenians or other Christians who "belonged" to such territories inside what was considered as the Muslim state system, *Iqtaa'* (feudal limits); (3) those who paid ransom and were allowed to leave Jerusalem to look for a refuge in one of the remaining Crusader's castles; and (4) those enslaved and forced to accept Islam under their new status – which was the largest group – some 15,000 men and women out of an estimated 40,000 Crusaders (Shakeel 1988).

The defeated Crusaders needed to save their lives and property from Muslim vengeance. Those who could not escape back to Christian lands, relinquishing estates they had cultivated for generations, had no choice but to embrace the religion of the new rulers. Most Muslims and Christians of Palestine trace their ancestry to some Arab tribe, but many Muslims also have some Mongolic, Kurdish, Seljokish and Turkish blood, while the Christians tend to have more of the Greek, Crusader and Jewish blood.

Christian and Muslim Arabs, living side by side for centuries, have even prayed together until recently, chanting the same "hymns" to ask for rain when drought or calamity threatened. Most lived in mixed villages, hired guards for all their village's fields and harvested on agreed dates, taking into consideration various religious holidays. In the village where I was born the only apparent difference between Muslims and Christians was the place they went to pray in. Only rarely did Palestinian Muslims observe the Muslim practice of polygamy and inheritance laws which gave brothers a double share of the inheritance from their sisters and an absolute authority on divorcing a wife for no reason or excuse.

Henry Rosenfield from Jerusalem's Hebrew University studied the habits and daily life of a mixed village in Galilee in 1954 and found 8% of the last five generations of Muslim men had more than one wife simultaneously (CBS ibid:44). He traced the *badal* solution for enhancing social and economic stability that Galilee peasants used to consolidate the family (and overcome the fatal economic issue of repeatedly dividing the land) where cousins exchange sisters in marriage. This study was conducted in Tura'an (a fact not disclosed in the book) and found that in 28% of Muslim marriages sisters from the same extended family were bartered. Christians were less inclined to this practice, but still some 16% of the families were formed according to this tradition. About 32% of Muslim couples married inside their extended family *(Hamula)*, while 21% of the Christians did the same (Rosenfield 1964).

Most Muslim women are divorced for not producing a male

heir. The stability of the Christian family offered women a peaceful and secure status in comparison which is reflected in a famous Palestinian folk I have heard Muslim women sing, *Ala Dala'ona,* whose surprising verse says, "Oh Dala'ona, O Dala'ona, Come through, O compassionate breeze of my homeland. How sweet is a Christian wedding, Unlike Muslims they don't divorce." Christians, unlike Muslims, do not have arranged marriages for the convenience of the family so young people need to meet and know each other. This forces the Christian community to be more open on courting issues. Young Christians can meet casually inside Christian neighborhoods, but outside their quarter they must dress and act "modestly" in the style of their Muslim neighbors.

A woman is far from being equal in the Arab society. Many are pressured into marrying someone who meets their parents' criteria. Unfortunately a long tradition of norms and practices that go back to biblical time is still operative. Rashid Ridha, editor of *Al Manar* and a student of the respected modern Islam "reformer" Muhammad Abdo, in discussing the status of Muslim women concludes that if a woman are to be treated "fairly" then it is the "man who is maltreated" (Ridha op cit:99). For these reasons the Christian community tends to do better in female education, since young men with education prefer to spend their life with a literate spouse. Since mission schools for girls were established two centuries ago has helped this process. It also follows that more educated women contribute more to a society's economy.

In the early 20th century Palestine was a rural land where industry offered livelihood to only 14% and trade to 10% of the workers. Muslims dominated farming with only 15% of the Jews and under 20% of the Christians in farming. Palestinian Christians gravitated to business and arenas requiring an emphasis on education. The 1948 war and the establishment of Israel changed everything for those Christians who managed to stay inside their homeland. They, like other Arab communities, lost most of their leaders who had lived in urban areas like Jerusalem Jaffa, Haifa, Ramleh, Lydda, Tiberias and Safad. Still the Christian minority maintained its status as being the most educated part of the community.

First, most Christian religious, monks and nuns, foreign nationals or natives, persevered at their posts and were calming influences in a time of turmoil. Monsignor Vargani, the Latin patriarch vicar in Nazareth and Archimandrite Basilius Samman, the chief Greek-Catholic cleric there are still remembered for their leadership roles. The Greek-Catholic paper, *al Rabitah* (The Link) resumed publishing. The Latin patriarchate moved their journal, *Al Salam walkhair* from Jerusalem to Nazareth. The Anglican church started their own publication, *al Raaid* in Haifa. All these publication kept exploring the social and political issues facing the Arab minority in Israel. The Christians also made up a large part of the left-wing Palestinian intellectuals who for the most part came from the ranks of the Orthodox and Anglican churches. This group tended to support the UN's Partition Resolution dividing Palestine between the Arabs and the Jews, and thus were persecuted by the Arab League states and were forced to stay in Israel which at some point was willing to welcome and treat them with respect.

Another reason Christians stayed within Israeli borders was that many Christian villages were in the upper Galilee mountains occupied during the 1948 war – which made them aware of the true military balance and that the official "Arab military intervention in the war" was nothing more than a slogan. They had no choice but to acquiesce to the new occupiers and face the consequences. For these reasons, 34,400 Christians of the 156,000 Palestinian Christians then in the Holy Land opted to stay in their homes inside Israel in 1949. Paradoxically, this has made the Christian community more Arab than they were before the war: the British soldiers and dependents evacuated the land and returned home; the Armenian, German and Greek communities who had lived in Jerusalem, Jaffa or Haifa were now either on the Arab side in Ramallah, Bethlehem or the Eastern sector of Jerusalem or had emigrated. Those who remained were almost entirely Arab except for a few hundred European religious and charity workers.

The Christians community also became more rural than previous since the city folk chose other options. Still Christians continued to contribute to urban life – producing the first publications for Arab readers in Israel: the *Al-Ittihad* communist weekly; *al-Rabitah* for the Greek-Catholic Melkites; *As Salam Walkhair* for the Roman Catholics and *Al Raaid*, the Anglican monthly. The short-lived economic monthly *Al Waseet* and the *Al Mujtamaa'* literary magazine were entirely Christian owned and edited. The Muslims and Druze communities had to wait for decades before anything similar was ventured. Under Israeli rule, the Arab school system served 25,750 pupils in 100 government schools with another 5,000 pupils attending "Christian" schools. The Compulsory Education Law enacted by the Israeli Knesset for all children aged 5-13 years was supposed to serve a potential total of 42,000 Arab pupils in schools inside the area allotted to Israel. Unfortunately the refugees were without any schooling. Because of the emphasis within the Christian community on education, they made up 44% of all teachers in the ranks of official government school teachers.

This gap continued another two decades for the 1983 census found Christians had kept their educational and economic superiority in Israel. Recent research found the 6,000 Christians in Jaffa to be more educated and affluent than their Muslim and Jewish neighbors. Christian educational system also attracts middle-class Muslim students. Thus Christians contribute greatly to the work force of the country – and this educational element probably is the reason why statistics show Christian women tend, two-to-one, to be employed as compared to Muslim or Druze women.

A brief exception occurred in the poorly paid textile industry when many Jewish-owned firms moved to Arab residential areas during the first *Intifada* disturbances (1988-1993) since they could not keep running in the occupied territories. For a time Muslim women found jobs more readily, but when the peace agreement with Jordan was established, most of these firms moved there from Arab townships inside Israel to take advantage of the abundant cheap labor available there. Currently there is a shortfall in the Israeli Arab community of about a quarter of their annual income. Which means they must be supported by welfare or outside donations. The government's policy of discrimination and the Arab community conservative social norms which do not encourage women to join the labor force are both to blame for this situation.

The Israeli policy is first to secure economic integration for new immigrants and to do this they encourage entrepreneurs to base new firms in the developing towns. Generous incentives (providing over 30% of startup costs) are paid out not only to increase Israel's economic product but its Jewish population as well. Thus Nazareth, the main Arab township in Israel which receives no such subsidies, is flanked by two Jewish towns – Migdal Haemek and Nazareth Illit – that are generously supported. Of course, it must be admitted that the Arabs' conservative and old-fashioned moral concepts and traditions contribute to Arab poverty.

Christians contribute to the country's gross national product as skilled and clerical workers, in academics, technical fields and at managerial levels. Thus Kafr Yaseef, the most academic Arab town in Israel, has the highest share of Christian population (over 60%). Statistics show that for the last three decades the average income of an Arab urban family is 60% of a Jewish family. Jews have access to jobs in the civil and military labor force and generally get the better and more lucrative jobs mainly because of a built-in bias of those in Israel who see this as "a Jewish state at war with the Arab world." So the country has a three-tiered society. The Muslims are always at the bottom and the Jews are at the top with the Christians in constantly deteriorating middle.

One problem is the level of dependents per worker. This number per Muslim worker has been steadily increasing as family sizes grow and jobs shrink, whereas for Christians and Jews the level of dependents has decreased. Households in Israel are becoming smaller for the past 40 years as women there are less fertile and spend more years in education pursuits, Muslim women continued to be the most fertile. In the 1950s they averaged 8.17 births, the Druze's average was 7.24, Christian women had a fertility rate of 4.56 and Jewish women were last with a rate 3.56. In 50 years this rate has dropped, but Muslims still have 4.65 births to the Druze's 3.84, the Jews now overtook the Christians with 2.62 to their 2.09 babies. One mitigating factor here is that the Christians' fertility dropped after Israel annexed of Arab East Jerusalem which contained some 1,000 nuns to skewer the statistics.

The annexation of the Arab sector of Jerusalem meant the natives there became residents of Israel, but unlike the Arabs who remained in Israel since 1948, they are not entitled to vote so the political parties have no incentive to court them and they remain marginalized from their own society. In contrast, the more prosperous Christians of Tarshiha who are natives, live on their own property, practice their professions and attend their own schools. Their Jewish neighbors are mostly immigrants from North Africa, the ex-Soviet Union countries or displaced Muslims from Bedouin tribes who finally conclude it is time to settle down. The Christian average household earns more for a smaller family, putting more at their disposal than the Arabs with larger households.

The worst demographic balance is inside the Christian community of Jerusalem. The share of aged pensioners (65 plus) is over 70% of their population, so the community is far from healthy – and its malady may prove fatal. The comparison of the 1972 and the 1990 figures is stunning. The first wave of the Christian exodus out of Jerusalem took place immediately after the Six-Day War in 1967 and this hemorrhaging of the community has maintained a consistent pace – which has done nothing to mitigate the fears that there is little future of a Christian presence in the Holy City.

From approximately 20,000 native Christians living in Jerusalem before 1948, by 1967 they were reduced to just 1,500 Christians living in the western, Israeli sector. Three months after Israeli forces occupied the Arab sector of town a census showed that East Jerusalem's population included 10,900 Christians and of this number over a third were refugees – or those driven out by the 1948 War from other areas that Israel came to occupy who had come to live in Arab Jerusalem. Over half of the Christians previous population had withered away – with no natural increase accounted for. So more than 70% of Jerusalem's native Christians had "vanished."

The Jewish forces conquering the Western sector of Jerusalem in 1948 where most middle-class Christians lived abolished many of their civil service jobs and forced them to look elsewhere for employment. Jerusalem's population dwindled in the ensuing years so almost a third of the parents canvassed in 1967 reported that some of their children were living abroad leaving an aging population behind. A third of these went to Jordan, almost half of them went to Arab countries such as Kuwait and Saudi with another sizeable number going to Europe and America – where a larger portion of the Christians ended up, as was to be expected.

The native Christian population in Jerusalem which had increased from 4,000 in the 1922 census to around 30,000 in the official estimate made in 1948, has been on a downward spiral ever since. One blip on this graph comes from an undefined number of Hebrew Christians who virtually live as an underground community plus many Christians from Galilee who come to study in the Hebrew University and then fall in love with this enchanted, haunted, colorful, spite-filled, but still very attractive town and decide to settle. While all this is happening, the Muslims have tripled their community from 60,000 to about 200,000 and the Jews increased about four times in the same period.

The emigration storms hit the entire population, but hurt the small Christian minority more, especially since they often had a bridgehead to welcome them into their new homelands because many had studied in other countries and put down roots around the world. These emigrated armed with the innocent and a naïve belief that American and European nations would embrace them as their prodigal children, but it does account for much of the growth of Eastern Christian parishes in major American and European centers.

Emigration, which has almost been fatal to the Christian community in Jerusalem, has not affected Nazareth as much, although a survey in 1989 found 65% of all families there had relatives in non-Arab countries. Over 40% of these had relatives in the United States – mostly in California and Texas – with about the same number in Canada. The rest have gone to Australia and Europe. Higher education has been a major factor not only giving people a chance to emigrate but leaving those behind in an improved standard of living.

The 1995 census showed 16% of the Jews, 13% of the Christians, but only 6% of the Muslims and less than 5% of the Druzes held university degrees. Unfortunately these Israeli official statistics also show that many Arabs find university gates closed to them because their *Bagrut* (matriculation) certificates fail to satisfy the authorities and stigma is placed on non-Jewish candidates, especially for doctoral studies. Of course there is less incentive for Arabs to pursue doctoral degrees since the civil service posts open to them do not require such—and young people say it isn't necessary to get a PH.D. to teach in a village school. Those who study medicine are not included in these statistics since most Israelis, both Jews and Arabs, study medicine abroad. All this produces an unfortunate widening chasm within the Arab community.

Even though Palestinian Christians were among the first to be alarmed at Zionist intentions to dominate Palestine and warn the other inhabitants about this, they took little part in Palestine's armed struggle against the Jewish-Zionist scheme. For most of the last 1400 years Christians had been "exempt" from military service and forced to pay the *Jizya*. Christian writers were the first to call for anti-Zionist plans, but only a few of their rank won fame as Palestinian fighters.

Exceptions to this include Fuad Nassar, a Nazarene Communist who led a small resistance force in the area of Hebron during the 1936-1939 revolt. A few Christians participated in the guerrilla war in Palestine trying to recapture their lost land during 1965-1993, but they seldom fought with the mainstream Palestinian organization under Yasser Arafat's leadership, but rather opted to volunteer under groups such the Popular Front for the Liberation of Palestine (PFLP) commanded by atheist-Marxists born in Christian families—Drs.George Habash and Wadia' Haddad.

Unlike Muslims, the Arab Christians tended to use "arms" made of paper and ink—writing, lecturing and trying to win foreign support for their cause. Farris Khouri in Syria, Charles Malik in Lebanon, archbishops G. Haggar and George Hakim from the Greek-Catholic Church in Galilee, Michael Sabbah from the Latin Catholics in Jerusalem, Archimandrite Atallah Hanna, the spokesperson of the Greek-Orthodox patriarchate in Jerusalem, Dr. Edward Said and Hanan Ashrawi in Palestine, Kamel Abu Jabber and Marwan Mua'asher in Jordan, Makram O'baid and Butrus Butrus-Ghali in Egypt and Tariq Aziz in Iraq, are just a few of the excellent writers and diplomats working for justice for Palestine.

Christian Arabs officially "lost" their status as *Dhimmis* 150 years ago, but they have never acquired the status of normal citizens. Because of their insecurity, they tend to be law-abiding traditionalists who behave themselves, keep the law, distance themselves from violence and work hard to excel in school and at work in order to obfuscate their inherent weakness as a minority. They have survived down through the ages by being hypersensitive to the wishes of those in control and by using their brains more than their brawn.

The Jewish and Arab educational systems are rather disparate, because the Jewish system is geared towards technology and hi-tech subjects whereas the Arabs concentrate on rote learning that emphasizes religious studies. Arabs also find it prohibitively expensive to set up the high cost establishments needed for technology schools. Christians tend to work extra hard at their studies and thus often outshine their Muslim neighbors.

The Jews, for generations *Dhimmis,* an oppressed and sometimes persecuted minority, now became rulers. The Muslims, no longer a dominant majority after 1948, have never adjusted to or accepted this role and try to cling to there power base. On the other hand, the Christians seem to love their traditional role of being Arab pioneers and an educated elite. Thus many Muslim pupils attend Christian schools, because especially the upper and middle classes consider these well worth the tuition, even when state-supported schools are available. The Roman Catholic nuns run the only boarding schools which Muslim conservative families will send their daughters to. Also, the health services in Nazareth, Haifa and Tiberias since 1862 have been the "monopoly" of Christian missions (Scottish, French, Italian, German and Austrian) – and they offer these services free of charge to all those in need – Jews, Muslims and Christians. Of course tensions and internecine rivalries exist because these operations are run by fallible humans.

15

Nazareth – A Case Study

When comparing Muslims and Christians in Israel one must remember that most Christians have lived in well-organized towns and villages with full modern amenities, while a goodly percentage of Muslims still live in rather primitive conditions where schooling is not readily available and even running water, electricity or sewage systems are absent. These conditions, in turn, ill prepare Arabs to find good jobs at a reasonable distance from their homes not does the infrastructure exist to help children get the education necessary to improve their lot in life.

In places like Nazareth where both Muslims and Christians have lived together for the last 400 years it is easier to assess how the two communities interact. It has only been in the last decades there has been much interaction. The vast majority lived separately in Muslim, Orthodox, Catholic or Maronite neighborhoods around their own mosque or church. They did meet in schools, marketplaces, at the water spring (before running water became available) and at social occasions like weddings, funerals or religious festivals. In times of crises, they would also meet for special prayers together, as in times of drought.

The relations between the two faith communities were quite peaceful, even more so than those inside the Christian churches—because they were not competing between themselves for the same turf. On the whole, the Nazarenes felt fortunate to have been under the influence of tolerant and rational leadership during the last two centuries when they had to deal with the tragic 1860 massacres in Lebanon and Syria and the historic turning point for the Jews and Arabs—the 1948 War.

In the 1920s Rev. Asa'ad Mansour wrote in detail about the unique "cousins' pact" signed by the town notables in Nazareth in the middle of the previous century. Representative of all the Muslim and Christian families in town (plus two Muslim villages nearby, Iksal and Mashhad) signed an agreement, the original of which was entrusted to the Franciscan monastery in Nazareth while signed copies were distributed to the signatories. This vouched that all who signed the pact and the families they represent became cousins and thus were entitled to the support of all others in case of being attacked. They are also bound to take part in any raid to wreak revenge on any who attacked their cousins and are likewise entitled to receive their share from a paid ransom or pay their part in case cousins were extorted for ransom. The names of those who signed this document, including the Nazareth Deputy Mohammed Aziz Al Fahoum, are borne today, 150 years later, by current members of the city council.

This coöperative move was a great boon for Nazareth during the sectarian disturbances that followed and which climaxed in the 1860 massacres. The town's historian cites a French military report written immediately after the massacres stating bluntly that the Nazareth Christians owed their lives to a Bedouin sheikh called A'aqila Agha Al Hassi who, out of warm friendship with a Nazarene notable, Tannous Qaa'war, tried to keep the Bedouin tribes from attacking the town and then warned the Christians of the imminent attack so these Nazarenes were able to gather a mixed group of Muslims and Christians and repel the attack.

The French report praised another Nazarene Muslim, Mohammed Safadi, who with Prince Abd Alqader Al Jazaeri, gallantly defended their Christian neighbors and stopped massacres in Damascus. Acre, an important center–as a walled castle and port town–was also rescued by Muslim leaders. Sheikh Abdallah Abi Al Huda Al-Taji, the city *qadi* (judge) refused to join the murderous mob who intended to annihilate the Christians there in 1860. Nazareth and Galilee were thus spared the fate suffered by most Christian towns and villages in the north as the massacres of 1860 passed by. Refugees from that era still remain in Nazareth because their family names indicate they originated from Shouf Mountains and are still known by this name.

Nazareth was similarly fortunate during the 1948 War because Israel's new government, sensitive to the world opinion – especially in Europe and the USA – warned the troops that occupied the town to behave in the most civilized way "since the eyes of the world are supervising you" (Lorch.1961:276). Thus when the Muslim mayor, Yousef Muhammad Ali Al Fahoum, and a small group of Christian dignitaries, surrendered the town unconditionally they were given in writing a pledge from the Israeli army that they would be granted equality in Israel.

Though this pledge was not honored during the 20th century, for the Nazarenes at the time, it was enough the Israeli forces permitted them safeguard in their town – and letting neighboring Galilean villages to remain as well. Some villagers managed to save their homes, others saved part of their fields as well, while many were driven out, as were Safforia, Maa'loul, Mjaidel and A'ilout, taking refuge in Nazareth. The villagers of A'ilout spent months in the Salesien monastery known as Abu al-Yatama (father of the orphans), and then managed to filter back to their partly demolished village on Nazareth outskirts with the help of the Salesian monks. The rest were forced to settle in Nazareth, like it or not.

The last to come seeking asylum after the 1948 war were Muslims and Christians from neighboring towns and villages who hoped the Nazareth shrines plus the presence of European observers in town would hold back the Israeli army from maltreating the population. One interesting result of this shared misfortune is that after years of living rather separately, Muslims and Christians mixed much more with Muslims living in traditional Christian quarters, and vice versa. This shared space was not exactly by choice, but by economic necessity.

So this small town of Nazareth, population under 15,000 in 1948, was faced with the major responsibility of being the only Palestinian urban center to survive as an Arab town in Israel. It immediately became the unofficial capital for Arab political and cultural life – where Arabs could buy basic necessities in a traditional market place with Arabic the lingua franca and where young people could study in an Arab setting. Nazareth was the only place in Galilee where an Arab owner of a radio receiver could recharge its battery long before electric power arrived in the villages and transistors were produced.

This also meant that Nazareth became the headquarters of the Israeli military government in Galilee and the seat for all courts – – military, religious or civil. It was the center for medical services, trade union activities and the first printing presses. Unfortunately, this cataclysmic combination was not exploited properly by the local leadership to sustain the town's unique character.

First Nazareth's population grew during the 20th century to more than 60,000 with another 150,000 residing in surrounding areas. These villages built schools and commercial markets to compete with those in Nazareth and its only nursing school at the French Hospital was closed and supplanted with two new schools established in nearby Dabboriya and Shafamr. A modern stadium in A'ielot replaced Nazareth's small soccer playground. The town's municipal government could not get the central government to subsidize needed civic buildings or maintain its basic needs. It celebrated the third millennium without a central bus station or railway station, without a modern sewage system or infrastructure needed to attract modern industrial entrepreneurs to invest in enterprises to provide jobs for the town's younger generation. A few new hotels and restaurants have been built for the tourist trade and the main street and some historic buildings have been

restored, but mainly this town is without such basic services as a public park or open plaza for cultural activities. Even the souvenirs that pilgrims and tourists buy are made outside the town.

The Israeli government, keen on outdoing Nazareth from its pivotal role in Galilee, embarked on the development of a Jewish substitute. Already by 1955 they had decided to establish a "Jewish" Nazareth. That town, Natzaret Illit, was built on top of the original historic town. The old shrines became nothing more than a destination for short visits. For most guests, Nazareth became a half-hour visit to the basilica, the purchase of a postcard and a return home. All this interference created the conditions for poverty and ill feelings to set the scene for the traditionally peaceful town of Nazareth to become the center of unprecedented hate in its Muslim-Christian relations.

In principle, since Israel created the first opportunity for Muslim and Christians in Palestine to be equals, one might expect they could live together more peaceably under a Jewish rule for the first time in history. This did not happen. Native Christians in Israel found they were suffering on both fronts–as Arabs, like their Muslim neighbors, and as members of a small, dwindling community facing daily hardships in a hostile and violent atmosphere. Although Israel is a parliamentarian democracy, this not much of a blessing because even if it is assumed there is equality and a separation of powers so citizens can appeal to the court against the government, this does not happen.

With the native Christian making up only 2.5% of the voters–and these divided into three fractious camps (Catholics, Orthodox and a few Protestants)–they have little political clout. The Christian minority is left with little choice other than to look for a new homeland elsewhere or to try to live in a closed community of their own. To adopt any of these options they need empathy-- both from their Muslim and Jewish neighbors and from the Christians in the West, especially those who care about developing ecumenical relations between Christian churches and interfaith cultural encounters with Muslims and Jews hoping to bridge the gap separating these three divergent cultures.

The many bells hanging over the holy shrines and already-empty churches in Jerusalem call for reconsidering future relations with their neighbors. Those of Bethlehem, Beit Jala and Beit Sahur face even graver dangers since these areas have become dangerous battlefields since the Second Intifada started in 2000. Nazareth and Galilee are relatively in better shape than their friends across the borders where their impact as a leading force is diminished in proportion to the community becoming more and more feeble.

The native Christians contributed to their own debacle by deciding to stand with their Muslim neighbors in the anti-Zionist struggle a century ago, but they had virtually no choice at the time. This was their country and struggle as well. They continue to aggravate their problems by immigrating, trying to improve their lives – a natural enough impulse. Others, too, have added to the calamity, i.e. the Nazi criminal regime, the anti-Semitic movements and those Zionist Christians who generously offer Zionism and the Israelis unconditional backing and support with no notice to those whom such support injures.

The Jews in Palestine, 50 years after the Zionist movement began, after building the first Zionist settlements and five years after the Balfour Declaration and the British mandate in Palestine, made up only 10% of the Palestinian population. (About the same size of the Christian natives). From then on their population increased from 700,000 in 1948 to 5,000,000 in 2000 – mostly from the massive waves of immigration the Zionists inspired, including over a million ex-Soviet citizens in less than a decade.

The Muslims increased without foreign intervention. Their high birth rate of 3.36% per annum, compared to the Christians' 1.45%, made them a significant part of the community – in spite of the persecutions waged against them. There were some "new" European Christians to arrive in Israel in the past few years from East Europe, but since many of them – from Russia, Romania or the Ukraine, had long lived under anti-Christian rule with a materialist education in a totalitarian state, they were ready to conform with the current and many converted to Judaism to solve their "problem" and become full-fledged citizens. Their religious commitment is rather tenuous, however, and the Jewish establishment was shocked when 25% of the new recruits for the military service in 2000 refused at their graduation ceremony to offer an oath of loyalty on the Old Testament, demanding rather they use both the Old and New Testaments.

Many of these new Israeli citizens will soon blend in with the large population of "secular" Israeli Jews who do not observe the Sabbath or the Halakha laws. Many Jews fast in public on Yom Kippur (Day of Atonement) and pay their synagogues a nominal annual visit. They may also eat Matzoth during the week of Passover (*Pesah*) like their Jewish neighbors, so these non-Jewish Europeans are not far off that model. They may face matrimonial and social problems from the religious establishment and eventually may opt to live outside Israel. Few are expected to become permanent Israeli Christians and will probably eventually join the Orthodox church out of nostalgic cultural motives. A few have already joined existing Armenian congregations; others are hesitantly crossing the threshold of evangelical or Roman Catholic churches.

As the Christian presence shrank in Israel, their leadership and representative posts in public life diminished, especially in politics on the national and local level. The Christians made up, during the first two decades of Israeli rule, around half of all Arab Knesset members. This has been reduced during the past two decades to 10 to 20%. The same is true of elected mayors and councilors—in a gradual but consistently diminishing role, emphasizing the failure of a Pan-Arab movement with its secular orientation and demise of Soviet-styled Communism. Of course the Muslim majority was now running for fewer posts and more emphasis was being placed on religion—where the Christians could not compete. Even when Christian candidates claim they are not religious or indifferent to religion, it does not make them attractive to religious Muslims.

During the first 30 years under Israeli rule, educated Christians led the Communist party and represented it in the Israeli Knesset. The ruling party, Mapai (now the Labor Party) made it a rule a Christian ought to fill one of their seats in the 120-seat parliament. Mapam leadership insisted on treating Arabs as religious groups.

The Muslim and Druze have occupied the seats allotted to them for the last 20 years, but Christian candidates have never managed to fill theirs because of the party's shrinking support among their electorate. The absence of a Christian in the ranks of the "ruling" party caucus reflects on their influence within the ruling circles. Unfortunately there has been a radical change in the demographic balance inside the Muslim-Christian Arab minority in favor of the Muslims. Thus the Israeli political parties have incentive to court the support of Muslims at the polls. On the other hand, many young ambitious Muslims discovered how attractive and lucrative is this trade. They use religious slogans en route to Knesset seats or a well-paid and influential local government position.

Ever since 1967 Palestinian Arabs in Israel, the occupied territories or in exile in Arab and non-Arab countries have been united in their aspirations for a national state to solve their basic common needs. Then in 1993 chairman Yasser Arafat and his Palestine Liberation Movement (PLO) surprised most people by declaring they had come to an agreement in secret talks in Oslo with the Israeli government. This became known as the Oslo Accords. What is not so remembered is the fact that these agreements ignored the million Palestinians living inside Israel, most of whom believed the Oslo Accords stamped their future as Israelis for a long time.

As Israelis they certainly felt no need for Arab or Palestinian slogans to cement their national unity. On the contrary, as Muslims or Christians, they gained some advantages in the Israeli system. The Muslims, with their numerical superiority, got more parliamentary seats and posts allotted to them in the elections. Christians also improved their image in the Israeli-Jewish public eyes by working hard to keep their distance from the dreadful Islamists, especially during and after the terror wave of the mid-1990s. This fatal wave was carried out by suicidal squads attacking civilians in public places in Israel's main towns.

Zionist leaders and thinkers, since the inception of their movement, have been aware of their numerical inferiority in the area they chose to build their national state. This drove many to search for a manageable plan for handling the anticipated Arab opposition. One basic idea was to appeal to the European colonial powers to adopt the Zionist Project as part of their imperial plans. Theodore Hertzel spent years attempting to get his project adopted by the German, French and British. He even managed to meet the Roman Catholic pope and the Ottoman sultan, but all in vain because the Zionists' offer was unrealistic.

The first who were willing to accept the offered Zionist help were the British. (A policy clearly influenced by some of their odd religious beliefs, such as the theory that the British are descendants of the "lost tribes" – an idea prevalent in England during the 19th century). In addition to such ideas, the British were aspiring to build their empire. Palestine looked like an essential station to guard the Suez Canal and the naval routes to India.

The Zionists, beside looking for European support, thought Israel should strive to create an alliance of non-Arab states in the region, i.e. Turks, Persians and Ethiopians. Many felt the Jews were uniquely qualified to lead the non-Muslim and non-Arab minorities in the Middle East, i.e. the Lebanese, Egyptian Christians, Syrian Druze, Alawite extreme Shiites, Iraqi Kurds and Southern Sudanese and others opposed to the Sunni Muslim/Arab hegemony. Thus for the past 50 years Israel has extended a helping hand to Iran, Turkey and the Lebanon. They also granted limited military aid to the Kurds in north Iraq, the Southern Sudanese and the Druze and Maronites in Lebanon on different occasions. In most cases these endeavors did not last. Today Turkey is the only ally Israel has in the region (with the exception of Egypt and Jordan with whom a "cold" peace agreement was reached).

The concept on which Israeli foreign policy is based differs little from the domestic policy towards the Arab minority. The religious chasm separating the Arab minority invites Israeli manipulation and some government officials have adopted the old colonial traditional system of "divide and conquer." Such a policy towards Arabs has been growing in Israel ever since 1948.

Nazareth's population was allowed to remain in their homes because Israelis believed Christian churches around the world would not tolerate the deportation of their faith community.

When attempts were made by army units to deport Muslims from Nazareth, the Christian clergy refused to coöperate and rallied to protect them. The Communists also, both Christians and Muslims, opposed anti-Muslim moves and at the time they were quite influential because they had warm relations with Israeli left-wing cabinet ministers and were the only Palestinians who supported the establishment of a Jewish state. Besides, their relationship to Moscow and the Soviet Union helped, because their comrades in Prague were Israel's main military hardware suppliers.

The "divide and conquer" strategy was constantly refined by Israel's first cabinet which included a minister mandated to carry out this policy–Bikhor Shitrit, minister of minorities. A native Jew from Tiberias, Shitrit was a veteran of the Palestine police force with a lot of experience with Arab communities. Israel's official archives called him the most liberal of Israel's first cabinet and often he interfered in favor of those whose homes and stores had been looted, preventing the Army from deporting others, including my village, and was busy trying to win Arab "notables" who could better serve Israel's intentions. His primary goal was to attain Arab recognition of Israel and the signing of a peace agreement with them, as he told me on many occasions, but he also wanted to weaken Arab solidarity to make this accord possible.

The first group of Arabs willing to spin off the Arab line were the Druze–a unique, extreme Shiite Muslim sect. They joined forces with the Jews during the 1948 war and most of their able-bodied men fought in Israel's army as well-paid "volunteers." By 1957 this military service was imposed as a regular duty on Druze males on lines much like those incumbent on Jews–except Druze women were exempt from service, unlike the Jewish women. The Druze notable who "asked" that Druze men be called for compulsory military service won a "prize" and they were recognized as a separate religious sect in Israel, independent from other Muslims.

Christians were also encouraged to follow suit, starting as well-paid volunteers in Israel's army. The Israelis launched this effort to "win" the Christians during the troubles in Lebanon of 1957-1958. At the time the Americans were attempting to build an anti-

Soviet pact, known as the Baghdad Pact. The Lebanese president, Camille Shama'on, joined this along with the Turks, Persians, Iraqis and Jordanians. Left-wing groups, backed by Egypt and Syria, were opposed to this coalition. Some interpreted this as a Muslim alliance against a Christian president. Lebanon became tense and war seemed imminent. Israeli specialists decided this was the proper time to launch their attempt to win native Christians to their side, since they tended to be pro-Lebanese since it was the only Arab state where Christians dominated.

I was one of the young Christians "invited"to join this new brigade. The military governor of my village Major Joseph Qidmi, in trying to persuade me, gave me his word as an officer that I would be given the chance to join an officers' training course and be an officer within a year. I had some other questions, so asked: Why did the minister of defense not call me, like every Israeli citizen in my age group, for compulsory military service? Why ask me to volunteer if I was just a potential mercenary? If I were to serve in the army, would my father would be able to once again till his fathers' land, which the Israeli government had confiscated prior to this for the benefit of a Jewish settlement? Major Qidmi was unable to answer my "political" questions, but could only assure me on his honor that if I were to accept his offer, he would see to it that I become an officer in the army. I refused.

Most Christians approached with such proposals also refused to join, on similar grounds. It was an obvious attempt "to divide and conquer" the Arab minority. When it couldn't manipulate the Christians, the Israeli establishment changed tactics and seemed quite successful luring Bedouin Muslim nomads into military service. The Israelis kept up their efforts to influence the Christians. When the Lebanese began to squabble over the Baghdad Pact, the Israelis tried to persuade Christians in Israel to "volunteer" for military service. They were still at it 20 years later during the early stages of the civil war in Lebanon. Even then, the attempt to recruit Christian Arabs in Israel to support Lebanese Christian-separatist tendencies was rebuffed by most.

Joseph Abu Khalil, editor-in-chief of *Al-a'mal,* the official organ of the Lebanese Phalange Party, admitted in a TV interview with Giselle Khouri that in November 1998 he had visited Israel hoping to establish a pro-Lebanese "lobby." Once there, he found some 80 Maronite students registered in Israel's universities, but all of them resisted for they were active members of national Arab groups supporting the P.L.O.

In spite of their poor track record, the Israelis once again in the eighties, as their troops occupied Lebanese territory (in alliance with the right-wing Christian militia "Lebanese Forces"), the prime minister issued a public letter calling young Christian citizens to volunteer for military service, assuring them the army in principle welcomed Christian volunteers. This "invitation" was doomed to failure because the horrific crimes known as the Sabra and Shatilla massacre (against the civilian Palestinian refugees) precluded any possible support for Lebanese Christian militias from their Palestinian Christian neighbors who lived in Israel.

When Israeli agents tried once again to recruit "volunteers" in September 1991, the local councils of the Christian villages, such as Mia'elya, felt they had to denounce this government policy publicly, not just reject it privately. This was to be expected for these were direct descendants of those Christians who were the first Arabic speakers who called for a united, Arab, secular, national state. Some of their Muslim neighbors were critical of such Arab nationalism, accusing them of embracing Arab nationalism to cover their anti-Muslim motives and that it was really an attempt to divide the Muslim *Ummah* (nation) into Arabs and Ottomans and rid themselves from the rule of Muslim religious caliphs. This accusation was not entirely off base, for the Christian minority was seeking a common denominator where all Arabs, despite their religion, could embrace a commonality that would lead them all to equality in the end.

Who knows when the Israelis will try to splinter the Arab Muslim-Christian bonds again? It would seem that the Israeli police's failure to defend the Christians in Kafr Yaseef in April 1981, in Tura'an 1997 and in Nazareth in December 1988 and again in April 1999 were obvious signs of an Israeli element which tolerates anti-Christian violence, hoping the resulting chaos and the violent attacks against Christians may serve in encouraging them either to emigrate from the country or bring them under the umbrella of the Israeli establishment which is ready to embrace them – only if and when they break their ties to their Muslim neighbors.

David Ben Gurion, Israel's first prime minister and the most prominent of its founders, was a firm advocate of the "divide and conquer" policy. He confided in his diary and to his aids what he really wanted was to "divide and convert" the Arabs of Palestine and thus was worried about the Christian clergy's reaction to such a campaign. A Ben Gurion aide, Yehushoa' Cohen, who served as his bodyguard, neighbor and personal friend during the time he lived in Kibbutz Sdeh Boker, told me Ben Gurion publicly discussed plans on how to encourage Arabs to convert to Judaism. Another aide who confirmed this to me was Israel's sixth president, Chaim Hertzog, who heard of this plan while he was an officer in military intelligence in the Southern Front Command.

Ben Gurion was a secular Jew who envisioned a homogeneous community within modern Israel. He was so keen on this, for over a decade he blocked the introduction of TV in Israel after such broadcasts were standard phenomena in most neighboring countries because he felt American, French, Russian and especially Arab films would prevent his national dream of a "melting pot" from coming true. He believed Jews coming from Arabic-speaking lands should forget their previous culture and become Hebrews, if not Jews as well. He established an official committee of inquiry that recommended Arab children should be driven to Hebrew boarding schools so they would become Hebrew. The reasons given for rejecting these plans were financial – and religious. Religious Jews were invariably opposed to intimate relations between Jews and Arabs, especially if it entailed any social relations between young men and women. Israeli financial reserves during the 1950s were being stretched to absorb the new immigrants – pouring out of the burning furnaces of Eastern Europe or from Arab countries.

The policy of pressuring non-Jews to convert in order to be accepted as Israelis still goes on today – especially with new immigrants from the ex-Soviet states, many of whom were non-Jews who arrived in Israel with their Jewish spouses. In case of divorce, they are given two options–convert to Judaism or be expelled from the country. The conversion policy is no longer targeted at Arabs officially. For them, Israel regards military–or security–service as sufficient proof as to their loyalty as an Israeli Arab.

Still, the Druzes main complaint in rallies and demonstrations asking for improved status and services is that they "serve as Jews, but are treated as Arabs." Their compulsory service in Israel's army since 1957 (voluntarily since 1948) has not given them equal status to the Jews. Certainly they are far from equal economically, educationally or in civil services. The Druze claim they have lost more than 600 dead in Israel's war–with twice that number injured and maimed. Some Druze officers have risen in the military ranks, but they claim they are not treated as equals. One Druze officer, Colonel Amal Asa'ad, a paratroopers' brigade commander claimed on Israeli TV during his electioneering campaign to Israel's Knesset in 1999 that he was barred from visiting a military base while on duty. He was stopped with his Jewish soldiers until he managed to contact the army's high command. Zayd Muhsin, known as "Yigael," another Druze colonel in Israel's reserve forces who served as an advisor to the late Prime Minister Yetshaq Rabin in 1993, told me he was shocked when the Israeli government rejected his proposal to give a small, deserted Jewish settlement on the outskirts of his village Jat to homeless Druze veterans.

In Israel the Zionist's original theme keeps being played out: Israel is an exclusively Jewish state where non-Jews are only tolerated and may become citizens provided their influence is too small to affect the Jewish hegemony. If the Arab community is divided on religious lines–or any other way–they must be treated separately to foster divisions and promote the Jewish policy of "divide and conquer." One sad illustration of this policy took place in April 1981 when a tragic, but quite common, squabble happened at a soccer game between two neighboring villages in Western Galilee which caused the death of a young Druze. Two days later, as a group of Arab leaders were negotiating a traditional peace agreement (*sulha*), a large police force was deployed in the fields separating the two villages—Julis and Kafr Yaseef. Suddenly a crowd of heavily armed Druze from Julis arrived seeking revenge against the Christian village. A police force of 60-armed officers virtually did nothing to prevent the ensuing pogrom. Houses, cars, stores and workshops were torched. Three people were shot dead, others were injured. Only one police officer behaved with honor for he blocked the entrance to the high school and told the mob's ringleaders they would only enter the school over his dead body.

This slowed the massacre, but the other officers refused to act claiming they had insufficient arms to do anything and were waiting for reinforcements—which did not show up for two long hours of terror and looting. I interviewed General Hayem Avinoa-'am, the north district police commander a few days later, who assured me the police knew the perpetuators and they would be brought to justice. Some 20 years have passed, yet not one of those criminals who acted in front of 60 armed police witnesses have been convicted in court. The World Council of Churches partly compensated the damage in Kafr Yaseef, but the cost of the rituals for the traditional "peace" was paid from the Muslims' Waqf reve-nues—collected to help needy Muslims, repair Muslim mosques, subsidize the maintenance of Muslim cemeteries or meet similar community needs. In Israel these funds are run by Jewish officials, so the ministry of religious affairs and the prime minister's advisor on Arab affairs decided to finance peace celebration between Druze and Christian from these Muslim funds—a typical demonstration of how the Israeli "civil servants" treat the minorities.

The pogrom against Christians of Kafr Yaseef was not an iso-lated incident. I know several similar cases where Israeli police watched or turned aside as violent anti-Christian mobs attacked. The police treated them as common crimes but investigations bore no fruit, even in Abu Snan near Acre where anti-Christian vio-lence went on almost nightly for months in 2000. Everyone except the police command knew a clandestine group was trying to scare a Christian activist from supporting a Druze candidate for the post of mayor. Similar crimes went on in Rameh and other villages––

with identical results. The police were either lazy or incompetent.

Nazareth faced a similar incident two decades later, but since this is the town of the Annunciation, even though the police force stood by while this pogrom went on for two days, the world's press was watching and this had an impact. It was soon public knowledge that Israeli police ignore Arab complaints and instead implement the government's policy of letting Arabs fight it out between themselves, the better to "divide and conquer." This, in spite of the fact that Nazareth was the only urban Arab town which went through the 1948 war virtually unscathed – mostly due to the coöperation between the elected Muslim mayor, Yousef Muhammad Ali Fahoum, of this largely Christian town and the Christian clergy and lay leaders.

Fahoum had few illusions about the dominating Palestinian national leadership and was one of many Arab leaders who were terrorized by the Mufti Haj Amin al Husseini's policy against the opposition. His home was burned after an attempt on his life had failed and he fled to Syria where he spent most of the 1936-1939 years of unrest. Because of his experience, Fahoum decided in 1948 that unlike many other Arab mayors of threatened towns, he was going to keep the townspeople from leaving when the Jews attacked. He physically implemented this policy, for among other ploys, his son A'atef admitted to me that his father ordered him and other aides to let the air out of the tires from the few cars still in town to load furniture or take refugees out of town.

Since most of Nazareth was Christian with a few dozen European monks, doctors and missionaries thrown in, there was good reason for the Israeli commander, Ben Donkilman, sent to conquer the town to give strict orders his troops remember that millions of Christians around the world considered the town a holy site and would be watching how they behaved. Many nearby villagers also ran here for shelter instead of going into exile. Donkilman had orders to occupy the town and force the civilians out of town, but according to his biographer, Peretz Kidron, he refused to obey these orders of his immediate commander, General Hayem Laskov, and General Moshe Carmel, commander of the northern front, "unless they come in an official written document signed by the prime minister and defense minister David Ben Gurion." Such orders never came, but Donkilman was removed from his post as military governor of Nazareth.

In any case, Nazareth's mayor and Msg. Vargani, representative of the Roman Catholic patriarch, organized this small city into Galilee's main refuge center and later the Arab's ad hoc "capital" inside Israel. This modest and ancient town, chosen as Jesus Christ's hometown, continues to play a vital role in world history. The most recent archaeological digs confirm that historically this small Christian community has included "Jewish Christians," (relatives of the Lord) and several cults—including some who worshiped the Virgin Mary. But the town's size remained pretty constant throughout the first millennium.

Under the Crusaders' rule, for the first time Nazareth became the see of a bishop. When the Crusaders were expelled, Christian Nazareth was demolished by Mamluk soldiers in the 13th century and it was deserted for more than 300 years, except for the occasional pilgrim, traveler or rare visitor. A permanent Christian presence in town was resumed in the 17th century when the Franciscans were given permission to build a monastery (1620).

The Muslim population slowly dwindled in Nazareth so by the 19th century with the Franciscan monks plus other Christian institutions from different European churches permitted by the Lebanese prince, Fakhr al Din, to erect shrines on the site of the Annunciation and the ruins of the house of the Virgin Mary. Even the good offices of a friendly prince did not keep these monks wanting to build from having to pay off their nomad Muslim neighbors who extracted their share of the "booty" from the church builders. It took awhile for the monks to figure out. The holes they dug during the day were filled with dirt and filth at night. The stones added to the walls in daylight were demolished while the exhausted monks slept. When the father superior of the mission appealed to the Maronite patriarch for help, he supplied a group of local Christians to guard the shrines—and they, in turn, became the source for modern Nazareth's Christian community.

Later other Christian missions arrived to build schools, churches, hospitals and orphanages. After the Franciscans built their traditional Casa Nova hostel for pilgrims, a German came to start the first hotel, Germania (still functioning as the Galilee Hotel). Other Germans built the first mechanized wheat mill to replace the old water mills, the road for wagons from Haifa to Nazareth and they introduced electric light here – before any others in Palestine. Later German officers arrived to train Turkish soldiers in Galilee and chose Nazareth as their headquarters.

As the town grew, native Christians made their living serving pilgrims as translators, guides, guards, horsemen and servants. They offered merchant and craft services in the region, producing and repairing tools. German advisors to the Ottoman forces during World War I lived next to the German Templars who built the first hotel, grain mill, hospital and orphanage in town. The Russians in an effort to win over the native Christian put their most advanced school in Nazareth in the 19th century and the British also built many institutions, including a hospital, orphanage and church – and then put their police and military headquarters in the Russian compound which had been built for pilgrims and students.

Nazareth was poised for its golden age under Israeli rule when, with the tragic exodus of most Palestinian Arabs, this small market town became Israel's main Arab community. After 1948 it had the first high school Arab students could attend, the only active cultural club, the only printing presses – all run by church institutions except the first municipality-run school. More schools followed established by the Franciscans and the Southern Baptists. The YMCA ran the first cultural club and the presses were established by Archbishop Hakim, head of the Greek-Catholic church in Galilee and later the patriarch under the name Maximos VI Hakim (1967-2000). This Christian presence remains today with three hospitals, dozens of educational institutes, NGOs, charities caring for the poor, the elderly, youth, the disabled – mentally or physically, Muslim or Christian. Besides these, there is the largest basilica in Asia, more than 20 churches and chapels serving all the major churches from east and west – the Orthodox, Melkites, Maronites,

Copts, Anglicans, Baptists, Brethren, Christ Church, Nazarene, Seventh-Day Adventists, New Apostolic Church – to name a few.

This massive Christian presence did not help Nazareth maintain its Christian majority after 1948 when Muslims fled neighboring villages looking for shelter. Their higher birth rate plus the Christians' tendency to emigrate changed the demographic balance. Muslims now account for 60% of the 65,000 population and are called to prayer five times daily from the minarets of twelve mosques – one built during Ottoman rule, none under the British and eleven now under Israeli rule. They have a handful of active NGO's – for Boy Scouts, a charity for women and a kindergarten which is the only Muslim educational institute outside a mosque.

The Israeli government stripped Muslims of most of their community assets in various Israeli towns after 1948 – declaring it "absentee property" since much of it was registered under the "absent" High Muslim Council (which ceased existing in 1948). The Israelis accepted some responsibility for maintaining a bare minimum services for the Muslim community, like cleaning cemeteries or repairing old mosques. Most of the new mosques were built by private donations. The consequences of these short-sighted policies has been a dearth of schooling available to educate a liberal, open-minded generation of Muslim clerics, so Israelis now face a Muslim clergy who arrived from the West Bank towns of Hebron and Nablus after the 1967 war and who had been educated in the hostile belligerent atmosphere of the occupied territories by the Muslim Brothers militant.

Subsequently Nazareth has become a main center for the Muslim community. Most of the local Arab newspapers and the only Arabic radio station operate from Nazareth. Both major civil and religious courts in Galilee are stationed here and it is the only Arab center with cultural clubs and tangible economic activity. All this means the Christian and Muslim camps compete daily for their presence in town. Some 40 pupils attend Christian schools (none go to the absent Muslim schools). The town contains two dozen active churches, most centuries old, but at least ten built since 1948. Christian missionaries own most hospitals that serve the Arab population and are run by Arab management which highlights in Nazareth the Christians' wealth and Muslim poverty.

Muslims, as a majority, occupy a minority of the top positions in the town – three hospitals and bank managers, judges and school principals and faculties. This leaves many Muslims frustrated and humiliated. Educationally Muslims must choose to send their children to Christian-run educational institutions – or to let them go to inferior governmnet schools. Muslims have no private schools in town and "lucky" Muslims who manage to get accepted to Christian schools – where they must pay tuition to attend – are treated as equals, but as Muslims, since these Christian institutions hire no Muslim teachers and refuse to teach Islam's principles, so these young Muslims feel alienated in a foreign atmosphere. Thus 90% of Muslim youth go to Israeli-run schools.

Since Christians tend to be better educated, they find easier access to employment. Muslims are plagued by a high unemployment, have high drop-out rates from school and are frustrated because they feel unable to confront the government and win back their rights. "When you can't hit your mad camel, you take revenge against the saddle" an Arab proverb goes. Often the Nazarene Christians are targeted as being "rich with so many churches and public institution, while they're just a minority in town."

This friction suits the Israeli officials just fine and they egg on the Muslims to demand the missionary-supported schools teach Islam for the Muslim students just as they teach the Christian faith. When they refuse, it build resentment among the Muslim students and increases the influence of Muslim fundamentalists.

In 1997 the Nazareth municipal and tourism officials decided to demolish a decrepit government school and turn the empty square in the town center into an open plaza to welcome the expected influx of Christian pilgrims during the millennium celebrations. A few days after the building went down, a group of Muslims occupied the square with a huge tent claiming the land belonged to Shihab Al Din Waqf since the demolished building had contained, they claimed, a Muslim pulpit (*mihrab*). They declared their tent a mosque to carry on the name of Shihab Al Din.

Just who Shihab Al Din was turned out to be ambiguous. Granted, a 15-square-meter mosque had stood outside the school yard for at least a century, but few ever took notice of the site. Shihab Al Din, to local tradition, was a soldier in Saladin's army that had conquered the Crusaders in Hittin in 1187. But Saladin never conquered Nazareth. The Crusaders in Nazareth were unvanquished until 76 years later when they fell to the Mamluk Baybars in 1263. The small mosque at the site seemed to indicate that Nazarene Muslims had at some time venerated a Muslim *willy* (saint) by this name (not obligatory that his tomb is at this spot), but no Muslim traveler had mention Nazareth as a Muslim shrine nor home to any Muslim great authority. Thus the Muslim governments that dominated the town for 1,200 years never bothered to build a significant shrine until these Muslims put up their tent.

Israel's land authority, official owners of the land, appealed to the court asking the intruders be removed. The Muslims were unable to produce any legal proof for their claim except some religious declarations (*fatwa*) that claimed most of the land in Palestine is Muslim-owned since it was obtained by force in the seventh century by Muslim warriors. In the two years it took for the courts to decide the case against the intruders, a larger group of Muslims began agitating for a mosque to be built near the basilica of the Annunciation. This pitted the Muslim population firmly against the Christians and when local elections did not go their way, they retaliated violently attacking Christian property – damaging cars, breaking store windows and insulting Christians from mosques' loudspeakers, culminating in vicious attacks on Easter morning worshipers in 1999. Again, Israel's "strong" police force stood by watching the scene erupt.

This pogrom went on for two days until the international press raised a hue and cry against Israeli law enforcement policies. Finally General Alic Ronn, the northern district's police chief, "confessed" on Israel TV that the police misbehaved and they would do better in the future if anything similar should. The victims' hopes that the police would bring justice and make the mob leaders pay were unrequited. None of these leaders was arrested nor made to answer to any court. This, of course, encouraged the unruly Shihab Ed Din group who felt triumphant and kept pressing their demands for a new mosque.

Benjamin Netanyaho's right-wing government called a committee to resolve the dispute. Its chair, Moshe Katsav, minister of tourism (now president of the state) made no proposals before it was disbanded by the new government of Ehud Barak, who replaced Netanyaho. A new committee was formed with Shlomo Ben Ami, minister of internal security and foreign affairs, as chair. They concluded the intruders' rights should be recognized on grounds which the court found it baseless. This seemed an obvious attempt to bribe the Muslim community and win their voters. The Ben Ami committee did stipulate a mosque could only be built a year after the provocative tent and pejorative slogans had been removed from the square.

When the committee was asked about the police failure to defend peaceful citizens on their way to worship at the Basilica of Annunciation, Ben Ami asserted he was in no mood to discuss such "trivial" issues. Still, he failed to appease the Shihab al Din demonstrators in Nazareth's town center. Although they removed some of their provocative placards, they never refrained from using their noisy loudspeaker to spread their "sermons" – even during Pope John Paul II high mass in the neighboring Basilica.

Whatever else this proved, it is clear Muslim fanaticism is expanding and winning support in the community. This a obvious attempt by manipulative Israelis to serve their own political aims – with dangerous precedents. The first time Israeli "experts" tried to use Muslim fundamentalists against the leftist factions of the P.L.O. was in Gaza in the 1970s. Sheik Ahmed Yaseen, a schoolteacher, was encouraged to organize a counter group to challenge Dr. Hayder Abd Al Shafi's left-leaning group. This game ended when Yaseen was found storing arms caches. He was arrested, but the seed he sowed grew rapidly to become known as Hamas (the Muslim Resistance Movement).

A similar effort some 50 years ago also underestimated Islam's anti-Israeli stance. Israeli "experts" then recommended that since few Arabs owned radio receivers, (which the "experts" needed to distribute Israel's point of view), they made the absurd recommendation to force Arabs in Israel to listen to religious programs on radio or from loudspeakers installed in public places which targeted Arab centers so official announcements would be transmitted along with religious readings from the Koran–to pacify Muslims. This kind of thinking extrapolates to the shocking report of *New York Times* correspondent David K. Shipler who claimed the Gaza Strip military governor, Brigadier General Yitzhak Segev, confided to him that Israel was, in Gaza, encouraging fanatic Muslims to attack the Red Crescent offices and other more moderate left-wing leaders. Shipler claims this high-ranking Israeli officer told him he himself had transferred Israeli funds to these extremists and tried to promote their situation. Israeli support for these fanatic groups eroded when so-called coöpted Muslims began forming anti-Israeli underground movements like *Usrat al Jihad* (Holy War Family).

Fortunately, the Nazarene Muslim community has not been carried away by waves of hate and many Muslims seem eager to maintain the warm, cordial traditions of coëxistence with their Christian neighbors even in most unsettling times. During the millennium celebrations, Israeli police violently confronted demonstrators–killing 13 young Arabs demonstrating against Barak and Ben Ami approach. Alic Ronn, the police chief who had failed to defend Christians on their way to church in April 1999, now ordered the police to confront the demonstrates not only with tear gas and rubber bullets, but with anti-terror special snipers who picked off demonstrators from the top of houses, killing the 13 Arabs plus scores injured. The government convened a judicial committee headed by a chief justice to investigate the police and their harsh treatment of the Arab citizens.

All this unrest generated in Nazareth forced the church leaders in the Holy Land into unprecedented coöperation. The leaders of all Christians churches–Orthodox, Catholic and Protestant–agreed to close the gates of the town's famous shrines for visitors in November 1999, declaring this was to call attention to Israel's glaring failure to rule according to the law. The next year during the pontifical visit of John Paul II, Vatican officials made it clear they opposed blocking the entrance to the basilica by a Muslim radical institute. The Israeli government, left with no place to hide, appointed yet another ministerial committee to find a "solution." In February 2002 they announced that no mosque was to be built on this site, although an alternative location could be negotiated.

Basically, the Israeli establishment takes little notice of the Christian population. No Christian has ever been appointed to a significant governmental post, not even in the ministry of religions' affairs. Two Muslim Arabs have served as deputy ministers of health and foreign affairs; a Druze was appointed minister without portfolios and another served as deputy minister of PTT (Post, Telephone and Telegraph) – but no Christian has ever risen that high. It seems hard to believe there is not a Christian civil servants that has risen in the ranks in the Jerusalem headquarters of Israel's ministries. The highest post held by a Christian in the Israeli bureaucracy was as manager of an Arab department for juvenile delinquents' rehabilitation – the late Dr. Sami Jeraysi, a graduate of London School of Economics and Brandies University in Boston occupied this "senior" post for 40 years.

Fortunately such a hostile, anti-Christian attitude is not universal to all Muslims. The Palestinian National Authority (P.N.A) enacted laws protecting religious minorities' rights. The Christians, with less than 2% of the Palestinian people, have seven reserved seats of the 88 in the legislative council. (The dwindling Samaritan community of 320 members was allotted a secured seat.) The first Palestinian cabinet included two Christian members – Dr. Hanan A'shrawi, the outspoken Palestinian rights advocate, and the late mayor of Bethlehem and minister of tourism, Elias Fraij. The head of Yasser Arafat's staff is the Christian Ramzi Khouri and staff's membership includes at least three Christian advisors. Arafat has seemed intent on calming Muslim-Christian clashes, allowing these two Arab sectors to work together for common cause.

The Nazareth crises stirred a wave of interest in Middle East. Muslim *Ulama* (religious scholars) from Palestine and Egypt published a *fatwa* (religious ruling) condemning the plan to build a mosque in front of the Basilica of Annunciation. Some critics claimed there were ulterior motives for this *Ulama,* but as officials in Egypt, Palestine and Jordan went on record against building the mosque, national Muslim newspapers in Lebanon *(As Safir),* Jordan *(al-Ray)* and Kuwaiti *(al A'Rabi)* published angry articles denouncing the initiative to build the mosque a "Zionist conspiracy" to divide the national unity. A Saudi prince promised to finance building the mosque at a new location away from the holy Christian shrine.

This wide-spread segment of open-minded Muslims includes those who enthusiastically promote a Christian presence in order to consolidate a pluralistic state; some want Christians in their neighborhood as a bridgehead for a dialogue with the Christian world; others simply feel affinity to their peaceful hard-working neighbors. The most common popular adage to justify and support good relations with Christians (and other non-Muslims) says: "The Prophet urged his followers (to maintain good relations) with neighbors, up to the seventh." The Koran states, "We have created you from a male and a female and divided you into nations and tribes that you might get to know one another. The noblest of you in Allah's sight is he who fears him most. Allah is wise and all-knowing" (Koran 49:13). In one Hadith Prophet Muhammad says "Those who cause injury to a *Dhimmi* are hurting me."

Islam's traditions of tolerance has not been lost. The exiled Algerian prince Abd Al Qader Al Jazaeiri, gallantly intervened on behalf of the Christians in Damascus during the 1860 massacres despite the fact that as a freedom fighter he had fought the "Christian" French colonialism in his homeland. Many other friendly Muslims have appreciated the benefits of a Christian-Arab community. Prince Hasan Ben Talal, previous crown prince of Jordan, published a friendly book on Arab-Christians urging them not to emigrate "since the current wave of what is called Muslim fundamentalism will come to its end soon, as in the case of any movement that consumes its driving power. And this is what was the fate of the waves of those movements fuelled by sheer sentiments." Prince Hassan appreciates the cultural, economical, and historical role of this minority: "The Christian Arabs commit a major mistake if they are driven by fear of future developments in the Arab World. Mistaken are those who voice fear of their future since these fears are threatening the Arab Muslims as well" (1995:134).

Another appeal was heard in the aftermath of the Copt massacre in al-Kasheh, the upper Egyptian township, on the last day of the 20th century. A most prominent Arab journalist, Muhammad Hassanain Haykal, appealed to Muslim Arabs not to underestimate this exodus of Christians from their country, for he warned this would completely change the human and cultural scene and impoverish the region if the Christians emigrated. Muslims need be aware, he said, of the unique sources of their heritage and diversified culture and what a disaster would befall the region if Christians felt, rightly or wrongly, they had no future in this region, leaving Muslims with no neighbors other than Jewish-Zionist Israel (Haykal 2000).

The accelerated emigration of native Christians from Egypt, Lebanon, Iraq and Palestine has made a wide circle of Arabs rather anxious. Prince Talal Ben A'bd Al Aziz (brother of King Fahd of Saudi) published a plea in favor of the native Christians, asking Arab regimes to study how to help them feel secure, and to discuss "if possible how to encourage those who emigrated to return." First published in the elite Lebanese newspaper, *Al Nahar,* this article was widely reprinted in many regional newspapers and received ample affirmation. There is growing support from prominent Muslim thinkers who proclaim rather vociferously how proud they are of their friendship with Christian Arabs and how Muslim-Christian co-existence is a yardstick to genuine patriotism and to a basic national, progressive, modern point of view.

Still, there is a long way to go to forge an Arab consensus on the basics tenets for a Muslim-Christian understanding. A major hurdle is the rejection of most Muslims for pluralistic ideas and a secular state. Dr. Yousef Hasan, a diplomat from the United Arab Emirates, calls for a dialogue between Muslims and Christians as two equal partners—yet he has nothing to say against Muslim states that restrict Christian teaching and blames those who accuse Muslim clergy of supporting terrorist groups but refrain from blaming Catholics and Protestants in Northern Ireland for similar behavior – ignoring the fact that spiritual leaders in Ireland meet often to pray together and condemn the violence, while Muslim spiritual leaders seldom condemn the use of violence.

Native Christians basically take three stands on Muslim fundamentalism: A few extremists justify the movement hoping it represent an anti-Zionist and healthy reaction. Israel's Knesset member Azmi Bishara represents this view. Many native Christian, because of the its all-encompassing dominance, are in total despair and have lost interest in any public discourse or hope to influence future. These want this storm to pass (and this is prevalent in Egypt where Copts don't care to run for political office or even to vote- – and then emigrate at the first possible opportunity "for the sake of their children's future." The other extreme search for allies – as did the Lebanese who allied themselves to Israel.

Inside Israel many Christians feel letdown from all sides – the Christian community in the West – especially the Americans – and the wider public inside their Muslim countries. In response they try hard to win favorable Jewish public opinion who are threatened by the same forces. Many, more in the past, volunteer to serve in the army or the border police force whenever there is a violent clash in their neighborhood – since by joining forces with the Israelis, non-Jew can win acceptance from Israelis.

Yet most Christians remain, at least for now, faithful to their own traditions. They partake in the general struggle to improve life for all their neighbors – Muslim and Jewish. Some feel fate has destined them to the wearisome role of being a bridge for different cultures and religious groups. This produces a lot of insecure in their midst and they are tired or annoyed that they constantly have to prove their loyalty.

Another writer who sees the current wave of extremism as unsustainable is W. Montgomery Watt. He finds that although Muslim religious scholars are enthusiastic regarding the revival of Muslims to their faith and their attempts to faithfully follow the example of the first Muslim community, "while for the masses the resurgence of Islam is essentially a reaffirmation of Islamic identity, for the conservative *Ulama* it is also a chance to recover the influence in the community which they have lost during the last century. Because of their deficient information about the modern world, this attempt, even if for a time successful, is bound to end in failure. A modern state cannot be run on the basis of medieval ideas" (Watt 1979:240). He is also sure the essential needs of the modern state will force society to change and predicts a liberal trend to come forward in the Muslim communities. The Israeli government made a step in the right direction when a decade ago it approved a Muslim college to educate teachers under the auspices of a Sufi order known for emphasizing peaceful principles. They hope such a school may provide an alternative to those Muslim clerics who came to the fore after being edcuated in Muslim Brothers' militant Islam in the West Bank towns of Hebron and Nablus.

For the time being we still are facing grim days. Christian Arabs in Israel, Palestine and neighboring states are misunderstood and have poor relations with both Muslims and Jews. They also suffer from internal divisions among Christian as well. The negligence of the Israeli government has boomeranged and it is living with the consequences of not promoting a liberal, open-minded generation of Muslim clerics in Islam's tolerant tradition. So the Israeli establishment has failed to provide an alternative to the Muslim clerics who came to the fore after the 1967 war after being educated in Muslim Brothers militant Islamic style from the West Bank towns of Hebron and Nablus.

The Israeli's failure to meet the basic needs of the Muslim community inside Israel and to demolish many mosques in deserted towns and villages—or use them for secular purposes—has created unnecessary hostility among frustrated Muslims who feel powerless and unable to confront the government and win back their rights. This, coupled with the Israeli's failure to offer Muslim children proper education in schools of their liking, added to the failure of the Israeli police to enforce respect to law and order, helped implode the pan-Arab secular ideology that united Arabs, increased the influence of Muslim fundamentalists and prepared the ground for conflicts such as the Shihab Ed Din crises.

16

Where to now?

"Fear not, little flock; because it is your Father's plea-sure to give you the kingdom" (Lk 12:32).

As we speed into the third millennium, a renewed interest in religion seems to swirl around us. Unfortunately the first victim of this turbulence in the Middle East may be the small native Christian minority. Those few children of the ancient Christians who survived over a millennia the long siege of the Muslim over-lords are about to be annihilated – not necessarily in a dreadful massacre or a sudden wave of violent oppression, but in a slowly eroding attrition from economic pressures and the loss of hope.

The tradition of tolerance in Islam is a sacred historic heritage for most Muslims. Thus Arab Christians were able to survive the struggle of being a minority faith in such a circumstance. Now insurmountable difficulties seem to be accumulating. Arabs – Muslims and Christians alike – see a widening gap between them and their neighbors and feel they are being left behind while others gallop ahead to new horizons. The Arab economy is worsening, despite huge quantities of crude oil discovered in many Arab coun-tries. The social conditions of a vast majority of Arabs are deteriorating. There is little popular participation in national public life in Arab states (except Lebanon) contributing to a feeling of alienation, stress and frustration for the educated, who begin to forsake their homelands in search of a voice.

The success of Zionists in creating a Jewish state (with some foreign Christian support) in the heart of the Arab region, cutting off Egypt and North Africa from the Fertile Crescent countries of Syria, Iraq, Jordan and Lebanon presses hard on Arab pride. Arabs have more contact now than ever in the past with advanced Christian nations, both from personal experience and from watching televised programs "pour salt on the open wound." The Arabs see, smell and feel how far they need to go to catch up with those who overtook them in the last centuries. To overcome their frustrations they dwell on their history, consoling themselves that for centuries Arab-Muslims were more advanced than Europe, their scholars introduced the ancient Greek philosophers to Europe and they led the world in astronomy, medicine, mathematics and chemistry.

Since the Zionist menace was so imminent, it seemingly was the "easiest" way to unite the government and the people – a glue that has held them together for 50 years. This was a fatal choice, for it widened the cultural gap between Arabs and the industrial communities – making the Arab despots even stronger. The foreign enemy became an ever-ready excuse to delay any political reforms. To rule by emergency regulations became the norm. The external danger justified military rule and the suppression of any opposition. A vicious cycle dominated the Arabs' public life. Religion became a soporific and ancient clerics armed with superstition and obsolete theories came to the fore and the results were soon in as the relations between the different religious groups became toxic.

And so the young, especially Christians, deserted the Middle East in search of clean air and a space to maneuver – which appeared to solve their personal problems. Yet such short-term solutions brought even more problems – of global magnitude. How can we hope for accommodation between the two billion plus Christians and Muslims of the world, if this small minority of 15-20 million native Christians who had helped shape Arab culture as law-abiding and hardworking citizens for centuries can no longer live side-by-side with their Muslim neighbors? Who will build the goodwill bridge over this seemingly unsurpassable hurdle on the road to human understanding? Unless something intervenes, the Christian shrines in the Holy Land will become museums where pious pilgrims travel to empty, cold shrines. Anti-Muslim prejudice, especially within the native Christian emigrant communities in the West, will instigate more hatred instead of encouraging interest and curiosity about Islam and its practices. Anti-Muslim acts are constantly being reported, in the USA, Europe and Australia.

We need to export the experience of the native Christian minority which survived for over a millennia years inside Muslim states and culture to those newly established Muslim communities inside the Christian world in Europe and America, so that they may also be given a chance to flourish and contribute to their new homelands. Scholars tend to agree the apogee of Islam's treatment of Christian subjects occurred during the early days of the Umayyad caliphs in Damascus in the seventh century. Samir Khalil, SJ, from the *Pontificio Instituto Orientale* in Rome claims that in Arab history when native Christians were allowed to play a major role in society and when Muslim leaders did not lapse into fanaticism or ostracism they would experience a period of national renaissance. Fr. Khalil warns that fanaticism has always led to cultural impoverishment, but assimilation of another culture needs to be done harmoniously or it will provoke rejection syndromes, not unlike those that happen with organs transplants in a body.

Major differences exist between the days of the seventh century Arab renaissance and today. During that stormy period Muslims were self-confident, having conquering much territory and living in the euphoria of those astonishing triumphs. Today Arabs are deeply frustrated because they find it impossible to keep pace with industrial nations of the West and simultaneously deal with the problem of Israel implantation in their midst.

Fortunately the lot of most Arabs is improving. For the first time in centuries most Arabs live in independent and sovereign states. The discovery of vast oil reserves in the region has brought huge social upheavals, mainly economic, but with this concurrent systems for modern education, new medical treatments and hygiene methods – all causing major demographic changes. The traditionally docile class of small land owners and peasants working in the fields of others – a class which formed the main spinal column of the Muslim state for centuries – has declined drastically both in numbers and influence. The world's exploding technological advances coupled with the region's population explosions and the failure of the ruling classes to move towards industrializing their states creating jobs for the masses of unemployed was a disastrous formula. Young people flocked to urban centers seeking new opportunities only to find frustration.

Expanded opportunities for education only heightened pressures building as each new dead-end eroded hope for prospective jobs. There was no way to compete with the West, because even as the leaders achieved fabulous prosperity, this did not trickle down very far to relieve the misery and despair of the majority – a class of hopeless proletarian and potential fuel for any revolution.

Remembering and boasting about the golden days of their great empire stretching from the Atlantic Ocean in the west to China in the east did little to assuage their frustration and a lot to whip up desires to return to a genuine Islam and a powerful Muslim nation. Religion has been a major component. When the "Young Turks" deposed the Ottoman sultan in 1908 to turn their multicultural empire into a Turkish national state, the implementation was, in fact, strictly along religious lines. The Armenian and Assyrian Christians were the first victims of this "secular" state. The Arab kingdom born out of the ashes of the World War I, the Arab Syrian State as the Hashimite Arab kingdom of Damascus was officially called, formed a cabinet composed entirely of Muslim notables. Christians were excluded (Ridha 1979:254-255) despite the fact it was declared to be an Arab state of all those who speak the Arab language – Muslims, Christians and Jews. Under strong pressure from the Muslim clerics, Royal Prince Faysal agreed the constitution would affirm the king must be a Muslim.

The Young Turks coup also brought Arab secular nationalism

to the fore. Muslim Arabs soon realized the Arab language and culture united them with their Christian compatriots. It had been a blow when the Ottoman empire lost World War I and was disintegrated in 1918. When the Turk national hero Ataturk abolished the caliphate in 1924, that Islam is a multinational faith became evident. Arabs are not Iranians, Turkish, or Pakistanis. Arabs are those who speak Arabic as a mother tongue and take pride in Arab history and aspire to advance mutual Arab interests. But the Arabs–Muslims and Christians–had more burning issues to wrestle with as they watched the partition of their Arab homeland into some 20 states with ensuing conflicts and border disputes between Arab regimes, the failure of the Arab League to produce the minimal coöperation between them, and the collapse of Arab solidarity in the war against Israel, especially in June 1967.

This predicament produced deep frustration on one hand with widespread Muslim fundamentalism. Others came to believe in mutual Arab destiny, but they had to face the repeated failure of their ideals–the disintegration of United Arab Republic in 1962 and the defeat of the Egyptian, Syrian, Jordanian armies in June 1967–which made high national expectations appear to be based on mirages. Then as Arab peoples were overwhelmed by deep humiliation and despair, almost accidentally a radical change in mainstream public opinion coincided with the "black gold rush" – the discovery of huge quantities of crude oil in most Arab deserts.

The nomads of Saudia Arabia and its neighboring Gulf states, who were the least educated and most conservative Arabs, were thrown into leadership roles. These sheikhs of newly acquired funds started to seek respectability and influence. They bought Lebanese newspapers and hired Egyptian, Lebanese, Syrian and Palestinian writers to run their new media outlets–which began to spout their conservative-religious views (Sharabi 1987:123). Millions of worshipers began to pack the mosques and women's dress changed instantly. Worshipers even began to flock to the churches. Faithful, pious Copts (and Muslims) daily gathered outside an old church in Cairo to see the apparition of the holy virgin, Mary.

The Israeli military triumph brought many changes to Middle

Eastern culture by giving the Jews for the first time a say in the region's power struggle, on both military and cultural levels. For the first time they had to be consulted on the fates of biblical sites disputed by the Muslim faith and connected to Jewish history and religion–Mount Moriah, Solomon's Temple, Hebron's Tomb of the Fathers as well as other holy and historic locations like Sheila and A'natot, major historical sites from the Bible. Moshe Dayan, Israel's minister of defense at the time, rather than risk further confrontations with the Muslims on religious themes, decided to leave the Temple Mount in Muslim hands because of its special place in the Muslim faith and because Orthodox Jews did not allow Jews to enter the area since such a walk might desecrate the Holy of the Holies. Dayan also decided Jews were entitled to share with Muslims the mosque built on the Cave of Machphela, the burial site their mutual father–Abraham, his wife Sara and others.

The 1967 Jewish victory drove both Arabs and Jews into the arms of Adonai-Allah, for contradictory ends. The Arabs went to seek help, while the jubilant Jews rejoiced that after 2000 years of exile they were able to return to Eretz Israel, the land of Israel, not just to the little state of Israel established in 1948. Now some Palestinian Arabs, both Muslims and Christians (a minority of about 150,000), were doomed to live with–and under–the first Jewish rule following the Nazi holocaust.

These Jews had gone to bed in the evening as unwanted aliens and discovered the next morning they were now in charge. The few Arabs who managed to escape becoming refugees faced a unique historical experience–living under the rule of historic victims who had reversed their roles to suddenly become colonial oppressor. The questions became: how does human suffering change people? Are they apt to become more empathic to minorities and their suffering, more attentive to the needs of others or do they turn a deaf ear to their cries? I witnessed the developing answers to these questions for more than four decades while working as a staff member of Israeli Hebrew newspapers, mostly the *Ha Aretz*. Jews who came from liberal regimes and communities were far more humane and restrained in their relations to Arabs–Muslims and Christians. Those from pre-Nazi Germany were entirely different from those who survived the Nazi atrocities and arrived later in Israel, as were those from the stable and "benevolent" monarchy of Morocco from those who fled tribal clashes and vicious military coups in Iraq or violence-stricken Algiers.

Over time I concluded that human beings are not "educated" nor tamed into becoming humane by suffering maltreatment and persecution, rather when they can, they try to flex their political muscles while maintaining control. Thus, after the 1967 war, Moshe Dayan, Israel's celebrated soldier, was planning to visit the USA and asked Prime Minister Levi Eshkol for advice on how to approach the American administration and public. Eshkol, one of the few wise and humorous Israeli leaders, advised Dayan to try to depict Israel as performing a role that mixed both the typical, miserable and scared Jew and the tragic, heroic, legendary Samson. "Simply try to play the role of miserable Samson," he said.

The Jewish-Muslim relationship has been subjected to extreme fluctuations throughout history. Jews of Yathrib welcomed Islam and supported the Muslim faith in the early days of Muhammad. The friendship turned bitter later with wild accusations exchanged, but overall Jewish-Muslim relations were usually better than those between Muslims and Christians or Jews and Christians. Both Muslims and Jews seemingly arrived at their mutual Golden Ages in Muslim Spain and when the Muslims were expelled from Spain in 1492, most Jews there fled for shelter to Muslim lands from North Africa to Turkey and other Ottoman colonies where Zionist leaders made a failed attempt to ally themselves to the Ottoman sultan—leaving unsolved the problem of Jewish relations with the mainly Muslim Palestinians and Muslim neighborhoods.

Until the mid-20th century Jews were forced into the classic victim role, but on being emancipated 50 years ago, they jumped to the other extreme and became oppressors—even though many Jews could not free themselves from the old mentality of the persecuted minority and victims of Gentile anti-Semitism. They had lived and developed such a mentality—and could not give it up.

Israel is the first practical test for the Jews after 2000 years in which Jewish moralists urged *others* to act within a moral code in treating those of a racial, national or religious minority. David Ben Gurion, Israel's first prime minister, was aware of this responsibility and rarely did he fail to reiterate the heavy yoke of Jewish morals and tradition he felt. His mantra was that Israel had come to fulfill the humane visions of the prophets and Jerusalem was to be a lighthouse to the nations. Yet he was a pragmatic statesperson who preached morals to his people wanting them to play role of an exemplar to the world. Unfortunately he turned a blind eye when his subordinate deported Palestinian peasants from their homes in 1948. Once he even instructed Yitzhak Rabin, then a young colonel, to force Arab civilians into exile out of their homes in Lydda and Ramleh and to justify this act, Ben Gurion invoke the traditional excuse of "security needs."

In 1954 I asked Ben Gurion what made him as minister of defense order the army to deport the friendly and peaceful Christian villagers from Iqrit and Kufr Bira'am two weeks after their villages were occupied by Israeli forces (without resistance). He answered this was a mistake and mistakes do happen. I pressed, "Then why was he opposed to permitting their return?" He claimed that if these villagers were permitted to return home, it would create a precedent and many other Palestinian villagers (who lived inside Israel, but away from their original homes) would ask for similar treatment. At the time I spent a day in his company (at his invitation) Ben Gurion was out of office and living in Kibbutz Sadeh Boker. He promised me that if he returned to the leadership of Israel he would do his best to compensate these "friendly" Maronites. A year later he became minister of defense and after few months was prime minister – but this pledge was never honored.

Uprooted Christian Arabs still struggle for compensation. In 2000 they welcomed Pope John Paul II and asked him to intervene on their behalf. The pope urged Israel to remedy this injustice and Israel's government gave one more pledge to do so – which did not materialize until 2004. Another Christian village deceived into leaving their homes for a short fortnight, Iqrit, appealed last June 2003 for the fourth time seeking help from Israel's high court.

Their plea was rejected on the grounds that the issue is political and the government used its legitimist discretion. Judge Dalia Dorner expressed hope the government might at some time in the future change her mind and allow them to return to their village.

Ben Gurion, though keen to follow in the footsteps of the Old Testament Jewish kings, was not himself religious so he used to meet regularly with Martin Buber, Israel's most famous modern philosopher who often advised the prime minister that the moral approach is the weapon of the frail, timid and weak and only the rare righteous and just king obeys with moral commands. Ben Gurion came to power less than three years after the Holocaust ended and he internalized the struggle for existence of the unarmed civilian Jews in Europe and the Jewish armed forces in Palestine. Within a few years Ben Gurion had openly allied Israel with the old imperialist states, Britain and France, in their last military attempt to extirpate the Arabs' hero – Gamal Abd al Nasser – and end his attempt to liberate Egypt from foreign military presence.

On the eve of the 1956 war, Israel's army imposed a curfew on villages near the "Jordanian border" – as it was at the time. Villagers at work in neighboring Jewish settlements the afternoon the curfew was declared – with no way of hearing about it – walked home after a long day in the citrus groves. They were stopped, identified and shot in cold blood by an Israeli soldiers who massacred 43 Arab citizens of Israel, including 15 children and women. Israeli military censorship prohibited local press from printing the news. A BBC correspondent flew to Cyprus to get the news out. Only then did Israel's censors allow news of the Kufr Qassem Massacre out locally. Ten officers were arrested and seven were convicted – but two years later they were back at home having been given a presidential pardon. At least one of these criminals was hired again to secure peace in a mixed Jewish-Arab township.

Ben Gurion's heirs were luckier because they were relieved of any immediate problems relating to the Israeli-Arab minority within their borders. From 1948 to 1967 the Arab League had declared their intent to "prepare" for a second round in the war with Israel. After the Arab's second disastrous defeat in 1967, Arab leaders met in a special summit in Khartoum and decided to adopt a policy "not to recognize Israel, not to negotiate with Israel and not to sign peace with Israel." This head-in-sand rhetoric offered the Israeli government the excuse to exclude the Arab minority inside Israel from playing any significant role in facilitating a dialogue between Israelis and Arabs on fears these citizens might become a Trojan horse in the service of the Arab side. The emergency regulations the British mandate authorities enacted in 1945 to suppress Jewish underground activities were now used by the Israelis to impose military rule on all Arab citizens up until December 1966.

Arab citizens of Israel who in 1948 were granted the franchise could elect or be elected to the Israeli Knesset and so they won back some of their basic rights as individual citizens by becoming integrated into Israel's political system. The opposition pledged to support their demands and the ruling party tried to win them, but for 55 years after Israel was established, no Arab citizen, Muslim, Druze or Christian, was appointed to a national post in the government, army, judiciary, police, banking system or any branch of academia, commerce or industry.

Finally in 2000 an Arab-Muslim was appointed chair of a government company responsible for youth, culture and sports' clubs (*Matnas* in Hebrew). His first week in office a postal carrier informed the new chair, Dr. Fayssal Azayzeh, a graduate of Harvard University, that he refused to serve him "since we don't serve in Arab villages." No Arab Christian has ever been appointed to a such a post because the Israeli-Jewish political establishment feels they can ignore the tiny Christian minority with impunity. The first Druze-Arab elected to a ministerial post (Saleh Tariff) in 2001 found himself a minister without a portfolio for few months (and later had to resign after accusations were leveled against him).

Unfortunately, the Christians problems are not just related to their Jewish and Muslim neighbors. They face too many internal struggles—between old and new churches. Their leaders carry grudges developed for millennia which precludes their coming together and forging a united front. Although for centuries most Arab-Christians were Orthodox, since Western missionaries and merchants came to the Middle East, many opted to go to new churches because the Greek overlords of the Orthodox church offered the faithful minimal care and spiritual guidance – causing many locals to turn for help to the Orthodox church of Russia, the Roman Catholics or the various Protestants. These Westerners were also in a position to offer help to those who accepted their doctrines – a boon in the short run, but after awhile this created rifts dividing the native Christian communities – contributing to the danger of its eventual elimination.

The first steps towards coming together to discuss coöperation took place during the last decades of the 20th century after Vatican II and the renewed emphasis on ecumenical relations with other churches (and monotheist faiths) and after establishing the World Council of Churches (and its regional Middle East Council of Churches). Unfortunately, this movement is still in its initial steps. Middle Eastern Christians are just as divided as the rest of Christendom – sorely demonstrated for all to see. The different Christian Boy Scout troops march under diverse banners, so Christians with 2% of the Israeli population, need six different organizations for their children's Scouting program – even though the Jews, Muslims and Druze manage one group per each religious community.

Then there is Easter and Christmas. The Catholics and Protestants celebrate Palm Sunday and Easter while the Orthodox are fasting and preparing for Good Friday – with a sad repeat on Christmas, to the dismay of all the faithful. The church hierarchy turned deaf ear to all appeals until finally most of the local communities in Galilee's villages agreed among themselves to celebrate Christmas' festivals according to the Gregorian (Catholic) calendar and Easter according to the Julian (Orthodox) calendar – a grass-roots ecumenical movement that works but still can't pressure those at the top to give up their intransigence.

The missionary offered much help to the natives – Christians and Muslims, alike – by introducing modern health and educational systems, but besides causing much of the splintering in the Christian community, in many cases those responsible for the education were such patriots of their homelands they followed their system was geared to make over the natives into model French, British, Italians, Russians or Americans. Students from Syria, Palestine or Lebanon were educated to live and love other lands, learn their language, history, literature and culture. In effect, missionary schools functioned as travel agencies promoting the Christian community's movement away from their homelands.

Such a divided house may appear headed towards extinction, but there are bright spots: the Anglicans, Lutheran and other Protestants, like the Latin and Orthodox churches, are involved in a long process of Arabization and seem to be trying to encourage their faithful to coöperate with their compatriots. The first Anglican Arab bishop, Najeeb Quba'in, was installed in 1976 and changed its name to the Arab Episcopal Evangelic Church. The 32 institutions of education and medical charity the Anglican missionaries founded are still serving, mainly Arab Muslims.

The Roman Catholic church went through a similar process during Pope Paul VI's historic pilgrimage in 1965 when he raised Fr. Hanna Kaldani to the bishopric, making him patriarchal vicar in Israel. After Vatican II, their educational institutes were revolutionized so French, Italian or English ceased to be the main tutorial language in the schools and emphasis was made on their own rich history, not just that of the mission-sending country. Currently Catholic schools in Palestine and Israel use Arabic as their first language with Hebrew as a second language. The climax of this revolutionary process came in 1988 when Pope John-Paul II decided a native Catholic should occupy the highest seat of the Jerusalem church and promoted a native of Nazareth, Michel Sabbah, as the first native to the post the Crusaders initiated in 1099. With this ordination, he became the leader of the Catholic church in the Middle East. Later on, the Assyrian Catholic Patriarch Ignace-Mussa I Daoud was promoted to the head of the Pontifical Congregation of the Oriental Churches, succeeding an Italian.

Other churches took similar, but essential ecumenical steps. The Roman Catholics included in their hymnal selections from Byzantine and Evangelical hymns to make it possible for guests from non-Latin churches comfortable. The Middle East Council of

Churches also brought those from various Christian churches together, encouraging them to discuss issues of mutual interest. Other grass-roots groups gathered laity and clergy to celebrate and pray together – like al Sabeel, the Theology of Liberation Center, launched by the Anglican, Reverend Naim Ateek. In Nazareth, some Mennonites, Orthodox, Catholics, Baptists and other churches worked together building a religious, cultural and economic site – a re-constructed village depicting where Jesus spent most of his life in the Holy Land. The Nazareth Village project is a wonderful coöperative venture, heralding a new era.

Unfortunately some Western Christian observers consider criticizing Israel's maltreatment of its non-Jewish citizens an "immoral" act. What is so immoral or "political" in condemning a government's racist policy of confiscating the lands of some citizens in order to build houses or soccer fields for the exclusive use of others? There is a misunderstanding of Christian values of any who condone governmental armed robbery of its citizens – especially when this policy is carried out for reasons of ethnic cleansing. Israel's own high court of justice ruled in 1999 in an unprecedented verdict against such practices.

In the Qaa'dan case the court ruled government lands should be accessible to any citizen on equal terms. For 50-plus years, the Israelis have prohibited Arabs from living in new Jewish settlement (built usually on Arab-confiscated lands). A young Muslim couple appealed to the court, claiming as Israeli citizens they had been denied the basic right to live wherever they choose in their homeland. The Israeli defense claimed the house in question was built in a Jewish settlement, Katseer, on Jewish Agency lands for Jewish settlers, and the Jewish Agency – as landowners – was entitled to serve exclusive Jewish needs. This argument was rejected in court since the land was government owned and later transferred to the Agency. The government is not entitled to allot public land for the exclusive usage of Jews or Arabs without securing the others' right on similar terms. The Zionist establishment is still struggling with its drastic implications and so seem unable to come up with new regulations preventing Arabs from living in new Jewish settlements.

Still, Israel is a unique Jewish state. Any observant Jew or atheist with a Jewish background, even if just one grandmother was Jewish, is entitled to automatic Israeli citizenship on arrival at the Israeli airport – in special cases even before arriving. They also receive financial grants to help them start life in their "old-new" homeland. A non-Jew, like myself, even a person descended from ten generations of those who lived and were buried in this country, needs to go through a long, tedious, red-tape-filled process to make it possible for an elderly law-abiding relative from Lebanon to come on a short family visit – even during the days Israel and the Lebanese Christians were allies. But the Israeli anti-Arab discrimination hardest to bear is the wide-scale confiscation of private farmlands – 30% of the Muslim Bedouin families, 50% of the Druze, 69% of the sedentary Muslims and 63% of the Christian families have suffered expropriation of some land (Smooha 1980:100).

The Israeli policy is quite consistent towards Christians and Christianity – far from friendly or fair. Native Christians have been treated as enemies since 1948 – despite the fact they tend to be a law-abiding and peaceful segment of society. Those deceived by the army into leaving their villages during the war have not been allowed to return, in spite of Israel's high court of justice verdict on their behalf in 1951.

Israelis officially accept the rights of individuals to change religion and permit foreign missionaries to enter the land, but once there missionaries are not free to preach. According to Israeli law missionaries face jail or deportation should they offer "any material help" to new believers or promise help to potential converts. Thus fanatical groups like the *Yad la akhiem* (who are officially and publicly supported by the Israeli establishment) specialize in harassing and persecuting any missionary who dares to offer hospitality to a potential convert or subsidy for a child to attend summer camp which they claim is nothing but a bribe. There are clandestine criminal groups who firebomb the synagogues of Messianic-Jews and even Conservative or Reform Jews – as well as worship centers of Catholics, Anglicans, Baptists, other Evangelical churches in Jerusalem, Tiberias, Jaffa-Tel Aviv, Acre and other towns.

Proverbs tells us "the wringing of the nose bringeth forth blood" which sheds a little understanding on why certain Muslim scholars today are able to make young people believe they become "martyrs" (*Shahid* in Arabic), entitled to special heavenly privileges when they commit suicide in the midst of a crowded bus. Current Muslim "revivalism" or "fundamentalism" is almost entirely unopposed, even within the ranks of the mainstream Muslim religious establishment, like that of Al Azhar University in Cairo. Even they insist the crime of apostasy deserves nothing less than death penalty and any sexual relations between two people (of the same or opposite sex) outside marriage bonds makes them deserve to be flogged. Stealing anything worth more than 4.6 grams of gold should be punished by having the thief's right hand amputated (Shukri 1978:490-495, Abd Al Fattah 1983:169).

Barbarity seems infectious. How else can you explain why Libyan leader Mua'amar al Qadafi supplies arms to the I.R.A. underground in Northern Ireland and finances the Muslim separatists' in the Philippines – and why Osama Bin Laden won a worldwide plebiscite held on Al Jazeerah Space TV Channel as the most popular hero of the Muslims in Arab countries, as well as in the non-Arab Muslim lands of Indonesia, Pakistan and Afghanistan?

Nor is tolerance promulgated. The leading Middle Eastern Muslim states of Saudia Arabia, Egypt, Kuwait, the United Arab Emirates, Libya and Iran all refuse to permit Christian missionaries practicing inside their borders and arrest any Muslim who converts to Christianity. Amnesty International reports these countries harass and arrest such "criminals" until they repent, repudiate their faith and return to Islam. The Taliban won wide acclaim as a most pious Muslim society in August 2001 by arresting German and American missionaries and a dozen Afghani converts whom they threatened to kill – with no opposition from any Muslim scholars.

Still Muslim public opinion and political establishment are changing somewhat due to the influence of mainstream culture. In most places they have stopped trading and keeping slaves and slave-concubines (except in Sudan and Mauritania), maiming shoplifters by amputating their limbs (except in Saudia Arabia and

Saddam Hussein's Iraq), stoning to death a young woman who ran away with her lover from a wicked husband who deserted, neglected or battered her (but most Muslim legal systems still recognize the right of a husband, father or brothers to lenient treatment – if they kill her). Muslim governments no longer officially impose on non-Muslims the *Dhimmis* status, the poll tax known as the *Jizya* or wearing distinctive dress. Christians are allowed to build new churches (not just repair old ones), celebrate prayers in public places and ring their bells (except in Saudia).

Egypt was not, according to its constitution, considered a Muslim state (except for the king) until after its humiliating defeat in the 1967 war against Israel. Many voices began demanding a change so the 1971 constitution decreed Egypt consider the Muslim shari'ah as a main legal source – which happened in 1981. This met with opposition from the Coptic church as well as many liberal citizens, because it meant Christians in Egypt were to be ruled by a system that refused to allow them to testify as witnesses – except when both sides in the dispute were Christians. The severe penal code, not to mention the severity facing children from seven to ten years of and flogging permitted to those ten to fifteen years of age, may be why Sadat, who called himself the faithful president, opted not to adopt these laws.

Jihad, as a religious duty to conduct military expeditions "to raise high the word of Allah," defend the Muslim *Ummah* (nation) from a potential danger, expand the land of Islam and "encourage" non-Muslims to convert is considered obsolete by many since such a duty can be carried out today by peaceful means, according to mainstream Muslim scholars. The Koran ordered Muslims to share in jihad to secure a place in paradise – but this order was not heeded any more than our Lord's injunction to turn the other cheek.

An early Muslim sect, al Khwarij, adopted jihad as their cardinal Muslim duty, but this led to their own persecution by other Muslims and total extinction within a century. The second Muslim sect to embrace this rule were the infamous 11th-century Assassins – who again were killed by other Muslims. Currently we face the al Qaa'eda-style group of Assassins who are also doomed to die at the hands of Muslims. We must recognize, however, that such Muslims need motives. Obviously today's frustration of the Arab and Muslim millions drives and feeds many to such extremes.

Some have attempted to reform Islam—like the Ahmadi sect who adopted a new interpretation of the Koran which said that since Muslims are free to preach their faith, this precludes a need for jihad. Other philosophers like the Sudanese scholar Mahmoud Muhammad Taha posited there must be a modern, peaceful understanding of the Koran. Taha divided the Koran into two parts—the first promulgating a peaceful faith because it was written in Mecca at the time Muhammad was a persecuted peacemaker and the second written in Medina when Muhammad was presiding over his newborn state and leading troops to war. Taha was hanged by the Jaa'far Numeiri military regime in 1985. The Ahmadi leaders were exiled out of the Muslim states to England.

Out of this turmoil come current arch-terrorists like Osama Ben Ladin who launch heinous crimes against innocent people. Until 9/11/2001 and later, most Muslim scholars refrained from condemning suicidal attacks, allowing the Taliban fanatics take pride in such things as destroying ancient works of art with impunity. Osama Bin Laden's "al Qaa'eda" group seem to be following a historical Muslim practice called *Taqiyya* (which turned them into an underground) for it recommended some Muslim Shiites sects pretend not to be Muslim if they lived in non-Muslim lands if their beliefs were life endangering or even in some cases if their faith endangered their economic interests. Thus the Assassins were followers of a sheikh who educated them and released them to fulfill his com mands— killing Muslim caliphs, princes, Crusader knights and mainly Sunni *ulama* (scholars) or *qadies* (judges). These terrorists caused havoc and anarchy in the Middle East until they were rooted out by the Mongols from the east and the Mamluk Sultan of Egypt. Unfortunately their legacy outlived them to our current millennium.

The first suicidal attack in modern times in the Holy Land was by a squad of Japanese terrorists who allied themselves with the left-wing Democratic Front for the Liberation of Palestine

(DFLP). In 1972 they hijacked Sabena airliner and massacred its passenger in Ben Gurion Airport, outside Tel Aviv. The first Arab suicidal operation happened in 1984 inside "Israel's safe belt" of South Lebanon when a Lebanese young woman called Sana Mehaidli detonated a truck into an Israeli military convoy killing herself with some 20 soldiers. Mehaidli was not a Muslim fanatic but a member of the secular political party, the Syrian Social National Party. Similar suicides began taking place – including a classic assassination attack by Suha Bishara, a Christian-born Communist young woman who attacked the Lebanese general, Anton Lahd, who had coöperated with Israelis. This killing frenzy was triggered in February 1994 when an American-born fanatic, Dr. Barukh Goldstein, attacked the Machphela Mosque in Hebron, gunning down 29 Muslim worshipers and wounding hundreds more before he was lynched by the survivors. By October 8, 2001, the day the USA started its war against the Taliban regime and Osama Ben Laden in Afghanistan, Israel's newspaper, *Ha Aretz*, published the count: 100 Palestinian Muslims had committed suicide on an anti-Israeli death missions.

We can conclude that Israel has failed to win Arab approval or force its will on a significant portion of them. The US' support for the Israelis has antagonized Arabs and radical Muslim circles. Many Muslims today feel culturally threatened, politically op pressed and economically exploited by a "Christian-American" system and seeing TV scenes of Israeli soldiers, tanks and planes attacking Palestinian civilians and children exacerbates this anger.

The famous American-Jewish scholar on the Middle East, Bernard Lewis, and the leading American evangelist theologian, Ravi Zakarias, have written books on the danger from extremists' Muslims – but neither found any reason to shoulder part of the responsibility for the hostilities (Lewis *ibid;* Zakarias 2002).The American government ignores all criticism. When Dick Cheney visited twelve Muslim and Arab countries of the Middle East in March 2002 to discuss establishing a coalition "against terror" in the region, he excluded Palestine from his tour. This negligence drives many Muslims into becoming anti-American.

Religious freedom is a consistent irritation in the area. Islam's laws prohibit Christians (and other non-Muslims) from preaching to Muslims. Every child born to a Muslim family is a permanent captive of the Muslim faith – on pain of being stoned to death. Whereas Islam recognize all "prophets" including Jesus Christ, since Christians refuse this title to Muhammad, all Muslims must fight Christian mission activities, differing only in the severity of their measure. Reforms, under these conditions, are rare. Some despots have made modifications – valid as long as the ruler lives. But since Islam is a universal faith without a binding high universal authority – interpretation of the Koran is the entire issue. How these holy orders are read in Afghanistan, Sudan, Algiers, Egypt, Syria, Tunis or Libya determines the success or failure of the world scene. With the impact of Saudia Arabia's crude oil, Muslim reformers have little hope for the future.

An Israeli law, enacted 50 years ago to grant women equal rights, is not being implemented for Muslim women. Another Israeli law permits Jews, Muslims or Christians to add another woman to their harem as long as she is only "known in public" (in Hebrew – *Yedoa'a batssebor*). This second wife does have equal inheritance, social or legal rights of a wife as long as she lives with her husband. Some 40% of Muslim nomads in the Negev desert still practiced this kind of polygamy in 2000, but Muslims living in the Muslim-Christian mixed regions of Galilee practice polygamy much less, but those in the Sunni-Muslim Triangle between Galilee and the Negev are more inclined to be polygamists.

Societal changes take place when social pressures force them. Thus Muslim communities in Israel let their adult females study in mixed schools and take part in the labor force side by side with males – when jobs and wages are encouraging. So what lessons can be learned from this narrative?

1 – Christians, Muslims and Jews can live in peace side by side – when certain conditions are met: They need to agree religion is a personal issue between the individual and God. While the homeland is a common topic and of mutual concerns, Saa'd Zaghloul, leader of the Egyptian revolt which united Egyptian Muslims

and Copts against the British occupation in 1919, coined the apropos slogan: *al dien lellah, wal wattan llel jamia'* (We owe faith to God but our homeland is common to all of us).

Middle East peace will be secure only if the leaders of the region can mitigate their conflicts and learn the value of compromise—allowing others to pray as they wish and give them enough space to live. Palestinians in the West Bank and Gaza Strip suffer a severe shortage of space and constantly are threatened by Israeli's encroaching policy of settlements. The world community unanimously opposes this misappropriation, but a majority of Israelis—based on religious and security reasons—forge ahead. All acknowledge for peace to be established, the Israelis must make an honorable land settlement, for just the demographics demonstrate that Palestinian Arabs, in the occupied territories since 1967, must have their national right for self-determination recognized and their free state established and practicing free elections, democracy and egalitarian concepts.

2—Palestinians and Jordanian Christians often receive preferential treatment from Muslim authorities because the Hashimite monarchs and Yasser Arafat, the Palestinian's leader, are eager to keep their Christian subjects and win their sympathy. However these communities continue to dwindle, for economic conditions plus the bleak public scene, influence young people to look for new homelands where they won't constantly face a state at war with little personal security plus economic hardships.

In Israel, despite the heavy-handed tactics of the government, generally people on the "street" find life rather friendly. The economic situation has, generally speaking, improved constantly over the last 20 years. Young Christians seem willing to try and stay in their homeland. Despite some waves of emigrations their population continues to grow. Palestinian Christians in Jerusalem, the West Bank and Gaza lack any signs of hope for any improvement in economic conditions which helps keep them at home.

3—Cultural affinity and national solidarity are great assets to a community divided on religious lines. That was true during Islam's early years and it still helps Christians who suffer under foreign domination. Though Western Christians, European and Americans feel some affinity to the native Christians of the Holy Land – none of their democratically elected governments is willing to endanger its own national interests to secure the survival of these Christians. The growing storm of religious fundamentalism endangers the well-being and social equilibrium of all societies. Hope rests in Christians banding together – not formally to establish union – but coöperating together to help one another actively serve their parishioners and maintain an atmosphere of hope in the face of enmity. This will also win their neighbors' respect and shine a beacon of faith on their corner of the world.

4 – Native Christians in Israel can certainly live today without charities coming from abroad to support them. Living generously and offering a helping hand to others in the Palestinian zones will be an example to all – especially working to make sure Israeli citizens, including Christians, are assured equal rights which the law grants them but are not always enforced by the agencies of the state. The establishment of an ecumenical council would enhance the Christians' presence in the Holy Lands. This council could organize Christian tours (from all churches) to celebrate together, and on the spot, the festival days of our salvation. Surely when thousands of Christian pilgrims from a score of countries celebrate the Annunciation Day festival in Nazareth with international choirs, or Christmas in Bethlehem or similar commemorations throughout the land, such colorful rejoicing crowds will leave vivid and joyful memories – on the participants and on the bystanders. This would also have a most positive affect on the morale of the local Christian community – if not cause a genuine spiritual awakening. One recalls the British traveler H.B. Tristam who told of the warm treatment that he received in 1863 when he passed through the Christian village Al Bassa.

5 – Native Christians can also welcome these visitors into their homes where friendships can be forged and mutual benefits derived for both the short and long term. How joyful for pilgrims to encounter those who share the Lord's earthly homeland. Such an ecumenical Christian experience might contribute to fostering a

new peace in the land.

* * * * *

Just the fact that Arab Christian communities have survived under different Muslim "Eastern despots" – to use Max Weber's term – for over a thousand years, and though isolated for generations have managed to practice a peaceful life-style (not following in the steps of those who have repeatedly fractured the church) is a miracle. The Muslim majority must be commended for their tolerance towards the Christian minorities in their midst.

Are we – as a Christian Arab community – on our way to extinction? I hope not, but many have their doubts and fears. The dwindling Christian presence sounds a warning. Yet, the Middle East is part of the new global village, not a world apart as it for centuries. In the age of Amnesty International, space channels and the internet, no political regime can escape scrutiny in its policy and treatment of religious or national minorities. NATO's intervention in Kosovo to rescue Albanian Muslims led to more interventions of the international community in East Timor to save the "Indonesian" Christians from disguised terror gangs. These international operations seem to signal a new era of global policy aimed at forcing recognition of the human and national rights of minorities and persecuted communities.

The tragedy is that for most of the 1,400 years of Islam, the followers of this faith have been in a state of war and conflict with Christian powers and communities – which has driven many to believe there can be no real coëxistence between the two religions. My community's experience would indicate there is common ground where both parties can meet and operate for their mutual interest. As a member of a peaceful Christian minority, I feel more secure in this open society than my parents were. The fact my Christian community is loyal to their rulers and its individual members are, often, more peaceful than their Jewish or Muslim compatriots gives me added security. That they are more peaceful, productive and law-abiding than their neighbors (inside Israel) causes the appreciation of friends and the envy of adversaries.

Bibliography

BOOKS

Abu, Laban Baha & Michael W. Suleiman (eds.), *Arab Americans-Continuity and Change,* Belmont: MA, 1989.
Aerts, P. Conrad, *The Franciscans in the Land of Our Redemption,* Washbourne: England, 1933.
Al-Masri, Iris Habib, *The Story of the Copts,* Cairo, 1978.
Al Asmar, Fawzi, *To Be an Arab in Israel,* London, 1975.
Antonius, George, *The Arab's Awakening,* London, 1965.
Ateek, Naim Stifan, *Justice and Only Justice: A Palestinian Theology of Liberation,* NY, 1989.
Atiyyah, Edward, *The Arabs,* London, 1955.
Attwater, Donald (ed.), *Catholic Encyclopedic Dictionary,* London, 1951.
Azouri, Najeeb, *Le Reveil La Arabe Nation,* Paris, 1905.
Bagatti, Bellarmino, *Ancient Christian Villages of Galilee,* Jerusalem, 2001.
Baldi, Paschal, *The Question of the Holy Places,* Jerusalem, 1918.
Briand, Jean, *The Judeo-Christian Church in Nazareth,* Jerusalem, 1982.
Burckhardt, John Lewis, *Travels in Syria and the Holy Land,* London, 1822.
Burge, Gary M., *Whose Land, Whose Promise?* Cleveland, 2003.
Cattan, Henry, *Palestine, the Arabs, Israel: The Search for Justice,* London, 1969.
Colbi, Saul, *Short History of Christianity in the Holy Land. Jerusalem,* 1966.
– *Christian Churches in the Holy Land,* Jerusalem, 1969.
Crag, Kenneth, *The Arab Christians,* Louisville, Kentucky, 1991.
Dalrymple, William, *From the Holy Mountain,* London, 1998.
Dawood, N.J., *A Translated Koran,* London, 1956.
Emmett, Chad F., *Beyond the Basilica,* Chicago, 1995.
Esposito, John L., *The Muslim Threat-Myth or Reality,* Oxford, 1999.
Falah Salman, *The Druze in the Middle East,* NY, 2002.
Goitein, S.D., *Jews and Arabs: Their Contacts Through the Ages,* NY, 1955.
Governanti, G., *The Shrine of Annunciation in Nazareth,* Jerusalem, 1962.
Guillaume, Alfred, *Islam,* London, 1956.
Haddad, Robert M., *Syria under Muslim Rule,* Princeton, NJ, 1970.
Haiek, Joseph R, *Arab-American Almanac,* Glendale, CA, 1984.
Hakim, Mgr. G., *Gospel: Pages Read in Galilee,* Brugge, Belgium, 1957.
Hilliard, Alison & Betty Jane Bailey, *Living Stones Pilgrimage,* London, 1999.
Hoade, Eugene, *Guide to the Holy Land,* Jerusalem, 1962.
Hourani, Albert, *Arabic Thought in the Liberal Age 1798-1939,* Oxford, 1970.
– *A History of the Arab Peoples,* NY, 1992.
Hurewitz, J.C., *Diplomacy in the Middle East,* Princeton, 1956.
Jansen, H., *Militant Islam,* London and Sydney, 1979.
King, Michael Christopher, *The Palestinians and the Churches, 1948-1956,* Geneva, 1981.
Lamond, John, *Modern Palestine,* Edinburgh & London, 1897.
LeStrange, Guy, *Palestine under the Moslems,* Beirut, 1965.

Lewis, Bernard, *The Assassins*, London, 1970.
– *What Went Wrong?* Oxford, 2001.
Lorch, Netanel, *The Edge of the Sword*, NY, 1961.
Lustick, Ian, *Arabs in a Jewish State*, Austin, TX, 1980.
Mackay, Runa, *Exile in Israel*, Glasgow, 1995.
Mansour, Atallah, *Waiting for the Dawn*, London, 1975.
McAlester, R.A.S., *A History of Civilizations in Palestine*, Cambridge, 1921.
Middle East Council of Churches (MECC) *Perspective*. Nicosia, 1998.
Nakhleh, Khalil, *Palestinian Dilemma-Nationalist Consciousness and University Education*, Detroit, 1979.
Newton, Frances E., *Fifty Years in Palestine*, Wrotham, England, 1948.
O'mahony, Anthony (ed.), *The Christians' Heritage in the Holy Land*, London, 1995.
Parkes, James, *Whose Land? A History of the Peoples of Palestine*, London, 1970.
Prior, Michael & William Taylor (eds.), *Christians in The Holy Land*, London, 1994.
Rantisi, Audeh, *Blessed Are the Peacemakers*, Guildford, Surrey, 1990.
Register, Ray G., *Back to Jerusalem*, Washington, 2000.
– *Dialogue and Interfaith Witness with Muslims*, Kingsport, TN, 1979.
Reiss, Nira & Judith Blanc, *Health Services to the Arab Population in Israel*, Tel Aviv, 1988.
Sabella, Bernard, Albert Aghazarian & Afif Saffieh, *On the Eve of the New Millennium: Palestine General Delegation in the u.k.*, 1998.
Said, Edward, *Out of Place*, NY, 1998.
– *Covering Islam*, NY, 1981.
Schlink, M. Basilea, *The Holy Land Today*, London, 1963.
Schulze, Kirsten E., *The Politics of Intervention: Israel and the Maronites 1920-1984,*, Oxford, 1994.
Schwartz, Walter, *The Arabs in Israel*, London, 1959.
Shabera, Apram, *The 7th of August – The Assyrian Martyr's Day*, London, 1994.
Shipler, David K., *Arab and Jew: Wounded Spirits in a Promised Land*, NY, 1986.
Smooha, Sammy, *The Orientation and Politization of the Arab Minority in Israel*, Haifa, 1980.
Spafford-Vester, Bertha, *Our Jerusalem*, Jerusalem, 1950.
Stendel, Ori, *The Minorities in Israel 1948-1973*, Jerusalem, 1973.
Stephens, John Lloyd, *Incidents of Travel in Egypt, Arabia Petraea and the Holy Land*, San Francisco, 1970.
Stock, Ernest, *From Conflict to Understanding*, NY, 1968.
Testa, Emmanuel, *The Faith of the Mother Church*, Jerusalem, 1992.
Tsimhoni, Daphne, *Christian Communities in Jerusalem and the West Bank since 1948*, London, 1993.
Thordson, Maria, *Christians 2000 A.D.*, Jerusalem, 1999.
Tibawi, A.L., *British Interests in Palestine 1800-1901*, Oxford, 1961.
Tritton, A.S., *The Caliphs and Their Non-moslem Subjects*, Oxford, 1931.
Twain, Mark, *Innocents Abroad*, NY, 1869.
Wagner, Donald E., *Dying in the Land of Promise*, London, 2001.
Waterfield, Robin, *Christians in Persia*, London, 1973.
Watt, W. Montgomery, *What Is Islam?* London, 1979.

Wessels, Antonie, *Arabs and Christians? Christians in the Middle East,* Kok Phros, Netherlands, 1995.

Westmo, Gustaf, *The Cross or the Crescent,* (n.p.), 1933.

Wilson, Sir Colonel Charles W. *The Land of Galilee,* Jerusalem, 1975.

Wrba, Marian, (ed.), *Austrian Presence in the Holy Land,* Tel Aviv, 1996.

Yazbeck-Haddad, Yvonne & Wadi Z. Haddad, *Christian-Muslim Encounters,* Gainesville, FL, 1995.

Zacharias, Ravi, *Light in the Shadow of Jihad,* Sisters, OR, 2002.

Zittrain-Eisenberg, Laura, *My Enemy's Enemy, Lebanon in the Early Zionist Imagination, 1900-1945,* Detroit, 1994.

Zureik, Elia T., *The Palestinians in Israel,* London, 1979.

ARABIC SOURCES

Abu A'amro, Zeyad, *Usul Al Harakat Al Seyseyya fi Qitaa' Gaza 1948-1967 (The Roots of the Political Movements in Gaza Strip 1948-1967),* Acre, 1987.

— *Al Haraka Al Islameyya fi Al Daffa Al Gharbeyya wa Qitaa' Gaza (The Islamist Movement in the West Bank and Gaza Strip),* Acre, 1989.

Al A'alem, Mahmoud Amin (ed), *Qadaya Fikreya (Ideological Issues),* Cairo, 1993.

Al Jabarti, Abd Al Rahman, *Al Gazwa Al Franseyya-Sadmat Al Gharb (The French Invasion-The West Shock),* Cairo, 1997.

Al Jarrah Nouri (ed.), *Rihlat Elias Al Moussalli ela America (1683-1668),* Beirut 2001.

Al Kheyami, Amir Muhana, *Zawjat Al Nabi Wa Awladoh, (The Prophet's Wives and Children),* Beirut, 1990.

Al Mahalli, Jalal Ed Din Ibn Ahmad & Jalal Ed Din Abd Al Rahman Al Sayouti, *Tafseer Al Jalayain (An Interpretation of the Qoran),* Damascus, 1969.

Al Nashashibi, Muhammad Isa'af, *Al Batal Al Khaled Salah Ed Din (The Immortal Hero, Saladin)* Jerusalem, 1932.

Al A'ora, Ibrahim, *Tarikh Welayat Suliman Pasha (History of Suleman Pasha Governate),* Sidon, 1935.

Al Qaysi, Abd Al majid Hasib, *Al Athoriyyon (The Assyrians),* London, 1999.

Al Razzaq, Ali Abd, *Al Islam wa Osul Al Hokm (Islam amd the Rule of Government),* Cairo, 1925.

Al Saleh, Subhi, *Mabahith Fi A'olum Al Koran (Research in Koranic Studies),* Beirut, 1965.

Al Sharfawi, Ibrahim, *Al Khala' bain Al Tradi wal Taqadi (Women Divorce in Conciliation and Court),* Cairo, 2000.

Al Tahtawi, Ali, *Al Khala' Fi Dawi Al Qoran wal Sunnah (Women Divorce in the Light of Muslim Scripture),* Cairo, 2000.

Al Turk, Nicola, *Al Hamla Al Franseyya A'la Misr Wal Sham, (The French Expedition against Egypt and Syria),* Beirut, 1990.

A'alwi, Hadi, *Al Eghtiyal Al Seyassi fi Al Islam (The Political Assassination in Islam),* Damascus, 1987.

Al A'aref, A'aref. *Al Mufassal fi Tarikh Al Quds (The Detailed History of Jerusalem).* Jerusalem, 1961.

— *Al Masseeheyeen Fi Al Quds (Christians in Jerusalem),* Jerusalem, n.d.

A'ashqouti, Raji, *Mihnat Al Masseeheyeen fi Lobnan (The Christians' Calamity in Lebanon),* Beirut, 1991.

Abd Al Fattah, Nabil, *Al Misshaf wal Sayf (The Koran and Sword),* Cairo, 1984.

A'bboud, Salim. *d.b. Vartin Waqreinataho (d.b. Vartin and his Wife)*, Beirut, 1910.

Abd Al Nabi Abd Al Fattah, *Al Ia'lam wa Hijrat Al Missreyyeen, (The Media and Egyptian Immigration)*, Cairo. 1989.

Abdo, Samir, *Al seryan Qadeeman wa Hadithan (The Assyrians in Ancient and Modern Days)*, Amman, 1996.

Abu Hanna Hanna, *Dar Al Mua'allimeen Al Rouseyya fi Al Nassera, 1866-1914 (The Teachers' Russian Seminar in Nazareth 1866-1914)*, Nazareth, 1994.

Abuna, Fr. Alber, *Tarikh Al Kkaneesa Al Seryaneyya Al Sharqeyya (History of the Assyrian Eastern Church)*, Beirut, 1992.

A'dawi, Kamal Nayef, *Al Hijra Al Filastinyya Ela America min Nehayat Al Qarn al-19 Wahatta 1945 (The Palestinian Immigration to America Between the End of the 19th century and up to 1945)*, Nazareth, 1993.

Al-Nayhoum, Al Sadeq, *Islam Ded Al Islam, Sharia'a Min Waraq (Islam Contradicting the Islam Law of Paper)*, London, 1994.

Al Masa'oudi, A'li Ibn Al Hussein, *Al Tanbeih wal Ishraf (Scholium and Attention)*, Beirut, 1968.

Al Remaihi, Muhammad, *Soqout Al Awham (The End of Illusion)*, Beirut, 1998.

Al A'ayeb, Salwa Balhaj Saleh, *Al Masseeheyyah Al A'arabeyya Wa Tattowareha (Arab Christianity and its Evolution)*, Beirut, 1997.

Al A'rawi, A'bdullah, *Mujmal Tarikh Al Maghreb.(General History of the Maghreb)*, Casa Blanca, 1994.

Al Ansari, Muhammad Jaber, *Al A'alam Wal A'rab Sanat 2000 (The Arab World in the Year 2000)*, Beirut, 1988.

Al Banna, Goerge Istefan Youssef, *Al Mughtaribun Wal Mohajiroun: Al Masseeheyyon Ela Ayn? (The Christians Who Live Abroad and Those Who Immigrated: Where to?)*, Amman, 1998.

Al Baz, Osama, *Misr fi Al Qarn Al 21: Al Amal wal Tahaddeyat (Egypt in the 21st Century: Hopes and Challenges)*, Cairo, 1996.

Al Hasan, Youssef, *Al Hiwar Al Islami Al Masseehi (The Muslim-Christian Dialogue)*, Abu Dhabi, 1997.

Al Bustani, Botrus, *Moheat Al Moheet (Encompassing the Circle)*, Beirut, 1870.

Al Hawaweini, Rafael, *Lamha Tarikheyya fi Akhaweyyat Al Qabr Al Muqaddass (A Historic Glimpse of the Holy Tomb Brotherhood)*, Beirut, 1893.

Al Hawwari, Muhammad, *Nimer, Sir Al Nakbah (The Secret of the Catastrophy)*, Nazareth, 1955.

Al Hawwari, A'irfan Abu Hamad, *Aiaa'lam Min Ardd As Salam (Famous People from the Holy Land)*, Haifa, 1979.

Al Jamali Faddel, *Dhikrayat Wa A'ibar (Memiors and Lessons)*, Beirut, 1965.

Al Kharsa, Mustafa (ed.), *Mudhakarat Al Malek A'bdullah (Memories of King Abdullah)*, Amman, 1965.

Al Nawawi, Mohyi Ed Din Abu Zakariya, *Riad Al Saliheen (A Collection of Hadith)*, Beirut, n.d.

Al Nimer, Ihsan, *Tarikh Jabal Nablus Wal Balqaa, Vol. I (History of Mount Nablus and Balqa)*, Damascus, 1938.

– *Tarikh Jabal Nablus Wal Balqaa, Vol. II (History of Mount Nablus and Balqa)*, Nablus, 1961.

– *Tarikh Jabal Nablus Wal Balqqa, Vol.III (History of Mount Nablus and Balqa)*, Nablus, n.d.

Al A'omar, Abd Al Karim (ed.), *Mudhakrat Muhammad Amin Al Husseini (The Memories of Muhammad Amin Al Husseini)*, Damascus, 1999.

Al Rifaa'i, Shams Al Din, *Tarikh Al Sahafa Al Soreyya (History of the Syrian Press)*, Cairo, 1969.

Al Samman, Nabil, *Botrus-Ghali Wal Hukoma Al A'alameyya (Botrus-Ghali and the World Government)*, Cairo, n.d.

Al Sharabi, Hisham, *Bahth fi Al Mujtama' Al A'rabi (A Stady of the Arab Community)*, Beirut, 1987.

Al Suwaidi, Towfiq, *Mudhakarati: Nisf Qarn Min Tarikh Al A'iraq Wal Qadeyya Al A'rabeyye (My Memories: Half a Century of Iraq's History and Arab Issues)*, London, 1999.

A'marah Mohammad (ed.), *Qasem Amin. Al Aa'mal Al Kamela (The Complete Works of Qasem Amin)*, Beirut, 1976.

Arafat, Jamil, *Min Qurana Al Mohajjara fi Al Jaleel (Some of Our Deserted Arab Villages in Galillee)*, Nazareth, 1999.

Arkoun, Mohammad, *Al Fikr Al Osouli Wa Estihalat Al Taaseal (Fundamental Thinking and the Impossibility of Fundamentalists)*, London-Beirut, 1999.

Ashqar, Ahmad, *Al Tadmeer Al Thati: Al Nassera Namoodhajan (Self Destruction: Nazareth as an Example)*, Nazareth, 2000.

Azzam, Abd Al Rahman, *Al Ressalah Al Khaledah (The Eternal Message)*, Cairo, 1964.

Badawi, Jamal, *Al Fitnah Al Taeifeyya fi Missr wa Asbaboha (Religious Strife in Egypt and its Reasons)*, Cairo, 1981.

Benvinesti, Meron, *Al Mashhad Al Moqaddas (The Holy Landscape)*, Ramallah, 2001.

Berthier A.L., *Rewayat Al Hamla Al Franseyyah A'la Misr wa Bilad Al Sham (The Story of the French Campaign to Egypt and Syria)*, Tripoli, (Lebanon), 1999.

Cheikho Fr. Louis, *A'olamaa Al Nassraneyyeh fi Al Islam (The Christian Scholars in Islam)*, Beirut, 1983.

Choueiri, Youssef, *Al Rihla Al A'arabeyya Al Haditha Min Auroba Ela Al Wilat Al Mottahida (The Arab Modern Travelers from Europe to America)*, Beirut, 1998.

Corbon, Fr. Jean, *Kaneesat Al Sharq Al A'rabi (The Arab East Church)*, Beirut, 1890.

D'aguilers, Raymond, *Tarikh Al Feranja Ghuzat Bayt Al Maqdess (History of the Europeans Who Invaded Jerusalem)*, Alexandria, 1990.

Dar Al Machreq, *Al Munjid Fi Al Lugha wal Aa'lam, (Al Munjid, A Dictionary of Language and Personalities)*, Beirut, 1987.

Deib Faraj Allah Saleh, *Al Masseiheyya Wal Masseeheyyon Al A'rab Wa Ossoul Al Mawarena (Christianity and Christian Arabs and the Roots of the Maronites)*, Beirut, 1995.

Farah, Rafiq, *Tarikh Al Kaneesa Al Osqofeyya fi Mutraneyyat Al Quds (History of the Episcopal Church in the Jerusalem Bishopric)*, Jerusalem, 1995.

Farid, Mohammad, *Tarikh Al Dawla Al A'aliya (History of the Sublime [Ottoman] State)*, Beirut, 1977.

Farsakh, A'wni, *Al Aqaliyyat fi al Tarikh Al A'rabi, (Minorities in the Arab History)*, London/Beirut, 1994.

Ghrayeb, Yousef, *A'ilot Ams Walyoum (Ailot, Yesterday and Today)*, unpublished ms, Nazareth 2000.

Habib Rauf, *Al Matareyya Wshagarat Al A'athraa (Al Matareyya and the Virgin's Tree)*, Cairo, 1979.

Hadidi, Subhi, *Edward Said, Taa'qiebat A'la Al Isteshraq (Edward Said: Comments on Orietalism),* Beirut, 1997.

Hamid Allah, Muhammad, (ed.), *Majmua'at Al Wathaiq Al Seyaseyyeh (A Collection of The Political Documents),* Beirut, 1987.

Heyer, Friedrich, *Tarikh Al Kaneesa fi Al Ard Al-Moqadasa, (History of the Church in the Holy Land),* Jerusalem, 1995.

Hitti, Philip, *Tarikh Al A'rab (The Arab History),* Beirut, 1958.
– *Tarikh Soriyya (History of Syria),* Beirut, 1959.

Hussein, Ahmed Amin, *Dalil Al Muslim Al Hazeen (The Sad Muslim's Guide),* Cairo, 1983.

Huwaidi, Fahmi, *Taliban, Jund Allah fi Al Maa'raka Al Kataa (Allah Fighters in the Wrong Battle),* Cairo, 2001.

Ibn Al Manthour, Muhammad Ben Kukarram, *Lisan Al A'rab (Arab Tongue),* Cairo, 1882.

Ibn Hisham, Abd Al Malek, *Seirat Al Rassoul (The Messenger's Biography),* Beirut, n.d.

Ibn Jubair, Mohammad Ben Ahmad, *Rihlat Ibn Jubair (Ibn Jubair Voyage),* Cairo/-Beirut, n.d.

Ibn Khaldun, Abd Al Rahman, *Al Muqaddamah (The Preface),* Beirut, 1964.

Ibn Talal, Hasan, *Al Maseeheyya fi Al A'alam Al A'rabi, (Christianity in the Arab World),* Amman, 1994.

Ibrahim, Hanna, *Hanna Naqqarah, Mohami Al Ard Wal Shaa'b (Hanna Naqqarah, Defender of the Land and People),* Acre, 1987.

Jana, Muhammad Towfiq (ed.), *Majmoua'at al Moa'ahadat Wal Wathaiq Al Tarik-heyyah fi Hayat Al Umam Al A'arabeyya (A Collection of Agreements and Historic Documents in the Life of the Arab Nations),* Damascus, 1937.

Jobran, Khalil *Jobran. Al Rasail (The Letters),* Beirut, 1994.

Khalid, Mansour, *Jonub al Sudan fi al Mukhayyala Al A'rabeyya (South Sudan in the Arab Fiction),* London, 2000.

Kalboni, Abdallah Saleh, *Tarikh Madinat Nablus (History of Nablus),* Nablus, 1992.

Kaldani, Hanna Said, *Al Maseeheyya Al A'arabeyya fi Al Ardun Wa Filastine (The Arab Christianity in Jordan and Palestine),* Amman, 1993.

Khaldi, Mustafa & Farroukh Omar, *Al Tabshier wal Istia'mar fi al Bilad Al A'ra-beyya (Preaching and Colonialism in the Arab Countries). Sidon,* 1964.

Khouri, Jiryes (ed.), *Al Hijra, (Emigration),* Jerusalem, 1991.

Khouri, Elias (ed.), *Al Masseeheyyon Al A'rab, (The Christian Arabs),* Beirut, 1981.

Khouri, Shehadeh & Khouri Nicola, *Khulassat Tarikh Kaneesat Ourashalim Al Orthodoxsseyya (The Essence of the Orthodox Church of Jerusalem),* Jerusalem, 1925.

Kishek, Muhammad Jalal, *Ala Fi Al Fitnati Saqato (Those That Dropped in the Strife),* Cairo, 1992.

Laurant, Shabri & Laurant Rani Awsa, *Siyassah Wa Aqlleyat fi Al Sharq Al Awsat (Politics and Minorities in the Middle East),* Cairo, 1991.

Lutski, Ivanov, *Tarikh Al Aqttar Al A'arabeyya Al Hadith, (The History of Modern Arab Countries),* Moscow, 1975.

Maa'louf, Amin, *Al Haweyyat Al Qatela, (Deadly Identities),* Damascus, 1999.
– Al Horub *Al Saleebeyya Kma Raaha Al A'rab (The Crusades as Seen by the Arabs),* Beirut, 1989.

Mahfouz, Fr. Youssef, *Mukhtasar Tarikh Al Kaneesa Al Maroneeya (Short History of the Maronite Church)*, Kaslik, 1984.

Manaa', A'adel, *Aa'lam Filastine 1800-1918 (The Personalities of Palestine 1800-1918)*, Jerusalem, 1986.

Mansour, Assa'd, *Tarikh Al Nassera (History of Nazareth)*, Cairo, 1924.

Mansour, Anis, *Al Lathien Hajaro (Those that Emigrated)*, Cairo, 1988.

Mansour, Johny Elias, *Al Motran Gregorious Hajjar (The Bishop Gregorious Hajjar)*, Haifa, 1985.

Murcos, Samir, *Al hemaya Wal A'eqb (Protection and Retribution)*, Cairo, 2000.

Mua'ammar, Towfik, *Daher Al A'omar*, Nazareth, 1979.

Muafaza, Mohammad Abd Al Karim, *Al Ordun: Tarikh Wa Hadarah (Jordan: History and Civilization)*, Irbed, 2001.

Murad, Muhammad, *Al A'olaqat Al Lobnaneyya-Al Soreyya (The Lebenese- Syrian Relations)*, Beirut, 1993.

Naff, Alexa, *Al Mughtaribeen (Becoming American)*, Damascus, 1988.

Nahhas, George (ed.), *Al Dean Wal Donya fi Al Masseehiyya Wal Islam (Religion and Wordling in Christianity and Islam)*, Lebanon, 1997.

Na'imeh, Michael, *Saba'oun: Hikayat A'omr (70: A Life Story)*, Beirut, 1959.

Papadopoulos, Chrysostom, *Tarikh Kaneesat Antakia (History of Antioch Church)*, Beirut, 1984.

Qajman, Hanna A'bdullah, *Bet Lahem min Aqdam Al Azminah Wahatta 1800 (Bethlehen from Most Ancient Times up to 1800)*, Bethlehem, 1992.

Qanawati, Fr. Goerge Shehatah, *Al Masseeheyya wal Hadhara Al A'rabeyya (Christianity and Arab Civilization)*, Cairo, 1992.

Rafiq, A'bd Al Karim, *Tarikh Bilad Ash Sham wa Misr min Al Fath Al A'othmani Ela Hamlat Napoleon (1516-1798) (The History of Egypt and Syria Starting with the Othoman Ocupation and up to Napoleon Campaign 1516-1798)*, Damascus, 1968.

Ridha, Mohammad Rashid, *Al Khilafah Aw Al Imameh Al A'othma (The Caliphate or the Great Imamate)*, Cairo, 1924.

Riad, Zaher, *Al Masseeheyyoun Wal Qawmeyya Al Misreyya (The Christians and the Egyptian Nationality)*, Cairo, 1979.

Sa'adeh, Anton, *Nushui Al Umam (Genesis of the Nations)*, Beirut, 1937.

Saa'id, Amin, *Tarikh Al Dawla Al Saa'udia (History of the Saudi State)*, Beirut, 1965.

Saghieh, Hazem, *Qaomeyyo Al Machreq Al A'rabi, Min Dreyfus to Garaudy (The Levant's Arab Nationalists from Dreyfus to Garaudy)*, Beirut, 2000.

Said, Edward, *Estishraq (Orientalism)*, Beirut, 1981.

Sakakini, Khalil, *Katha Ana Ya Donya (Oh World, That is What I Am)*, Jerusalem, 1955.

Salamah, Adib Najeeb, *Al Injeelyon wal A'mal Al Qawmi (The Evangelists and the National Action)*, Cairo, 1993.

Salibi, Kamal Sleiman, *Tarikh Lobnan Al Hadith (Modern Lebanon History)*, Beirut, 1970.

Sarraf Faraj Bishara, *Al Masseeheyya Wa Ghazza (Christianity and Gaza)*, Gaza, 1993.

Sayigh, Rosemary, *Al Fallahon Al Filastinion min Al Iqtelaa' ela Al Thawra (The Palestinian Peasants from Uprooting to Revolution)*, Beirut, 1980.

Sharab, Muhammad Hasan, *Ma'jam Buldan Filastine (Dictionary of Palestine Sites)*, Medina, n.d.

Shabera, Apram, *Al Ashoriyyen: Fi Al Fikr Al Iraqi Al Moa'aser (The Assyrians in Modern Iraqi Thinking)*, London, 2001

Shukri, Ghali, *Al Malaffat Al Serriya Lil Thaqfah Al Misreyya (The Secret Files of Egyptian Culture)*, Beirut, 1975.

—*Al Thawra Al Muddadda (The Counter Revolution)*, Beirut, 1977.

Tamari, Salim (ed.), *Al Quds 1948, Al Ahyai Al A'rabeyya wamaseereha fi Harb 1948 (Jerusalem 1948. The Arab Quarters and its destiny in the 1948 War)*, Beirut, 2002.

Tudebud, Botrus, *Tarikh Al Rehla ela Bayt Al Maqdes (History of the Travel to Jerusalem)*, Alexandria, 1998.

Waqf, Shihab, *Al Din, Al Nawahi Al Tarikheyya, Al Qanonyya, wal Shara'eyya (The Historic, Legal, Religious Aspects)*, Nazareth, 1998.

Yaseen, A'touf Mahmud, *Nazeef Al Admigha: Hijrat Al A'qoul Al Arabeyya (The Hemorrage: The Arab Brain Emigration)*, Beirut, 1984.

Yateem, Fr. Michael & Aghnatious Deek, *Tarikh al Kaneesah Ash-Sharqeyya (The History of the Eastern Church)*, Harrissa, 1991.

Zaki, Izzat, *Kanais Al-Mashriqeyya (Churches of the East)*, Cairo, 1991.

Zain, Nur Al Din Zain, *Nushoi Al Qawmeyya Al A'rabeyya (The Birth of the Arab Nationality)*, Beirut, 1968.

Zeyadeh, Nicola, *Al Masseeheyyah Wal A'rab (Christianity and the Arabs)*, Damascus 2000.

Zuraik, Costantine, *Nahnu wal Mustaqbal (We and the Future)*, Beirut, 1977.

—*Ma Al A'mal (What to Do)*, Beirut, 1998.

HEBREW BIBLIOGRAPHY

Alon, Yegal, *Betahbolot Milahamah (Contriving Warfare)*, Tel Aviv, 1990.

Assaf, Michael, *Hita'orerut Haa'raveem Be Aretz Yesrael Vi Breehatam (The Arab Awakening in the Land of Israel and their Flight)*, Tel Aviv, 1967.

Aliav, Pinhas, *Hamaa'rakha Hamedineat a'l Yerushalem (The Political Battle over Jerusalem)*, Jerusalem, 1992.

Bavly, Dan, *Halomot ve Hisdamneyot Shehohmitso (Dreams and Missed Opportunities)*, Jerusalem, 2002.

Ben Artsi, Yosi, *Me Germania Le Eretz Yisrael (From Germany to the Land of Israel)*, Jerusalem, 1996.

Ben Gurion, David, *Anahno Ve Scheneno (We and Our Neighbors)*, Tel Aviv, 1936.

Ben Or, Y., *Yedia'ot Misrad Hakhenokh (News of the Ministry of Education)*, Jerusalem, 1951.

Benziman, Uzi, *Yerushalalim, A'er llow Khuma (Jerusalem, a Town without Walls)*, Jerusalem/Tel Aviv, 1973.

Benziman, Uzi & Atallah Mansour, *Dayarei Meshneh (Sub-Tenants)*, Jerusalem, 1992.

Cohen, Aharon, *Hamizrah Ha Aravi (The Arab East)*, Merhavia, 1955.

—*Ha Mizrah Hateekhon Shel Yamaino 1918-1958 (The Middle East of our Days 1918-1958)*, Merhavia, 1958.

Eish Shalom, Michael, *Masaa'e Notsreem Be Aretz Yesrael (Christian Travels in the Land of Israel)*, Tel Aviv, 1965.

Goren, Asher, *Haleaga Ha A'raviet (The Arab League)*, Tel Aviv, 1954.

Kamen, Charles, *Akharie Ha Ason: Ha Aravim Bemedinat Israel (After the Catastrophe: The Arabs in Israel)*, Haifa, 1984.

Lazaros-Yafeh, Hava, *Praqim Betoldot Ha Aravim Vha Islam (Chapters in the History of the Arabs and Islam)*, Tel Aviv, 1967.

Landau, Yaa'cov M., *Ha A'raveem Beyesrael (The Arabs in Israel)*, Tel Aviv, 1971.

Layish, Aharon, *Ha A'ravim Beyesrael-Ratsifout ve Tmoura (The Arabs in Israel-- Continuety and Change)*, Jerusalem, 1981.

Mayer, Thomas, *Hita'orirot Ha Muslimim Beyesrael (The Muslim Awakening in Israel)*, Giva'at Haviva, 1988.

Moshe, Gabai, *Kidma Mizrache, 1936-1939 (Kidma-East 1936-1939)*, Giva'at Haviva, 1984

Morris, Benny, *Lidata Shel Baa'yat Hapliteem Ha Falastineem 1947-1949 (The Birth of the Palestinian Refugees Problem 1947-1949)*, Tel Aviv, 1997.

Olmert, Yosi, *Mia'oteem Ba Mizrah Ha Teekhon (Minorities in the Middle East)*, Tel Aviv, 1986.

Osteski-Lazar, Sarah, *Iqrit wa Bira'am: Ha Sepor Ha Malai (Iqrit and Bira'am: The Full Story)*, Giva'at Haviva, 1993.

Prawer, J., *Hatsalbaneem : Dioqana Shell Hivra Qolonialit (The Crusaders: A Portrait of a Colonial Society)*, Jerusalem, 1975.

Rabinovich, Itamar, *Ha Shalom Shehamaq: Yahasaie Yesrael A'rav 1949-1952 (The Road Not Taken: Israel-Arab Relations 1949-1952)*, Jerusalem, 1991.

Rosenfield, Henry, *Hem Hayo Fallahim (They Were Peasants)*, Tel Aviv, 1955.

Segev, Tom, *Hayesraelem Harishoneem 1949 (The First Israelis 1949)*, Jerusalem, 1984.

Shima'oni, Yaa'cov, *Arvie Eretz Yesrael (Arabs of the Land of Israel)*, Tel Aviv, 1947.

Stindel, Uri, *A'ravei Yesrael-Bain Hapatish ve Hasadan (Arabs of Israel, Between the Hammer and the Anvil)*, Jerusalem, 1992.

Ya'ari, Avraham, *Massaa'ot Eretz Yesrael (Travelers of the Land of Israel)*, Ramat Gan, 1976.

NEWSPAPERS AND PERIODICALS

Al Ahram, Arabic daily newspaper, Cairo.

Al Ahram Al A'rabi, monthly magazine, Cairo.

Al Akhbar Al Kanaseyyah, Episcopal Church of Jerusalem, Arabic monthly

Al Ayyam, Palestine National Authority organ, Ramllah, Palestine.

Al Hikma, Arabic and Assyrian bi-lingual quarterly, Jerusalem.

Al Hilal, Arabic monthly, Cairo.

Al Ittihad, Arabic daily, Haifa, Israel.

Al Jaryda, Special monthly issue. Beirut, Lebanon, June 1982.

Al Kotob, Weghat Nazar, Arabic monthly, Cairo.

Al Manbar Al Islami, Al Awqaf Ministry monthly, Cairo.

Al Massarah, Arabic Catholic monthly, Harrissa, Lebanon.

Al Montada, Middle East Council of Churches (MECC) Arabic monthly, Beirut, Lebanon.

Al Quds, Arabic daily newspaper, Jerusalem.

Al Rabitah, Melkite Church Arabic monthly, Nazareth, Israel.

Al Salam Wal Khair, Arabic Catholic monthly, Nazareth and Jerusalem

Cornerstone, English quarterly. Sabeel Center publication, Jerusalem.

Eastern Churches Review, biannual, Oxford, England.

Haa'ayen Hashvia'eat, Hebrew media affairs monthly, Jerusalem.

Ha A'olam Hazeh, Hebrew weekly, Tel Aviv, Israel.

Ha Aretz, Hebrew daily newspaper, Tel Aviv, Israel.
Holy Land, Illustrated quarterly of the Franciscan Custody of the Holy Land.
Majmaa' Al Bohuth Al Islameyyeh, Al Azhar monthly magazine, Cairo.
Maqor Rishon, Hebrew right-wing weekly, Tel Aviv, Israel.
MECC Perspective, English monthly. Nicosia, Cyprus.
Leqet, Prime minister's monthly newsletter published 2/1981-7/1984.
Qardom, Hebrew bi-monthly special issue, *Nazareth Ve Ataraiha (Nazareth and its Sites),* Jerusalem, 2/1982.
Rose Al Yousef, Arabic weekly, Cairo.
Qaddaya Fikriyya (Ideological Issues), Cairo, 10/1993.

ARCHIVES

A'atef Fahoum & the author papers – Nazareth.
Central Zionist Archive – Jerusalem.
Labour Movement Archive – Beit Berl.
State Archives – Jerusalem.

ARTICLES

Abd Al Karim, Khalil, "Mahmoud Amin Al A'alem," *Qadaya Fikreya,* Oct. 1993:-445.

Al Sulh, Menah. "Al A'rabi," *Kuwait,* Oct. 1994.

Barnea', Nahum, Benziman Uzi (ed.) *Haa'ayen Hashvia'eat (The Seventh Eye),* May 2002:5.

Hanafi, Hasan, "Misr fi Al Qarn," *Osama Al Baz,* Cairo, 1996:157.

Kattar, Elias, in *Jaryda Beirut,* 1982:115.

Qladeh, William, "Suleiman," in *Osama Al Baz, Misr fi Al Qarn,* Al-21, Al Amal wal Tahadeyat, Cairo, 1996:171

Rabatt, Edmond, in Elias Kouri(ed.) *Al Masseheyyoun Al A'rab,* Beirut, 1981:26

Shukri, Ghali, in Al Aalem Amin Mahmoud (ed.) *Qadaya Fikreya,* Cairo. 1993:193.

Sivan, Emmanuel, in *Hava Lazaros-Yafeh Praqim Be Toldot Ha A'ravim Ve Ha Islam,* Jerusalem, 1967.

Son, Tamar, in Abu Laban & Michael W. Suleiman (ed.) *Continuity and Change,* 1989.

Zakaria, Fuad in *Al Arabi Monthly,* Kuwait City, June 1993.

Zraik, Costantine in Elias Kouri, *Al Masseyyoun Al A'rab (The Cristian Arabs),* Beirut, 1981.

Index

A History of Arab Christians

Additional copies of this book may be obtained
from your bookstore
or by contacting
Hope Publishing House
P.O. Box 60008
Pasadena, CA 91116 - U.S.A.
(626) 792-6123 / (800) 326-2671
Fax (626) 792-2121
E-mail: hopepub@sbcglobal.net
www.hope-pub.com